Wholly Dev

180 Devotions written to help you fully receive and walk in God's purpose for your life

Judy Nichols-Prouty

This book is dedicated to the Lord Jesus, the One Who Loved me...and gave Himself for me.

Acknowledgements

To My Niece, Rayna: Your belief in me many years ago was far greater than my own. It's because of that belief that this book was birthed. Thank you for "gifting" me with the amazing blog...it became a reservoir to me...a place that I could dive back into whenever I needed encouragement. Your beautiful heart has inspired me (and I'm sure countless others) to be the best that we can be!

To Ellie: You have been so much more than just an amazing mother-in-law. You have been a friend...and a support to this project...along with innumerable other projects (some of them just crazy ideas!). Your help, encouragement and prayer have been a blessing to me all along this journey. To have such a beautiful and trusted woman of God in my life has truly been amazing. Thank you for the gift that you are to me.

To the May family - Ryan, Alexis, Jeff and Cynthia: You were the first people I ever met who modeled what you believed, and walked it out daily in your own lives. Seeing that walk of faith, which was so genuine in all of you, was life changing for me. You reminded me often to go boldly to the throne of God. I believe that you will see some of that boldness come through in the pages of this book. Thank you for loving people, right where they are in life, and for bringing the message of hope to so many right now, who truly need to hear it. Y'all are a blessing!

To My Wonderful Writers' Group - Leslie, Marylin, Nancy and Denise - I will always remember the phone call from you, Leslie, and your words that day, "I think you are a writer." And then you went on to say, "I think there is a book in you." Those words struck my heart like an arrow that had found its' way to the target... (in a good way)! Desire, along with a newfound confidence, were birthed that day in my heart...and it has only grown since then! I am so grateful for the instruction, the encouragement, and for your perseverance, as you brought together this incredible group of women. I have received so much from every one of you very gifted ladies. Our times of sharing, not only what we'd written, but our hearts as well, were precious to me, and I was so incredibly blessed to be part of such an amazingly talented and creative group of women. Thank you all for your input, your friendship, and your encouragement. I love you all...and may I say to each of you as Leslie said to me...I think there is a book in you!

4

To Dan and Nancy Thompson, my outstanding pastors, and dear friends: You have taught us, poured into our lives, stood with us during difficult times, prayed for us, seen the best along with the challenges we've faced, and loved us through them, encouraged us in our faith, modeled your own faith, and challenged us to soar...and to never give up! Your heart for the Lord and for His people has both inspired and propelled us to trust God and take the leap into new territory. I see you like two mighty oak trees, firmly planted in the Lord. As Jeremiah 17 says...you don't even notice when trouble comes, because your roots go deep and you are being continuously fed by the Living water that brings strength and nourishment into your lives. Thank you for standing strong for Jesus and for never giving up, or giving in to pressure. You are both deeply loved.

To Brian and Monica: I have watched you both grow into the amazing people you are...strong, courageous, full of life, willing to "take the high road" and make a stand for what's right. I have learned so much from watching you. Seeing you pour into the life of your son and giving selflessly has deeply impacted my own life as I watch him grow into a young man with direction and purpose. I'm immensely proud of you both.

And to Kaleb: I remember the day so well when your dad let me know that your mom was pregnant...with you! I literally danced around the kitchen that day! We were overjoyed at the idea that you were coming! I just want you to know that your life was well thought out and purposed by God. You were born at the perfect time in history and to the most wonderful and loving family imaginable! You have been an amazing gift to all of us - a gift that has never disappointed - a gift that has brought life, smiles, fun, laughter, and joy to everyone! You are deeply loved!

To Andrew Wommack: I doubt that you'll ever see this - but just in case - Ten years ago, I was recovering from a serious illness and didn't know how, or even if I could go forward in life. The Lord led me to one of your books, and I began to receive understanding about the deep love of God, and about who I was in Him because of that love. It was life changing. For all of your years of study and pouring into the lives of so many, I am grateful. I am one of the lives that has been profoundly changed.

To Ray: You truly are the love of my life, and I see Jesus in you every day. You loved me into wholeness, kind of like Jesus does! Your quiet strength has been a constant source of encouragement to me. You have always wanted all that God has for me. You have listened intently to all of my silly ideas, and then encouraged me to pursue them. You have loved me, loved my family, and stood by us in all of life's difficulties. I have never doubted your love. Thank you for that. Thank you that every day when I wake up, I am secure in it. Thank you for daily living out your love for God in such a way that it has had great impact on me. You have inspired and encouraged me more than you will ever know. I love you with all my heart, and I am honored to be your wife.

To Bill and Joni Rose: Thank you so much for your Saturday phone calls, and emails to see how you could better walk us through this. Knowing that you were there for any questions, as well as to hold us up in prayer was such a blessing. We are so grateful.

To Matthew and Nathan: You have always been loved.

If even one person had been missing from the above group of people, it would have changed the outcome...not only of my life, but of this book. It's like a recipe that is missing an ingredient. The finished product would be different. There would be a change in flavor - or perhaps something would seem to be missing. I am so grateful for every one of you. Each of you have uniquely added a key ingredient that have given this volume what I believe to be an unmistakable flavor. I only hope that you will enjoy it, and be blessed immensely.

Prologue

I'm thinking that it was about 11 years ago now that I received a very thought provoking, and eye opening email one day. It was actually designed to be fun...one of those where you answer questions about yourself like, "Which do you prefer, coffee or tea?", or "What would be your dream vacation?" After you filled in all the answers, you would 'reply all' to send to everyone on the mailing list. Then you would wait for all of their emails to come to you. It was a great way to learn fun facts about your friends...things that you probably didn't know. I was finishing my questions, and really enjoying this...until I came to the final question..."Describe yourself in one word." A bit of panic started to rise up in my heart. I tried to brush aside what my first thought was. But, it seemed to be my only thought...especially if I was going to be truthful. And, as much as I tried to dismiss it, it kept coming back...Hopeless. What a terrible word. Without hope...that was me. That was the word that would best describe me. And I wondered how I could have ever gotten here.

I was a born again, Bible believing Christian. I had a good life, a good marriage, and a decent job. I was active in my church and I ministered to other hopeless people frequently. I was putting out a daily devotional to try to encourage people that I knew. But what no one knew about me was that I was facing my own battle with discouragement. Those who knew me best probably didn't see through my smiling facade. My husband knew. You see, he had been there, when together, 25 years earlier, we had gone through the most unthinkable ordeal that I could imagine a couple go through. Nothing could have prepared us for what was about to happen in our lives. We went through a loss that was unbearable. It felt like something had literally drained the life right out of me...like with every breath I took, I was on borrowed time. I didn't know how to put one foot in front of the other to keep going. This was devastating, not just for me, but for my husband. I didn't see us being able to survive this. I thought that my body would simply expire...but I kept waking up every morning. I had a little boy who needed a mom. And even though I wasn't a very good one...as I had pretty much checked out of the human race, he was my reason for living. I needed him as much as he needed me. The days turned into months that became years. I didn't understand how we could continue to push forward. I looked for help from anyone who would listen, in the church we were attending, and in people.

I was told by a friend that somewhere along the way, I must have sinned greatly, and that whenever I could figure out what I had done, make it right, and then learn whatever God wanted me to learn from this, possibly the situation could change.

This news was almost more than I could take, because I had sinned. I had made some terrible decisions as a young woman...decisions that I couldn't now change. And now I believed that this loss that we were confronted with was my fault. There really was no way to fix anything, or change it for the better. It was done. And now, so was I. To try to move past the regret and the guilt also seemed impossible. It just became part of who I believed I was, and what I lived every day. I coped with all of this by staying busy, working 3 jobs, and being active in the church. I knew that all of this was not normal. I had heard about this wonderful, forgiving God my entire life. I had been taught that God IS love. I wanted to know Him. I wanted to have a relationship with Him that was genuine. I wanted to understand where that love and forgiveness fit in to my life. What could I do if I could not make restitution for a sin such as mine? Who could I turn to if I could never make things right? I felt trapped. I believed that God was angry with me, like I'd been singled out as the lone person who would never be able to make Him happy. Did God love me? Did He just tolerate me? If He IS love, then He MUST love me...right? At least a little bit? And would a God who loved me want to teach me through the torment that I was enduring? If Jesus had died for my sins...was this particular sin that I had committed just too despicable, even for Him? I wanted so much to hear His voice, to have Him tell me that everything was going to be all right and that I wasn't the biggest disappointment in all of creation. Most of all, I wanted to hear Him say "I love you." I wanted to sense His presence. I wanted to be held. I wanted to intimately know this God Who had laid down His life for me. I wanted to be able to trust Him. And I knew that somehow the journey that I was on had to change. If anything I've described here represents in even a small way how you may have felt at some point in your own life, then I hope that the pages of this book will be an encouragement to you, and a healing balm for your own heart. I spent so many years believing that I had to "work" for God, to make amends for the mistakes I'd made in my life. But my journey WAS about to change. And I was about to embark on a life changing trek that brought the hope that I so deeply desired...and along with it...the intimacy with Jesus that I had longed for. But for now, here I was, sitting in front of the computer screen...unsure how to answer that last question. I asked God to begin to reveal Himself to me in a way I'd never known before. Something seemed to come alive in me as I presented that request to the Lord. Then, I typed in my answer, and pushed send.

8

Stretch Your Roots Deeply Into The Life Giving River of God

Jeremiah 17:7-8 *"Blessed (with spiritual security) is the man who believes and trusts in and relies on the Lord. And whose hope and confident expectation is the Lord. For he will be (nourished) like a tree planted by the waters, that spreads out its roots by the river; and will not fear the heat when it comes; but its leaves will be green and moist. And it will not be anxious and concerned in a year of drought nor stop bearing fruit."*

This is probably my favorite verse in the entire Bible. Beloved of God, you are BLESSED. I get a picture in my mind of a beautiful old oak tree next to a river. The top roots that you **can** see around the circumference of the tree are a reminder of the deep roots that you **can't** see. The roots that are reaching down into the depths of the earth are fed by living water, nourished and sustained.

Because of the constant feeding that the tree receives, its leaves remain green and healthy, and it continuously bears fruit. The heat does come, but the tree doesn't notice it. The tree has no fear. It has no anxiety. It has no concern. It simply remains. It is whole, nourished, healthy...fed.

Isaiah 61:3 likens us to trees. We are called trees of righteousness, strong, magnificent, distinguished, and filled with integrity. And when we are planted in Jesus, the Living water, we too are fed, nourished, and strengthened. We are blessed, because we are connected to a Source that brings life! This verse was looking ahead to Jesus, the One in whom we place our trust, the Author of our Hope and the One on whom we rely. Our confident expectation is in Him and Him alone. There is no other in whom we could or would place our firm belief. There is no copy. Jesus is the Original, the Only. He stands alone.

Remind yourself today of this truth, as well as the promises found in this verse. Meditate on them. In doing so, you will be stretching your roots deeply into the life-giving river of God.

Our Job Is To Trust Jesus - Part One

2 Chronicles 32:10 "Thus says Sennacherib, king of Assyria, 'In what do you trust, that you remain under siege in Jerusalem?'"

As I write this, not only our nation, but the entire world is facing one of the most difficult and challenging situations that we could have ever imagined. The coronavirus has rocked our world, our lives, our homes...our way of life. I, like most of you, am currently under quarantine. I made a decision early on that I would need to stay busy, if possible, in order to not "think" too much about what is going on around me. There seems to be no escaping it. I'm guessing we all have that same sense. If we turn on the television, news of it is on every station...and we do not always know what is true. If we look at social media, it's the same thing. If we call a friend, it's what most people seem to want to talk about. I understand it. It's frightening. People want answers. They are looking for hope.

I started to feel like I was going into survival mode...which is never a good thing. I am a child of God...born again. I've been made New by the blood of Jesus. His Word is filled with hope. It is alive, and when I read it, I can trust that the words I'm reading are going to stream beautiful rays of truth into my soul to bring hope, and healing. I never have to wonder if I am being led astray. I trust the word of God. It's what I stand on. It's what I have stood on at other times...through life threatening illness, through serious poverty, and in the worst loss imaginable. I trust God.

Several years ago, we received a call that the dam near our home was about to break, and that in the ensuing flood, we would probably lose everything. We sought the Lord through a friend that we trusted. God began to speak to our hearts that He had dispatched His angels and that our home would be fine. It was difficult to stand, to believe that we'd heard from Him, because many that we talked to said otherwise... but the peace that we experienced truly did pass all understanding. We chose to stop watching the news, and to turn our attention to God, the Author and Finisher of our faith. Our friend spoke life into us, revealing that she believed that God's angels were literally holding back that water. I could see it. Not physically. But I knew in my heart, and through the eyes of my spirit that the water was being supernaturally held back

And it was true. The dam held strong, and the homes of thousands of people were saved.

So many times in my life, I have known that the hand of God has protected us. In every situation where things looked extremely grim...we believed God. We trusted in what we could not see with our physical eyes because we knew that there is an unseen world...a world that is actually more real than the world we can see.

On the second day of quarantine, I opened my Bible. God knew my heart. He knew that like most others, I was looking for hope. I was seeking answers. My Bible happened to open to 2 Chronicles 32:10. If you get the chance, please read this passage. It goes through verse 22. As I sat and read the story, the words began to penetrate the fear that had crept in, and to replace that fear with hope. And why not? God's word IS alive. This passage is a story about Sennacherib, the king of Assyria. He, along with his army, had besieged the surrounding cities, and taken many lives. And now they were coming for Jerusalem. As if that wasn't bad enough, Sennacherib sent some of his forces ahead to King Hezekiah, the king of Jerusalem, to taunt him, as well as to frighten all of the inhabitants. The story of Sennacherib is one of an evil man...almost an evil presence, if you will. And it began to remind me of what we are currently facing. There is a presence in this world that is anti-God. It comes through the news media, and through some well meaning people as well. It's purpose, just like Sennacherib's, is to taunt us, to frighten us into believing that our God will not help us.

Sennacherib reminded the people that the gods of the other nations did not help them in any way. He had destroyed these other cities, almost effortlessly. This godless man, Sennacherib, also wrote letters insulting God and telling the people not to follow Hezekiah or his God. He incited fear into every heart in Jerusalem. His object was to frighten and terrify the people so that they would simply give up and give in to his demands without a fight.

But Hezekiah knew God. He had a relationship with the True and Living God. He knew that the heart of God was to love and protect those who were His from any and all enemies.

11

Hezekiah, along with the prophet Isaiah went before the Lord and cried out to their God. And the Lord sent an angel, who destroyed EVERY warrior, commander, and officer in the camp of Sennacherib.

And when Sennacherib entered the temple of his god, some of his own children killed him with a sword.

The heart of God hasn't changed. He still wants to love and protect. He still wants to fight our battles and guard us from our enemies. And as I have experienced in my own life, He still dispatches His angels into our own situations to fight on our behalf, and to protect us. My hope is that you will see that in the pages of this book. And that you'll learn that when we pray, the Lord is quick to respond!

Our Job Is To Trust Jesus - Part Two

2 Chronicles 32:9-32

The story of Hezekiah and Sennacherib has really come to life for me recently. The words seem to jump off the page for me, and the hope that comes to my heart is what I want to share with you.

There is so much fear mongering going on right now in the news...so many "what ifs". We don't know what is true and what isn't. I have chosen to not watch the news at all. I do receive news from a couple of ministries that I trust...and I receive hope there as well.

Beloved, what are we trusting in? I can tell you...at almost 67 years old, I have learned some things. One of the most important is that the word of God can be trusted. We can look to the news and easily be misled, and even distracted...from the truth that is in the Word of God.

First of all, let me say that God did not send this virus. He did not give His stamp of approval for it to take place so that He could teach us something. If that were true, then why, if we came down with it, would we go to the doctor? Why would we want to get out of God's will - if that's what we believe His will is? Why wouldn't we just want to stay sick so that we could allow God to teach us whatever it is we think He wants us to learn? Why do we blame God for the awful things that happen in the world? How can we call Him a loving Father, when out of the other side of our mouths we blame Him for all the murder, sickness, evil, and perversion that are going on? Do you see that if we were blaming our earthly fathers for these types of things, we would think it criminal...and yet we see fit to blame God.

Most of this "blame game" comes from a lack of understanding. We believe what we've been told by our pastors, or other teachers, who...God bless them...didn't have a correct knowledge of God's word either. Beloved, we live in a fallen world. God is not the sender of evil. The devil roams about seeking whom he can devour. Much of the evil we see comes directly from him. Man also has been given free will. We are free to make choices, and sometimes the choices we make aren't the best. Some of them can cause a snowball effect in our lives, where maybe the thing we were dealing with begins to grow. And we see that God didn't bring this "thing" on at all. Our own choices are what did it. Ask yourself this question. If God controls everything...does He control you?

Did He control you when you were speeding, or when those harsh words came out of your mouth at someone? Did He control you when your anger got out of control or when you made that decision that wasn't for the best? I'm not trying to condemn anyone. We have all made bad choices. We know that God is sovereign. But look up the definition of the word sometime. It means to be crowned as the person in top order, to be the supreme ruler, to be unlimited and absolute. It doesn't say anywhere in the definition…to be all controlling. I am trying to help you see that God is good…and He is always good.

In the story, Sennacherib taunted Hezekiah and the people of Israel. His purpose was to frighten the people into succumbing to his demands. Beloved, in our own story, we get to choose who to listen to, and how we will react. The Lord has given us free will. We get to decide what, and Who we pay attention to. We make decisions daily as to what we allow into our minds, and how we react to things. If I could advise you, it would be to stop listening to the news. Get in the word of God, where you will never be misled. Put your trust firmly in the Lord, and in nothing else. You have been given a free will, beloved. The choice is yours. You will never regret choosing Jesus.

Stay tuned for part three.

Our Job Is To Trust Jesus - Part Three

Blessings to you, most beloved of God! I'd like to continue today from a teaching that I started on 2 Chronicles 32:9-22.

I spoke yesterday about the true sovereignty of God. The Word speaks of the fact that God has complete dominion, authority and power. There is nothing that can defeat Him or even stand...against the power of God. Nowhere in the definition does it say that God controls everything.

Again, our God is a good Father, and He is not "allowing " all of the evil that is taking place in the world. Psalm 115:16 says " The highest heavens belong to the LORD, but the earth He has given to mankind". He spoke of it in the book of Genesis. The Lord gave dominion over the earth to man, when in Genesis 1:26, He said, "Let Us make man in Our image, according to Our likeness; let them have dominion over the fish of the sea, the birds of the air, and over the cattle, **over all the earth** and over every creeping thing that creeps on the earth." God prepared the earth as a place for man to dwell, to be enjoyed by man. He has made all on earth subject to man. All of this, He has given to us. If you follow this verse through in the original Hebrew, it means to bestow, as a gift. I hope this helps someone. I believe that much of what we've seen unfold in this world in recent months has been at the hands, (and hearts) of men.

Getting back to our passage, verse 21 tells us that God sent His Angels into the situation. We don't generally see angels, but we know that they exist. They are ministering spirits, who work on our behalf to protect us. In the story of Sennacherib, the angels were dispatched, and they destroyed every one of Sennacherib's warriors, commanders and officers. " Thus the Lord saved Hezekiah and the inhabitants of Jerusalem from the hand of Sennacherib, and from the hand of ALL others. And, He gave them rest on every side."

How many others did the Lord save the children of Israel from? ALL! How many sides did He give them rest from? EVERY! Beloved, as this passage came to life for me, I realized that God is a God Who wants to fight our battles for us. Hezekiah asked the Lord into his situation. What about us? He trusted God with it. He handed it over to Him, casting his cares, and trusting God with the outcome. Our job is also to trust Him. Our job is to seek Him, to build our faith, to cast out unbelief.

God wants us to believe in Him completely, so that even when we truly are in the most difficult of circumstances, we know that He is fighting our battles for us...and we can rest in that.

One last thing. When Sennacherib went back home with his tail between his legs, the Bible says, ashamed because everything he had planned backfired, he entered the temple of his god, and some of his own children killed him with the sword.

Sennacherib in this story to me represents evil. He represents the demonic influence that we face, even today. Sennacherib was taken down with the sword. We have our own sword. The Bible, according to Ephesians 6:17 says that the word of God is our sword. I believe that we can take down the evil (Sennacherib) that may exist in our life. I'm speaking of a modern-day evil...and we can demolish it...with the word of God! It is our sword. May we use it to bring down the giants in our lives. May we stand on the truth that is in it, and not be persuaded in any other direction. May we hold high our shield of faith, believing in the protection that it offers. May we wear the helmet of salvation, that stops all untruth from being able to penetrate our minds. May we remember daily who we have been made to be in Christ, putting on the breastplate of Righteousness...and having done all of these, we strap on our peace, the ability to stand firm with sure footed ability and readiness, that is produced by the good news of the gospel.

The Lord bless you all.

Let's Have The Audacity To Believe God

John 11:25 "Jesus said to her, 'I am the resurrection and the life. He who believes in Me, though he may die, he shall live.'"

Jesus' friend Lazarus was clinging to life when He received the message from Mary and Martha to come, for their brother was ill. He didn't seem at all troubled by the news. In fact, He declared that this sickness would not end in death at all, but that He would be glorified through it. Jesus then went on to do the unexpected. He stayed where He was for two more days! He didn't go to Lazarus immediately. It seemed unthinkable that He would have healed so many others before Lazarus, but in the case of His friend, He waited.

Has it ever bothered you when you had a plan for God in your heart that He didn't follow? I'm sure that most of us, at some point in our life, have run into a similar situation. And we wonder...where was God? This is what Mary and Martha, the sisters of Lazarus, were thinking. They questioned Jesus upon His arrival, as by that time, Lazarus had died. In their hearts, they were disappointed. They believed that He was too late, and that He had let them down. They loved and believed in Jesus...but they didn't understand, and were confused by His lack of action.

This verse seems to be one of the cornerstones that we stand on as believers. It is part of our theology. But theology doesn't help confusion or grief when it's very real. Life does. Truth does. And so, Jesus, the resurrection and the life, the bringer of truth, walked up to the tomb and called Lazarus forth from the grave. His statement of Who He is, along with His power to raise Lazarus teach us that everything the Bible has to say about the promise of eternal life is wrapped up in the person of Christ! He holds eternity in His hands!

The story teaches us something else though. It's an amazing picture of how God is certainly moving in our situations...even when to us, it may appear that He is doing nothing. He could be doing more than we might imagine. Jesus didn't do what the sisters were expecting of Him. He did something even better!

There may be times in the future when God doesn't do what you are expecting. He may not do what you have imagined or think that He should do. However, in each situation, if what you are looking for isn't happening...then you can expect something even better.

I believe that God has an expected end for each of us. Even though we may not understand at the moment, we can trust the outcome to our heavenly Father, who will breathe new life into any situation.

This story ends with Lazarus coming forth from the grave. The grave clothes that Lazarus had been bound with, were loosed. Death could no longer bind him. One day, Jesus will speak our names, calling us to Himself, and forbid death to bind us. But what about now? I believe that in this present time, there are those who need to shake off the grave clothes. Jesus died that we might have life, and have it **abundantly!** Let us get rid of those grave clothes, women of God…and have the audacity to believe God!

God Is Our Protector

Genesis 3:22-23 *"And the Lord God said, 'Behold, the man has become like Us, knowing how to distinguish between good and evil; and now, he might stretch out his hand, and take from the tree of life as well, and eat its fruit, and live in this fallen, sinful condition forever'. Therefore the Lord God sent Adam away from the Garden of Eden, to till and cultivate the ground from which he was taken."*

These verses have been so misunderstood or overlooked, at least in the circles of folks that I know. Somehow, we have been led to believe that God is an angry God, that He was angry with Adam and Eve, and that they lost fellowship with Him over the incident where they ate of the fruit. Yet, the Bible clearly continues to reveal Him speaking with them in future verses. I've been taught that they were kicked out of the garden because God could no longer stand to put up with them. But please, look closely.

Now that they had disobeyed, their eyes were opened. They knew that they were naked. And the danger became...what if they now stretched out their hand and ate from the tree of life? Then they would live forever in this fallen state! God was trying to protect them!

Can you imagine what would have happened if they eaten from the tree of life at this point? That fallen state would have continued...FOREVER! The power of sin and sickness had been released. What would it have been like if they had developed cancer, and had to live forever in that state? What if they had migraine headaches, and could get no relief? What if their minds began to stray from God and depression set in? They would have to live with it forever. What if, as the generations went on, crime began to develop and there was nowhere to hide from it? What if fear and torment never ended? I could go on and on, but you get the idea.

God was not trying to punish them. He was trying to protect them. Our Father is a good Father, and He has protected us also in many ways that I'm sure we haven't even seen, the greatest of which was that He sent His Son Jesus, Who laid down His life for us. He came that we might be able to live life fully, and in abundance. We are indeed a people most blessed

19

We Have The Right To Call Him Abba

Romans 8:14 *" For as many as are led by the Spirit of God, they are the sons of God. For ye have not received the spirit of bondage again to fear.... but you have received the spirit of adoption, whereby we cry, Abba, Father."*

There are a lot of different names used in the scriptures that are actually the Names of God. He is Jehovah Jireh...which means that He is our Provider. He is Jehovah Rophe, who is our Healer. There are many more, but the one that really stands out is Abba. This is one of the most significant names that speaks to us about how God deals with His children. The word "Abba" itself is an Aramaic word, and it would most closely in our English language be compared with the word "daddy". It signifies a deeply close relationship that a Father has with his child, and the intimate trust that a child would be able to put in his

"daddy".

We, as born again believers, have a right to call Him Abba...to walk in that closeness with Him on a daily basis, to think of Him as the "daddy" Whose lap you would sit on and pour your heart out to, while at the same time, being loved and protected. Because you are His child, He will never let you out of His sight.

It's also life changing to understand fully what it means to be an adopted son or daughter of God. It is probably the highest privilege imaginable in this life. It means that we can live confidently and walk boldly because of the Indwelling presence of the Holy Spirit, who directs our steps and the path that we take. Children who were adopted during the time this passage was written were given all the full benefits that their full blooded siblings had. They were joint heirs. And we have been accepted, forgiven, redeemed, and sealed with the Holy Spirit of promise. Being adopted through faith in Christ is the source of our hope and the security of our future.

As we come to know the true nature of Who God is, we should be amazed that He not only allows, but encourages us to call Him Abba...Father. We are His! It was His good will to make us accepted. We have been given an inheritance through the blood of Jesus and we are sealed by the Holy Spirit of promise. We have not received a spirit of bondage that we should have anything to fear or be afraid of. We have been adopted and we can live boldly and with complete courage because our trust is not in ourselves...it is in the One who is our Daddy...our Abba...our Father...and He will never fail one of His children.

We Have Been Called To Be His Holy People

1 Peter 2:9 *"But you are a chosen race, a royal priesthood, a consecrated nation, a special people for God's own possession, so that you may proclaim the excellences (the wonderful deeds and virtues and perfections) of Him who called you out of darkness into His marvelous light."*

Many of us spend our entire lives trying to earn acceptance. We seek it from our parents, our friends, and our co-workers. This desire to be accepted can affect the way we think, the type of clothes we wear, the kind of car we drive, and even the career we choose. We were created to be loved. And we love to know that someone has chosen and accepted us. God accepts us. And He accepts us just as we are. He loves us despite our imperfections, our weaknesses, our skill level, or lack of it. There are no conditions with God, no restrictions. We do not have to get cleaned up, stitched up or made up.

Your value to God is proven in the most significant event in history...by the cross. God said "I love you this much". Then He stretched out His arms and gave His life. He says we are a chosen race. Chosen by whom? Chosen by Him. He calls us His own possession. As believers, we have a special place in God's unfolding plan of redemption. God has selected you and me out of all the people in the world for a special reason. We have been anointed with the oil of gladness to serve as His representatives on earth. We have been selected, called, chosen, consecrated, and set apart for a very particular purpose, "that we may proclaim the excellences of Him, Who called us out of darkness into His marvelous light."

We are not a chosen race of earthly people. We are a spiritual body of believers, lovers of God, who have been called forth from every nation and tribe, as well as every language. We have been made citizens of heaven, the redeemed of God, a holy nation. We are kings and priests unto God. We have been declared righteous in His sight, and because of our union with Jesus, all that we say and do should be a reflection in keeping with the heavenly privilege that has been bequeathed to us.
Don't ever see yourself again as that person who is weak or imperfect. See yourself as He sees you, that He may be glorified and exalted in your life.

The Difference Between Milk And Meat Is In How You Receive It

1 Corinthians 3:2 *"I fed you with milk, not meat, for you were not yet able to receive it."*

I recently heard one of my favorite Bible teachers talking about this verse. He spoke about how a cow chews its' cud, and then brings it back up. It chews again, swallows, and then brings it back up again. I believe a cow has four stomachs, and it takes a lot of chewing, swallowing and regurgitating before the food finally makes it to the fourth stomach.

What we receive from spiritually is important, and sometimes needs to be chewed on, more than once. Just recently, as we have been dealing with a pandemic, not just in the United States, but all over the world, I opened my Bible one morning, and the word, which is alive, began to jump off the pages and into my heart. The Lord was speaking to me. The word that He gave me that day has carried me through the last 3 months, so that I was without fear, and I knew that He had dispatched His angels into the situation. I was completely at peace.

That hasn't always been the case. It's amazing to listen to great Bible teachers. There is often so much insight into the word that we might not have seen for ourselves. Often, I have had an "aha" moment when someone has been teaching, especially if it's on a topic where I have not had clear understanding.

But there was nothing like that day when God Himself spoke to me from His Word, and I knew that I knew that I'd heard from Him. I was aware that even though we were in a difficult season with something that none of us have ever faced before, God had not left us. Just as He had promised, He was working in ways that we cannot always see. I became very aware of His presence with me in everyday life.

I was fully persuaded of His word being true, and of His peace that does pass all understanding.

The difference, child of God, between milk and meat, is in how you receive it. It's amazing to go to teachers and be strengthened through the milk of the Word.

22

But when you want meat, you walk right up to the cow (or go right into the grocery store and pick out that steak).

The real meat is going to come as you seek Him for yourself. Deuteronomy 4:29 says "But from now on, you will seek the Lord your God, and you will find Him, if you search for Him with all your heart and all your soul."

You WILL find Him! What an incredible promise! Let the seeking begin!

Faith Requires An Object

Luke 8:25 *"And He said to them, 'Where is your faith (your confidence in Me?)' They were afraid and astonished, saying to one another, 'Who then is this, that He commands even the winds and the sea, and they obey Him?'"*

Jesus and His disciples had gotten into a boat to cross over to the other side of the lake. As they were sailing, Jesus fell asleep...and a great storm arose. The boat, and its' occupants, were in great danger. The disciples were afraid, and woke Jesus. He got up and rebuked the raging, violent waves, and the sea became perfectly calm. This is when Jesus asked them where their faith was.

I have asked myself that question many times. Where is your faith, Judy? Why are you struggling to see that God is with you in this situation, just as He was in that boat with the disciples? I think that part of what happens to me is that as long as I can still somewhat control whatever situation I am in, I might tend to rely on self, rather than relying on the Lord. The storm that these disciples were in was real...and there wasn't anything physically that they could do. And notice that the storm didn't just happen to them. It happened to all who were on the Sea of Galilee at that time. I'm guessing that's when fear really set in.

We can keep fear at arm's length as long as we can fix the problem. But when the flood waters rise in our lives, when the doctor gives us a bad report, when an unexpected tragedy lands at our door, we too feel the desperation of the disciples, "Master, we are perishing! Don't you care?"

This is when faith is imperative. Think about it. When our resources and skills are equal to the task, we don't really use our faith. But when the storm is out of control, we all have a need for faith. And that is what Jesus was asking. "Where is your faith?" It was a pointed question. I believe that He was actually trying to awaken something in His followers. WHERE IS YOUR FAITH? You see, faith is the antidote to fear. We can all fake it in calm waters. But this storm had brought them to the end of themselves. And now, they needed to act quickly.

Faith has to have an object. In other words, there is something (or someone) that your faith is in. Their faith was in Jesus. The boat was not about to sink with the Son of God on board.

The plan of God was not about to change. Jesus is the King of Kings and Lord of Lords. His kingdom was not about to falter.

The lesson for us is that when Jesus is in the same boat with us, we cannot sink, even when we are surrounded by the storm, and even when the boat begins to take on water. He promises never to leave us or forsake us. (Hebrews 13:5) He says He is with us and will watch over us wherever we go. (Genesis 28:15). He reminds us to be strong and courageous. (Deuteronomy 31:6). He tells us not to fear or be dismayed, for He is our God. He will strengthen us, help us, and uphold us with His righteous right hand. (Isaiah 41:10) He says that as we pass through the waters, they will not sweep over us and that as we walk through the fire, the flames will not set us ablaze (Isaiah 43:2). He tells us that we can do all things through Him (Philippians 4:13).

Where is our faith? It is in His Word. It is in knowing the character and true nature of God, and then standing on what we know to be true, over whatever circumstance may be surrounding us. We cannot stop the storms of life, but the marvelous truth contained in this story is designed to calm any fear and to give us peace. He is with you and will handle the events that are raging out of your control. He is in the boat with you...and He loves you.

Don't Reject His Embrace

Deuteronomy 33:27 *"The Eternal God is your refuge and dwelling place, and underneath are the everlasting arms"*

No matter where you are or what is going on around you, you are safe in the arms of God...because He is your refuge. He is your dwelling place. You may be facing the most challenging circumstances you have ever faced, but you are not alone. He is there...and His arms never tire of holding you.

Remember that. Remember that the arms of God are everlasting arms. Resting in that awareness of Him will bring you to an even deeper place of trust. He cares for you. He sees your circumstances. He knows your heart. He knows those who would like to hurt you...but those arms that long to embrace, also desire to protect.

Your dwelling place is in His very loving and capable arms. You can trust that the concerns of your heart are held firmly in the provision that He has made for you. He wants you to lean on, trust in, and confidently hope in Him.

Yesterday, we got to spend the afternoon with our precious grandson. He was tired and fell asleep in my husband's arms. I loved the picture...it wasn't just that he was comfortable and confident enough to rest in the arms of his grandpa...it was that his grandpa was fully devoted to holding him, making sure he was content, holding him tightly so he didn't fall. We have a God Who is fully devoted to us. He loves us. He wants to carry us through whatever difficult circumstance we face. He will not let go.

Beloved, don't reject His embrace.

We've Been Justified By His Grace Alone

Galatians 5:4 *"You have been severed from Christ, if you seek to be justified (that is, declared free of the guilt of sin and its penalty, and placed in right standing with God) through the Law. You have fallen from grace (for you have lost your grasp on God's unmerited favor and blessing)."*

This verse is so clear, and yet is very often taught so incorrectly. I was told for years that we were still somewhat under the law. As Gentiles, we were never under the law. I was also taught that we have to add to what Jesus has already done for us. Jesus came so we could have eternal life with Him, but I learned incorrectly that we had to continually make ourselves right. If we failed in some way, we had lost our right standing with Him, and then had to add to His work. The trouble is...His work was perfect. I used to wonder how that was possible. What could I possibly add to what He had done for me at the cross? Was His method actually imperfect...so that I, in my flesh, should somehow make restitution...when He had died for the very thing that I was trying to make restitution for?
The verse is one of the most astounding in scripture, but if we aren't seeing it through the eyes of our Spirit, then we are going to attempt to "fix" what we see as the "flaw" in what Christ has redeemed us from. And beloved, we were redeemed! Period! Legalism devalues and belittles the glorious grace of God by erroneously requiring some sort of human merit to secure God's unconditional, free gift of salvation! Paul at times needed to correct doctrinal error that had infiltrated the various bodies of believers. The Galatian gospel replaced Christ with the false gospel of human effort, and an unscriptural, works-based salvation. And it is still being done today. Legalism requires one to follow the entire law of Moses, with its 613 indivisible regulations. Failing to keep even one of these regulations results in the entire Law being broken. When an unsaved man or woman seeks to be made right with God through keeping the Law, they have cut themselves off from the one and only true way to be saved...as a free gift of God's grace...by faith in the Lord Jesus Christ. You have been severed (cut off) from Christ if you seek to be justified through law keeping. You have fallen from grace. You have moved away from God's favor and His blessing. May we never stray from the truth of the glorious gospel of grace - that we are justified by His grace alone, through faith alone, in Christ alone!

God Can Use Small Things to Bring Big Change Into Your Life

1 Corinthians 1:27 *"But God has chosen the foolish things of the world to put to shame the wise, and God has chosen the weak things of the world to confound the things that are mighty."*

When you are faced with a big challenge, do you automatically look for the most powerful means to solve the problem? This isn't always the way that The Lord operates. The Bible tells us that it pleases God to use what the world considers weak, foolish, base, or even despised...to bring to nothing...things that are mighty.
Think about it! In Exodus 4:2, God used a simple rod in the hand of Moses, a simple man...to perform miracles and confound the might of Pharaoh. Think about Esther, a simple Jewish woman in the Old Testament, who saved an entire nation! In John 6, The Lord used a simple little boy who happened to bring his lunch that day.... five loaves and two fishes. With that little boy's lunch, Jesus fed over 5000 people, and His disciples gathered up 12 baskets full of leftovers. In Judges 15, Samson slew a thousand Philistines who were the enemies of God's people, with the jawbone of an ass.

And then there is David, the least likely of all his brothers to be King. With five stones and a sling, he brought down the giant Goliath. Lastly, there is the message of the cross. It cuts to the innermost part of pride or self centeredness. It silences the brilliance of the highly educated. It eliminates the self will of those who might be elevated in their own eyes. The power and wisdom of God is from above and can only be found in Jesus, and Him crucified. God's way of salvation seems foolish in the eyes of the world. But it will be eternal loss to those who do not recognize that Jesus is the one and only path to everlasting life with Him.

Beloved, do not despise what may seem weak or insignificant in your life. God can use small things to bring down giant situations!

Healing Is A Legal Part Of Redemption

John 3:17 *"God sent not His Son into the world to condemn the world, but that the world through Him might be saved"* (sozo) meaning - delivered, preserved, healed

I'm curious about something. I wonder why we find it harder to believe for healing than we do for deliverance. Salvation includes all aspects of our lives - spirit, soul and body. Healing is a legal part of redemption and is available to all who believe. If healing is not a part of redemption, a different Greek word would have been chosen and the evidence for physical healing in the New Testament would have been explained as a temporary phenomenon,

If the type and shadow of Christ on the cross, the serpent on the pole, was sufficient to heal the children of Israel physically, shouldn't we believe that Jesus Himself, who accomplished redemption for us and became sin and a curse for us, has provided both spiritual and physical salvation for the world?

Several years ago, when I was in Bible college, we had a Saturday picnic at a local park. We prayed for the community and invited them to stay for lunch. I was with two classmates praying for a woman who showed us the deformity in her left arm. She had been born with one arm shorter than the other, by several inches. We began to pray for this woman. I had my arm around her, my hand resting on her left shoulder. All of a sudden, I felt something start to move in her shoulder. I opened my eyes, while one of my classmates continued to pray. And it happened. This woman's arm had grown out, and was now the same length as the other arm! I saw a lot of people healed of all kinds of maladies, and my understanding about healing began to change.

I had believed for years that God picked and chose who He wanted healed. Now I started to realize that healing (sozo) is part of salvation. The kingdom of God operates by faith. But when we haven't been taught to believe for healing, a great deal of unbelief can creep in, which can certainly negate our faith. Unbelief is the believer's greatest enemy. Most of us live with some level of it in our lives.

When we discover those areas that are keeping us from fully living in the abundant life that Jesus died for us to have, we need to go before the Lord and ask for His help in purging those areas of unbelief with a revelation of His love and goodness. Revelation from God is the answer to unbelief.

Beloved, when we choose to believe what the Bible says about us, we will begin to experience the full gamut of all Jesus died to give us. Dedicate yourself to believing what is written for you and about you. That is life!

What Season Are You In?

Isaiah 55:10-11 *"For as the rain cometh down, and the snow from heaven, and returneth not thither, but watereth the earth, and maketh it bring forth and bud, that it may give seed to the sower, and bread to the eater, so shall my word be that goeth forth out of my mouth; it shall not return unto me void, but it shall accomplish that which I please, and it shall prosper in the thing whereto I sent it"*

Without the changing of seasons, vineyards would never bear fruit. Flowers wouldn't blossom. Each season offers something that the vine needs for continued growth. Spring brings rain to stimulate growth that will come to maturity in the warmth of summer. Summer is a time of strengthening, while Autumn is the time of harvest and winter brings much needed rest. Without this rest, the vine wouldn't be strong enough to go through the cycle again to harvest.

Ecclesiastes simply says, "There is a time for everything and a season for every activity under heaven". Would it be fair to assume that there are also seasons in our Father's vineyard? That is often the way I interpret change in my life. I've experienced seasons of growth, seasons of quiet, seasons of sorrow, seasons of boldness, seasons of sheer happiness. And in all the many changes in my life, one thing I know for sure. God does not change. He is faithful always... in every season. I can rely on the fact that with whatever change that is going on around me, change that I may not want, change that I may not understand...God is faithful. I can count on this. I can stand on this truth and not fall.

As I said previously, vineyards are able to bear fruit because of change. Likewise, our spiritual growth requires an ever-changing climate...seasons when whatever is happening in our lives is used by our Father, Who nourishes our lives toward fruitfulness in each season. Your change is not going to throw Him for a loop. No, He will use that time of change to bring growth, nourishment and new provision into your life.
We must learn not only to embrace the season we are in, to enjoy its' gifts and confront its' challenges, but also to let go when the season changes. The cycle of God's care is always dependable. That never changes. Even when we cannot see it, He is behind the scenes, working to bring fruit into our lives. He understands the seasons of our lives, and knows when to prune, when to feed, when to harvest. We are the branches on His vine, privileged to grow and blossom and bear fruit...to follow Him through all the seasons of our lives.

31

Paul Entrusted Everything To Christ

2 Timothy 4:7-8 *"I have fought a good fight, I have finished my course, I have kept the faith. Henceforth there is laid up for me a crown of righteousness, which the Lord, the righteous judge, shall give me at that day: and not to me only, but unto all them also that love his appearing"*

I recently finished a study in the life of Paul. I have always loved the writings of Paul, but I have learned and begun to understand some things about him that I didn't know before. Paul's life was completely changed, from a man who followed the law and persecuted Christians, to a man who knew Christ, and who loved Him. The depth of that love is nearly indescribable. He KNEW God. He trusted Him. He trusted God's plan for his life. He spent his life pouring out to people, and took no thought for himself, always being obedient to the call of God that was on his life. He had entrusted everything to Christ...every effort, every tear, every drop of sweat, every mistake, every victory, every ability, every sermon. Paul had placed all he had into the hands of his Savior. No matter how difficult his circumstances grew, and believe me, his circumstances were often difficult, he remained obedient till the end. As the chains gripped his hands and feet, the stench of death was all around him, and he said, "I am convinced that He is able to guard what I have entrusted to Him" II Timothy 1:12

The book of II Timothy has become even more precious to me lately. Paul had chosen to trade his life of honor and respect for one of rejection and tribulation...but His choice was to follow Christ. Faced with humiliation, Paul proclaimed, "Yet I am not ashamed, because I know whom I have believed". Paul's sanity was protected by his certainty in his Savior. He KNEW the One in whom he believed...He knew Him with the kind of knowledge that was worth any loss he might go through.

If we are going to survive the trials and circumstances of this life, we must KNOW the One in Whom we believe. No matter what loss we may have suffered, no one can take what we know away from us...no one can take WHO we know. Paul looked at life through the window of Philippians 1:21 "For to me to live is Christ and to die is gain".

We can learn so much from the life of this man. My desire for every one of us is that we would KNOW the ONE in Whom we have believed...that no matter what we may face in this life, our minds and our hearts would be firmly planted in Him..

32

My prayer for each of you today is that we would simply be in agreement with His prayer... "That He would grant you, according to the riches of His glory, to be strengthened with might by His Spirit, in the inner man...that Christ may dwell in your hearts by faith, and that all of you, being rooted and grounded in love, may be able to comprehend with all saints what is the breadth and length and depth and height, and to know the love of Christ, which passes knowledge, that you might be filled with all the fullness of God."

Which Power Are You Releasing Into Your Life?

Romans 6:16 *"Know ye not that to whom ye yield yourselves servants to obey, his servants ye are to whom ye obey; whether of sin unto death, or of obedience unto righteousness?"*

Most people recognize that our actions are very important in the physical realm. We understand that there are consequences for what we do. If we drive too fast on the freeway, we may get a ticket. If we say something harmful about someone, we can cause pain for that person. If we overeat, we will gain weight.

But there is more to life than just this physical, natural world. There are spiritual dynamics that are continually at work. When the person that you're speaking negative words about doesn't even know about your words, YOU still do! You will be affected. When you are venting frustration, anger and unforgiveness, the words that you are speaking go out into the atmosphere, not only for those in your direct path to hear, but for YOU to hear. You can convince yourself of someone's guilt, just by your words. We may think that if they don't know what we said, it's no problem. This verse reminds us otherwise. When we react with anger or bitterness, we've just yielded ourselves to the devil. Whether or not we recognize it, he is the one who influences us to respond in the wrong way.

James 3:16 says "Where envying and strife is, there is confusion and every evil work." This verse didn't say "some" evil work. It says every evil work. When we get into envy or strife, we are opening a door for the devil to work in our lives. We are drawing a target on our back that shouldn't ever be there. Our thoughts, words and attitudes are either releasing the power of God in our life, or they are releasing the devil's power. Then we wonder why things are happening in our lives that we can't explain and don't want to see happen as believers.

You should know, beloved, God is good and He's done all He could to save, bless, heal and even prosper you. We need to set a watch before our mouths, as well as take every thought captive to the obedience of Christ. We need to recognize that there is a realm that we do not see, and that if we allow a door to be opened to it, the devil may come, seeking whom he may devour.

We want to recognize the spiritual dynamics in our lives. God wants us yielded to Him. He wants His blessings and power to be released in us.

Every time we act, we are releasing spiritual power into our lives. Think about this, beloved. This is serious business.

What kind of power would you say you are releasing into your life, and the lives of those around you? Remind yourself daily that you are a sweet savor unto God. I'm convinced that for most of us, this is our desire. Now, go enjoy your day, sending out that sweet aroma of Christ wherever you go.

You Have Been Made Righteous

Isaiah 64:6 *"But we are all as an unclean thing, and all our righteousness are as filthy rags..."*

What do you believe that our righteousness's are? Please...you may need to do a double take here. This verse is not saying that it's our unrighteousness that is as filthy rags. It is saying that it is our righteousness, our goodness, our virtues, the quality of being morally right in the eyes of God, that are as filthy rags. There is a Hebrew word in this passage, and it is the word "ED", which was translated in this verse as the word "filthy". The literal meaning of the word is "menstrual cloth". In other words, all of the great things that we think we are doing for God, and that includes our own self-righteousness, are as a soiled menstrual cloth in the eyes of God. Everything that we do on our own to obtain some type of right standing with God is disgusting in His sight.

I remember a church that I attended years ago. We had altar calls every Sunday. The whole purpose was to "get our hearts right with God". I was often leading the pack. I was down at the altar, week after week, because I felt that my heart was desperately wicked. Maybe I'd had an unclean thought that week or said something I was sorry for. Beloved, I am not saying that we should not go to God when we feel we have failed in some way. But what I am saying is...What about Jesus? What about what He did to make us right with God? What about the fact that we are IN Christ? Does that come and go any time we fail? Can we trust in His ultimate sacrifice being permanent or was it for naught?

We must remember that the folks in the Old Testament were not born again. They did not have the Spirit of God living in them, as we have today. Christ had not died and risen from the dead yet. Things are different for us on this side of the cross.

When we come to Jesus, and receive His salvation, we are given His righteousness. It is a free gift. And from that point on, being seen as righteous is the only way the Father sees us. As believers, it would not be correct to say that all our righteousness is as filthy rags. Jesus is our righteousness. We are in Him, and He is not a filthy rag! We aren't even currently sinners, saved by grace.

36

We WERE sinners, but now we are in Christ! We have been saved by grace...NOW.

We are the righteousness of God in our born-again spirit, and this too is because of Jesus. We are not just in the flesh. We are spiritual beings. We are no longer unclean. We have been made clean by the blood of Jesus.

Today, my hope is that you will remember. Because of Jesus...you have been made clean, and your righteousness does not depend on you. It depends entirely on Him. You can trust fully in the One Who will never fail you.

You Were Created To Soar!

2 Timothy 1:7 *"For God did not give us a spirit of fear...but of power, love and a sound mind"*

Fear is a spirit. It does not come from God. If we are experiencing fear, it should be a clear indication that somehow our thinking has gotten out of whack. I've known people who have dealt with this spirit all their lives. They truly do not know what life would be like without it. People fear all kinds of things...failure, rejection, pain, even death. People fear speaking truth, because they want to be accepted and loved.

Fear can trap us. It takes away our power...the very thing the Lord gave us! When fear comes on the scene, it will try to stop us dead in our tracks. Fear will keep us tethered, like a ball tethered to a pole. It can only go in circles. It can't really fly...and the Lord wants us, as believers to soar!

In Paul's statement to Timothy, you might note that he doesn't say that God is referring to those "strong, courageous, powerful, or influential people". He simply refers to "us". The Lord did not give "us" a spirit of fear. He is speaking to you and me.

I believe that the Lord wants us to look fear straight in the eye and see it for what it is...and for what it isn't. The spirit of fear is not something that has come from your Maker. It is something the devil uses to stop you in your tracks. It can literally put a roadblock in your life, as you find yourself tethered to it. The Bible says at least 365 times, "Fear Not". I wonder if that was because God knew that every day we would need a reminder that He is with us...that whatever we fear, we need to respond to quickly. Don't let it develop into something bigger. When fear of any kind tries to invade your mind, and your life...it is not the time to succumb to it. It is the time to stand against it. We can do that in a couple of ways. The first is to fill your mind with the truth that will revoke that fear. Often, just knowing the truth about something will be like pressing the delete button on fear.

But the other thing is that perfect love casts out fear. If you are dealing with fear, then bathe yourself in the love of God. When you are fully aware of how greatly you are loved, you will begin to realize that the fear has no place to reside in your heart. There is only room for Jesus in there. Remember that fear is a spirit...and that it doesn't come from God.

God is your Creator. And, He created you with a spirit of POWER, LOVE, and a STRONG MIND. Fear is not of God. Today, bring it before His throne. This fear has to go. Don't be gentle with it. Go after it. Stand on His Word! Speak to this mountain!

And Remember... that your God created you to soar!

Paul's Preaching Never Downplays The Power Of The Cross

1 Corinthians 1:18 *"For the preaching of the cross is to them that perish foolishness; but unto us which are saved, it is the power of God"*

Paul divides the world into two groups, those who are perishing, and those who are being saved. Those who are perishing are destined for an eternity apart from God. Those who are saved are destined for an eternity sharing in His glory.

To the first group, the cross is "folly". It is foolishness. To them, the preaching of the cross seems moronic, or idiotic. The literal meaning of the Greek word "folly" is the word moron. And to those who cannot, or will not see the truth in the gospel, we appear to be "morons". Ungodly people often think that believers, along with their faith, are stupid, and even crazy.

But for those who are being saved, the cross is God's most amazing, most powerful act. Jesus, in spite of His limitless power and authority, laid down His life to pay the price for sin. For all who believe, we understand the exchange that was made that day at the cross. Jesus exchanged His righteousness for our sin, so that we might become righteous.

God embraces humanity through the cross. Both Jews and Gentiles are called into relationship with God through the finished work of Jesus at the cross...and suddenly, that which seemed weak, or moronic to some, becomes divine revelation, power and salvation to all who will receive.

We do not get to God by our own human efforts. Rather, God has come to us, and establishes faith in the proclamation of the cross. Paul's preaching never downplays, disguises, or dismisses the power and wisdom of God manifested in the cross of Jesus Christ. Does ours?

Celebrate Being Reborn From Above And Rejoice That You Are His

John 3:6 *"What is born of the flesh is flesh...of the physical is physical...and what is born of the Spirit is spirit"* (Amp)

Did you know that you have been regenerated by His Holy Spirit? When you are in union with Him, His Spirit molds you into His image...in order that you may inwardly share His likeness. You no longer have to live by the flesh. You now live your life in His Spirit, which dwells in you, and directs your life.

Everything connected with the flesh, is fleshly. Our flesh is associated with our human nature, character and senses...and our human nature is fallen. Our physical birth rendered us incapable of entering heaven, because tainted flesh and blood cannot enter into God's perfect kingdom. This is why we must be reborn. Once we have been spiritually reborn, we look with excitement to entering that heavenly realm. You've been born from above.

You are different now because though you were born of the flesh, you were reborn of the Spirit of God when you opened your heart to Him. Others around you may not understand that He has made you a new creation in Christ. The world may not celebrate your new nature, but You, as His child, should never stop celebrating!

He is your Lord and Messiah, and you are His child...Not only are you His child, you are now a citizen of the kingdom of God. You are not an outsider or an alien to His kingdom. You are not excluded from the rights of heavenly citizenship. You are different from the world. You now share citizenship with the saints...His own people, consecrated and set apart. You belong to the household of God.

The world around you may groan, fight, destroy, complain, gossip, and hurt...serving Satan's purposes, but YOU are different. You are not of the world. You are no longer bound by its' limits. You are no longer a slave to it. You are a child of the Most High. Celebrate it. Rejoice that you are different. Rejoice that you partake in His divine nature. Rejoice that you are His.

The Heart Of God Is For Restoration

Joel 2:25 *"I will restore to you the years that the swarming locust has eaten, the crawling locust, the consuming locust, and the chewing locust."*

Restoration. The word itself is beautiful to me, because it is such a sweet picture of the heart of God. Much of the time when we have lost something or had something stolen from us, we look at it as injustice. And God is a God of justice. He is not all right with it when one of His beloved children has to endure unfairness of any kind. His heart is to restore whatever it is in your life that has been lost or stolen.

I will never forget the time surrounding the death of my mother. She was my closest friend. We talked most days, and she knew all of my deep dark secrets. Okay, not that I had many deep dark secrets, but my point is, I could tell her anything. She was my confidante, and I was hers. She loved me. She was the person in my life that I could and did trust with absolutely anything. After she moved to heaven, I was lost. I was happy for her, because I knew she was in the presence of Jesus. And I knew that what had been taken from her in this life - her health and happiness - were being completely restored now! I knew that the love she longed for in this life was now being fulfilled in the arms of Christ.

But I missed her. I missed the friendship that we had. I missed her voice. I missed the daily phone calls to ask me what I was making for dinner. I missed being able to open my heart to someone who would never criticize me, only love me. It seemed like there was a big hole in my heart, and in my life. Then, about a year later, I met my wonderful husband. After a few weeks, he introduced me to his mom. She has become my best friend. We have shared a wonderful friendship for over 35 years now. I am so grateful for her in my life. And I am so thankful to God for that restoration. He knew I needed it.

God longs to restore to you what the locust has eaten. The locust is a picture of the enemy. You may have lost a friend, someone you loved, or maybe you lost time. If you have regret over time wasted in worry, anxiety, depression, bondage of any kind, guilt, doubt, or whatever it might be, God can restore and redeem that time. Speaking of time, He lives outside of it. We count the days and the hours waiting for things to happen. But God simply lives in eternity...and reminds us that we do as well. Don't give up, beloved.

You can choose today to relinquish all the pain, all the disappointment, all of the betrayal or hurt, or even rejection that you may have dealt with. You can trust Him with these things. Put them into His very capable hands. And then, choose to remember. Remember He loves you. Remember His promises. Remember that He never breaks His word. You can trust in His unfailing faithfulness to take whatever you have handed to Him, and completely restore it. Hallelujah!

Put On The New Man

Ephesians 4:17-19 *"This I say therefore, and testify in the Lord, that you should no longer walk as the rest of the Gentiles walk, in the futility of their mind, having their understanding darkened, being alienated from the life of God, because of the ignorance that is in them, because of the blindness of their heart, who being past feeling, have given themselves over to lewdness; to work all uncleanness with greediness."*

This passage is pretty eye opening. Paul is giving us a warning. He is telling us not to become like the unbelievers, who walk in the futility of their minds. That word "futility" is the same word that is used 36 times in Ecclesiastes and is translated to be "vanity". It comes from a Hebrew word meaning *breath* or *vapor*. It refers to anything frail or lacking in substance. Solomon had tried to find satisfaction through knowledge, wealth and all that it affords, and through the pleasures of art and women. He had houses and land, anything he could have wanted, but he observed that even if you have all these things, it's futile without God, like striving after the wind.

Paul says that to live in the futility of the mind is to think and live without any regard for God, or for eternal things. It is to live selfishly or for fleeting pleasure. It is to live without regard to the consequences, living by the world's philosophies, that completely leave God out. God doesn't want anyone to live that way. He doesn't want anyone to live without Christ. He doesn't want us to live in the futility of our minds or just drift through life. The Lord has given us purpose, and YOU are of great value, not only to Him, but to others.

I have known believers also, who have begun to slowly fade in their walk with God...and none of them got up in the morning and simply made a decision to forsake God. It's been one step at a time. Folks begin to get discouraged and fall away, or get offended, or they get pulled by the things of the world to a place that they don't know how to get back from. Many feel too guilty, too ashamed, too discouraged, or too overwhelmed to cry out to God.

As believers, we want to continuously walk in the Light, as He is in the Light. We don't want to take steps away from the One, who IS Truth, thereby having our own understanding darkened. We want to be continually renewed and transformed in our minds and thinking. Unbelievers lack a new life from God. The Bible says that because of the ignorance that is in them, they are alienated from the life of God. I can't imagine anything worse.

Paul traces their spiritual ignorance to the "hardness of their hearts". The person whose heart is hardened ignores God. It results in him not knowing God, not having a relationship, and being cut off from the very life that God wants him to have.

Paul admonished us not to live like this. It can, for some, get easier and easier to make poor choices. Beloved, don't go there! This kind of life never satisfies. It always enslaves! Just look at the life of Solomon sometime. What started out as a heart that loved God, and was completely sold out to Him, ended on a slippery slope, as he, step by step, decided to make decisions to marry foreign women, many of them, who the Bible says, turned his heart from God. He eventually did evil, and did not fully follow the Lord.

As a believer in the Lord Jesus, we should live a very intentional life. We have an eternal purpose here on this earth, to glorify God through serving others, worshiping our heavenly Father, and bringing light to those who are living in darkness. If you are a child of God, let your light shine brightly in this world that is getting darker. Put off the old man and be renewed in the spirit of your mind. Then put on the new man who was created in true righteousness and holiness. Hallelujah!

Whose Report Will You Believe?

Numbers 14:24 *"But since my servant Caleb has a different spirit, and has remained loyal to me, I will bring him into the land where he has gone and his descendants will inherit it."*

The Israelites had been set free from centuries of bondage in Egypt. Now God was leading them by a pillar of cloud by day and a pillar of fire at night. Pretty incredible! He had spoken to them about a land flowing with milk and honey. He wanted to bless them. He wanted to take them to a land in which they did not have to labor, with cities that they did not have to build, and vineyards that they did not have to plant. He wanted to be good to them. But He desired that they trust Him. He wanted them to believe His promises. He wished for them to look to Him, instead of whatever they were seeing with their eyes. And the people struggled to do so.

The majority of the population of Israel shrank back in fear. They chose a route that was safer, one with less risk in their eyes. They could have taken the course that would have led them into victory, not only for the adults, but for their children as well. But they believed a negative report. Moses had sent men in to spy out the land. Ten out of the twelve sent returned with a report that there were giants in the land. Fear gripped the entire nation of Israel. However, two of the spies came back with a positive report, relating to the Israelites that even though the giants were there, God was with them, and He would certainly go before them.

My question for you today is simple. Whose report will you believe? So many of us have been stopped dead in our tracks by negative reports and comments. I remember years ago, my husband and I wanted to foster a child. Our hearts were set on it. We knew that many kids needed a good home with loving parents. We were aware that the foster system wasn't always easy to work with, but we knew the love of God in us to take on such an endeavor. We went to someone we trusted for counsel, and we were stunned at his advice. This person cast a vision over our lives that day that caused us to completely change directions. And the dream died.

Have you ever had a dream that died? Beloved, this shouldn't be so. The Bible says that Caleb (and I know Joshua as well) had a different spirit. They were men who didn't need to fit in with the crowd. They didn't have to be liked. They based their conclusions on truth rather than majority report.

They believed that the same God who brought down Pharaoh, could do the same to any other enemy who stood in the way.

Jesus died so that we might have a life of abundance. But abundant living requires different living... where your thought processes, self-disciplines and difficult decisions carve out a narrow road that isn't often traveled. You may feel like you are walking alone...but you are never really alone. The Lord is with you and goes before you. Ask the Father to show you the astounding courage that He has instilled in you, and to lead you by it day and night. The difference will be worth it.

Surely, He Has Set Them In Slippery Places

Psalm 73:9 *"They tell their cohorts, 'God will never know. See, He has no clue of what we're doing.'"*

This is a psalm of Asaph, who was one of the singers commissioned by David to be in charge of worship in the house of the Lord. He was a gifted individual, and he understood where that gift came from. He knew it came from the Lord, and he used music to praise Him and communicate His Word to the needy world around him.

But Asaph was also dealing with something that was deeply troubling to him. While he knew that God was good to Israel and to the pure in heart, it also seemed that God was good to the boastful and to the wicked. And this seemed unfair to Asaph...so much so that it made him nearly stumble and slip. It seemed that the godly alone should prosper. But that's not what Asaph saw. And it's not what we see either. We see scoundrels getting rich, being paid well, and very much sought after. In the current world we live in, we see that right is wrong, and wrong is right. We see those in power judging and ruling cruelly over those who might be considered to be 'the least of these'.

Together with Asaph, we get a picture of the wealthy, famous, proud, showy, violent and even greedy...enjoying their wickedness. And to go even further, as the verse says, these wicked men murmur against the Lord, saying "God will never know. He has no clue what we're doing."

For Asaph, all of this brought him to a place of wondering. He began to question the value in holiness. He felt that while the wicked enjoyed wealth, along with ease, he had to endure being 'plagued and chastened every morning'. It surely seemed to him that God was easier on the wicked than on the just. Asaph couldn't deny the evidence that shows that the wicked and ungodly often have good lives. He could not deny that his own life was hard. He came to the conclusion that all of this was too painful for him to even talk about.

But then something happened. Asaph went into the sanctuary of God. It was there that he gained perspective, and began to see things from an eternal viewpoint. Asaph went to church! And in doing so, he came into possession of some gripping convictions that steadied him, and enabled him to begin to walk with firmness, and with assurance. Asaph received understanding.

Asaph began to see that the ease and security of the wicked was really only an illusion...and that they were actually "set in slippery places", ready to fall at any time. He had worried earlier on that his own feet might slip. Now he was realizing that the wicked are the ones in "slippery places".

Beloved, I hope that you can begin to see, as Asaph did, that what we have seen happening in our world will not be allowed to continue forever. It may appear to us that the wickedness we have been surrounded by is almost going unnoticed by God. But I can assure you, He sees every heart. He knows what is happening. And He is NOT asleep! We can trust that God is actively pursuing righteousness, and like Asaph, we can EXPECT God to guide us through these difficult times, with His counsel. God is the strength of our own hearts, and He is our portion...forever!

Words Once Spoken - Cannot Be Retrieved

Psalm 73:15 *"If I had said, "I will say this," (and expressed my feelings), I would have betrayed the generation of your children. "*

It is implied here that Asaph did not give utterance to the thoughts and feelings that he was having regarding his impressions of how the evil surrounding him was seemingly "being allowed", with no actions by God to stop it. He was confused by this, and simply didn't understand why. That is so often the case with us as well. We don't understand why, as we watch the world around us unraveling. And for many people, watching news, trying to make sense of what they don't comprehend, and then thinking about it and talking about it with anyone who will listen, becomes their way of dealing with the unrest in their heart.

But Asaph, even in the midst of utter chaos, realized something. He knew that to "give utterance" to these thoughts might set off a chain reaction that could actually do damage in the hearts of those around him. He could see how people might be led to feel as if no confidence should be placed in God. His words had the power to suggest ideas which wouldn't otherwise occur and would only tend to fill their minds with distress. Unsettling thoughts can shake the foundation of faith, of peace, of hope, and even of the joy that someone might be walking in.

The phrase, "I would have betrayed" means 'to treat in a faithless manner'...a manner that is even treacherous. Asaph knew that he ought to not say anything that would lessen anyone's confidence in God, or anything that might even bring distrust, or that would disturb their peace, and their hope. He especially understood that to speak of his own doubts, especially within earshot of the children of that time, would be a betrayal and an offense to them. He knew that the minds and hearts of the youth were especially tender, and that to speak of his own troubles would be an act of injustice, as it would plant seeds of doubt in their lives that would not be easily overcome.

Years ago, I used to teach Sunday school. One of the things I used to do was bring a tube of toothpaste to class, and then squeeze some out onto a piece of fabric. Then I would have the kids try to put it back in the tube. It can't be done. It only makes a mess. And words spoken, can't be taken back either. Once they are out...into the hearing ears of those around us...they can easily make a mess.

Asaph used wisdom with his words. His commitment to not hurt those around him with the words he spoke were an act of justice. May each of us remember that words plant seeds in the heart of the hearer. May the seeds that we plant bring only life and hope to those around us. We can begin to see a crop of expectation, trust, desire, and ambition...simply by the words that we've spoken. Now THAT is exciting!

He Is Your Portion...And That Is Enough!

Psalm 73:26 *"My flesh and my heart may fail, but God is the rock, and the strength of my heart, and my portion forever."*

In the first 16 verses of this Psalm, Asaph was nearly disoriented by what he saw. He was looking at gross injustice from the wicked around him. But in verse 17, his outlook starts to change as he begins to have clarity into the situation...and it happens by entering into the presence of God. "It was too great an effort for me, and too painful...until I came into the sanctuary of God; Then I understood their end." In the presence of God, his perspective changed. He not only gained wisdom, and Godly perspective...but he began to realize his own bitterness and ignorance of soul...and that's when things began to change.

Asaph went on to ask, "Whom have I in heaven besides You?" The question was also the answer, because we know that we have NOTHING apart from the presence of God. Asaph realized that all the riches of this earth pale in comparison to the satisfaction of knowing God. He also came to understand that there is no lasting joy or satisfaction found outside of knowing Him. With this renewed perspective, all the worldly gain of the wicked becomes tiny, in comparison to knowing Him. All worldly happiness that is absent of God becomes fleeting and worthless.

We have all experienced the same sense of injustice at one point or another, as we observe things going well for those we esteem to be wicked. But these verses invite us in to a Godly perspective that shows us that we can find true value and reward in simply knowing God Himself.

Then we are reminded that that we do not have to depend on our own human faculties, for they will certainly fail us. But Christ is the Rock on which we can place our trust. He is enough! He is our Portion in this life.

We have the Lord's assurance that the sufferings of this present life cannot be compared to the glory that is about to be revealed to us, and IN us! And, we have a blessed hope that is anchored in Christ, as well as an inheritance that has been secured for us. Let us draw near to God, catching hold of His eternal perspective.

May we trust in His unfailing love with all our hearts. May we not allow the circumstances that surround us cause us to doubt the goodness of God.

And may we not allow our failures to define us, because the One that made us never makes mistakes! You are who you are...because He made you that way! You are perfect in His sight. He is your Portion...and that will always be enough!

The Door Of Rest Is Open To You

Hebrews 4:9 *"So there remains a full and complete Sabbath rest for the people of God."*

God has spoken it in His word and that is enough for us. We can take Him at His word and rely on it. It was unbelief that prevented Israel from enjoying the rest that God offered. That doesn't negate God's promise of rest, however. Believers in Christ are the ones who have entered into that rest. The word "entering" is the Greek word "eiserchomaetha" and it informs of a present ongoing action. It is a statement of present experience in which believers enjoy this position of rest. People enter in by recognizing that Christ's work of redemption has been completed. The invitation is for you to believe, "today". God has invited us to share in His presence.

Paul stated that it was the grace of God (His power working in us to do the things that we cannot do ourselves) that was the source of all that he had or could ever be. He fully depended upon that grace to have its full effect in his life through seeking Jesus continually. It is a labor of love but also a labor of the flesh to rest in the grace of God. We trust in and depend upon God's ability to work in and through us. We are aware of His presence in us, and we stand on His promises. When we are weak, we trust in His strength. When we are uncertain about which direction to go, we rely on the fact that His sheep hear His voice. Paul's confidence was in Christ. Ours should be as well.

We can make the choice to trust God and to be restored from things that have come against us. If we have been disappointed, deceived, hurt or even gone through great loss, we can and should expect restoration.

God is still true to His promises. His word abides forever. We enter into His rest because His promises still stand. Christ is seated at the right hand of the Father, and He is at rest. All who are in Christ are seated with Him in heavenly places. By faith, we rest in His word. We have entered into Christ, and Christ Jesus IS our rest. He is the Sabbath rest for His people.

There is a door of rest open to you today. The door is not shut. The time is not past. You have not missed a beautiful opportunity. Resting in God is a weapon. It is spiritual warfare to receive His promises, believe them, and stand in them. The door is open, beloved. The time is now.

54

Because Of Jesus, You Are MORE Than A Conqueror!

Romans 8:37 *"Nay, in all these things we are more than conquerors through Him that loved us"*

There is so much in this one verse that I could literally write a book...and I'm sure someone has! I want to focus though on who you are as a believer...because of Jesus. He has made you More Than A Conqueror! If you begin to read the verses leading up to, and following this verse, you will not only be amazed, you will be encouraged. The word of God is ALIVE with hope!

What was Paul referring to when he said that we are more than a conqueror "in all these things"? I believe he was literally saying that in whatever you may be going through in your life, you are MORE than a conqueror, as it is impossible for us as believers to be separated from or live without Christ in any way! A conqueror is someone who wins...someone who is victorious...someone who is a champion. This is how God sees you! When you are facing tribulation, when you are feeling distressed by the situation you may be in, when you have been persecuted, when you have experienced hunger, lack, or even threats of any kind, your God is on your side! He is for you! So I ask you...who or what, can come against you...when nothing, Nothing, NOTHING can separate you from His love! Sickness cannot separate you from His love. Death cannot separate you from His love. Nothing in life can separate you from His love. Nothing angelic or demonic can separate you from His love. Nothing today and nothing tomorrow can separate you from His love.

Beloved, it may at times not FEEL like you are more than a conqueror. But the word of God is alive and powerful...and it's true. It overrides those feelings of doubt and despair. It gives us something to stand on that is never shaky. When suffering comes, don't let it drive you away from God...but allow His love to penetrate your heart, knowing that it is because of that love, and the fact that He IS love, and He lives IN you...that you are MORE than a conqueror! You will never look at hardship in the same way if you are standing on the solid ground of the word of God!

We've Been Blessed With Every Spiritual Blessing

Numbers 13:23 *"Then they came to the valley of Eshcol (cluster of grapes). and from there cut down a branch with a single cluster of grapes; and they carried it on a pole between two of them, with some of the pomegranates and the figs."*

I read something recently that was so interesting. The fruit of the land in Egypt was cucumbers. melons, garlic, and onions. All of these grew on the ground. A person would have to bend and stoop to pick them. But the fruit in the promised land was pomegranates, grapes and figs. All of these hung from either trees or vines and were easy to pick. Harvesting fruit from Egypt had to have been backbreaking, but in the promised land, you could simply reach right up and pick it. It's a beautiful picture of the promises of God being so simple to partake of.

Knowing us better than we know ourselves, God was aware that seeing is believing. He wanted to give the Israelites a glimpse of their inheritance, as well as a taste. Like our spiritual ancestors, we are blessed with a beautiful foretaste of glory divine in the life and promises of the Lord Jesus. God also told the children of Israel that the land He would bring them into would have beautiful, large cities that they didn't have to build, and that there would be houses filled with good things that they didn't have to fill. He told them that there would be wells that they didn't have to dig and vineyards along with trees that they didn't have to dig or plant. This was all a picture of what God wanted for them.

He has always been a good Father. Today as well, He has given us so much. His heart has always been to bless His children. We have the name of Jesus, the Holy Spirit, the beautiful promises of God, the power that is in the blood, the armor of God, faith, the Word of God, the keys of the kingdom, the Spirit of power, love and a sound mind, and the gifts of the Spirit. We have been blessed with every spiritual blessing, and when we walk in those blessings, we are fully equipped to be the overcoming, more than enough, power filled Christians that God purposed for our lives.

When Moses sent the 12 spies in to evaluate the land, ten of the spies came back with a negative report. There were indeed giants in the land, but two out of the twelve spies, Joshua and Caleb, told the people not to fear them because, "they are our bread". They believed God. They believed His word. They believed in His faithfulness. They knew that He was with them.

56

Joshua and Caleb had a different spirit. They had a spirit of rest, and it was because their faith was not established on the giants they saw, but on the promises of God.

We face the same types of things today. There are giants in our land. But we have the promises of God. And just as the children of Israel were informed to go forth and take the land, God's promise has not changed for us today. Believe Him, beloved. Trust in His Word. Know that He will not leave you. Know that His love is unfailing and that He is calling you to simply rest in it.

But That Is No Concern Of Mine

2 Timothy 4:14 *"Alexander the coppersmith did me great harm; (but that is no concern of mine) for the Lord will repay him according to his actions."*

We have no way of knowing for sure if this is the same Alexander mentioned a couple of other times in the scripture, but one of those times was in 1 Timothy 1:20. When Paul spoke of this person, he said that "some people have made shipwreck of their faith", and then he mentioned Hymenaeus and Alexander, who he had handed over to Satan, so that they would be disciplined and taught not to blaspheme. Then in verse 15 of our passage, Paul warned Timothy to be on guard against Alexander because he had vigorously opposed Paul's message.

These are the words of someone who had been greatly hurt. And they are some of the last recorded words recorded, by the Apostle Paul. As he gave final instruction to his son in the faith, Timothy, he instructed him to be on guard, because of Alexander's vigorous opposition to his teaching. The word 'harm' is the Greek word *kakos*, which means "something evil or depraved". The word translated as "much" can mean "a large amount or something which occurs many times". Whatever Alexander had done was no small thing.

By cautioning Timothy, Paul was not dwelling on what had happened. He was simply relating a warning, something that Timothy needed to know. Paul was not throwing himself a pity party or trying to gain sympathy. He wasn't allowing bitterness or hatred to crawl into his heart. I get concerned that sometimes when we are explaining forgiveness to people, we make it sound as if we should just allow people to abuse us, but that is not the case.

What Paul did here in the second part of his statement was to release Alexander the coppersmith to God. Paul knew the great harm that had been done to him. He warned Timothy. Then he did the most amazing thing imaginable. He trusted God with the situation. I love the way the Amplified Bible states "but that is no concern of mine". Paul wasn't even concerned about HOW God would handle the situation. He just knew that He WOULD handle the situation. He stated that the "Lord will repay him according to his actions."

58

Living in the crazy world we live in, I can almost say with 100% certainty that every person reading this devotion has been hurt by someone.

We all have experienced the loss of trust with someone we thought would never fail us. Probably every one of us have had words spoken to us that were cruel, or words spoken about us that weren't even true. Whatever was done to Paul, was "something evil or depraved." It was no small thing. But Paul is the model for every one of us. He knew how to handle what had happened. He warned Timothy. Then he went to God with the situation.

Beloved, I don't know what kind of harm may have been done to you in your life. But I know how you can handle it. If there is a need to warn someone, do it quickly, the less words, the better. Then entrust the situation to the Lord. Pour your heart out to God. He is listening. He is trustworthy. He will never fail you. And He WILL repay, however that needs to be done. By allowing God to take over for you in the situation, it frees you up to go on with life, and continue to walk in the love, joy and peace that Jesus died for you to have. What an amazing God!

When You Know The Truth, You Will Certainly Be Set Free

John 8:32 *"Ye shall know the truth, and the truth shall make you free"*

Pilate had a problem. The Jewish leaders kept bringing Jesus Christ before him and demanding His crucifixion. He could not find any justification for it, but he needed to keep the peace between the Jewish people and the Roman government. Pilate's brief interrogation of Jesus brought little clarity to the problem because Pilate was viewing things from a human perspective while Jesus was operating on a spiritual level.

Pilate asked Him about the accusation that He claimed to be a king.

"You are right in saying I am a king," Jesus replied. "In fact, for this reason I was born, and for this I came into the world, to testify to the truth. Everyone on the side of truth listens to me."

Frustrated, Pilate responded with a common philosophical question of the day, "What is truth?"

Some things never change. For over 2000 years, mankind has asked, "What is the truth?" And, like Pilate, so many people have missed it (even though it was right in front of them) because they were asking the wrong question. The question is not *what* is truth, but rather *who* is truth.

Jesus made it amazingly simple for us. He said, "I am the way and the truth and the life." But instead of asking, "Who is truth?" we continue to echo Pilate's words, "What is truth?" When that is the question we are asking, we will continue to leave as empty-handed as Pilate.

Jesus is the source of all truth. He is dependably correct in all matters. He is the reality in which we stand firm. Since Jesus is the truth, He is the most reliable source for the truth. He began his teachings in the New Testament with the phrase, "I tell you the truth."

In that light, it's interesting to look at other scriptures related to truth and substitute Jesus' name:

"Show me your ways, O Lord, teach me your paths; guide me in your truth (*Jesus)* and teach me, for you are God my Savior, and my hope is in you all day long." (Psalm 25:4-5)
"The sum of Your word is truth (*Jesus*)" Psalm 119:160

"They perish because they refused to love the truth (*Jesus)* and so be saved." (2 Thessalonians 2:10b)

"This is good, and pleases God our Savior, who wants all men to be saved and to come to a knowledge of the truth (*Jesus*)." (1 Timothy 2:3-4)

Philosophical theories of truth often attempt to answer the "nature question": *What is the nature of truth?* Properly stated, it should be: *What is the nature of Jesus Christ?* People look to the stars or the hills for truth, but they are focused on creation instead of the Creator. People look to the world for truth, and only become more confused. Some look to themselves to find truth. In the worst cases, people look toward unholy spirits for guidance. But Jesus clearly said that He is "the truth," not "a truth," and followed it with "no man comes to the Father but by me."

That's why Paul warned the church, "So then, just as you received Christ Jesus as Lord, continue to live in him, rooted and built up in him, strengthened in the faith as you were taught, and overflowing with thankfulness. See to it that no one takes you captive through hollow and deceptive philosophy, which depends on human tradition and the basic principles of this world rather than on Christ." (Colossians 2:6-8)

Truth, according to the world, is relative or unobtainable. Jesus, however, is an absolute. He is present and He is faithful. He is the only way. Any other "path" to truth leads to destruction. But when you know The Truth, He will set you free.

Don't Fear Tomorrow. God Is Already There.

Exodus 14:13 *"Do not be afraid. Stand firm and see the deliverance the Lord will bring you today"*

I think my favorite word from the passage above is "today". I am so thankful for the fact that I was delivered at Calvary...and for the assurance of heaven one day, but it is so comforting...and what peace it brings to think about the deliverance that I can experience "today".

Whatever we are facing, small things to big, we can bring them to God...and He hears our prayers. He not only promises to comfort us...but He will sustain us and carry us as we go through whatever situation we are in. What a great lesson to learn that no matter what enemies are pursuing us, the Lord is mighty to save. God is our strength, and our stay...a very present help in time of trouble. What peace we often forfeit when we leave God out of the equation and try to address the issues of life on our own, instead of depending entirely on the word and the promises of God.

Billy Graham's daughter Ruth, recently wrote a book called, "Fear Not Tomorrow. God Is Already There". The title alone was comforting for me. Whatever tomorrow may bring for my life, God is already there. When tomorrow gets here, it will become "today". He was in my yesterdays...and He is most certainly with me now.

When we look too far ahead, it is easy to get overwhelmed and anxious...but remember that your future is just a series of..."todays"...and you have been promised His deliverance through each one. Knowing that, it is completely possible to overcome any fear that might try to work its' way into your mind.

Beloved, *Stand Firm.*

Is Your Prayer Life Controlled By Faith...Or By Sight?

James 5:17 *"Elijah was a man just like us"*

Thank God that Elijah was just like us! We can learn something from his life. He sat under a tree and complained to God, expressing his unbelief...as I'm guessing many of us have done. Sometimes it is difficult when we haven't seen the answer we are looking for. That verse continues, however. It says, "yet he prayed earnestly"...the literal meaning of that in the Greek simply means that "he prayed in prayer"...or in other words "He kept on praying". The lesson for us today is simply that we must keep praying as well.

When Elijah was on Mount Carmel, he had called down fire from heaven to defeat the prophets of Baal. Rain was needed for God's prophecy to be fulfilled. The Bible says that Elijah bent down toward the ground and put his face between his knees. I think he was literally shutting out all the sights and sounds around him. He put himself in a position to not be able to see or hear anything...but GOD!

He told his servant to go and look toward the sea, to see if the needed rain was coming, but when the servant returned, he told Elijah that he saw nothing there...NOTHING! Beloved, how often have you prayed, and then and then waited, but saw NOTHING? Can you imagine what most of us would do under the same circumstances? Many of us would give up, thinking this was just what we expected! Elijah, however, had a different expectation...and even though he didn't see the answer yet, he DID NOT give up! In fact, six times, he told his servant to go back and check again.

Each time, the servant returned saying there was "nothing". Yet the seventh time, the servant came back with the report that there was a small cloud, the size of a man's hand rising from the sea. What a perfect description, for a man's hand had been raised in prayer to God before the rains came! Then the sky became black and the rains came in abundance! (You can read this story in I Kings 18...)

This is a story of faith and sight...faith that cuts itself off from everything else, except God...and yet sight...that sees nothing. But in spite of hopeless reports time and again received from sight...faith continued!

Do we prevail in prayer? Even when things seem darkest, do we let our prayer life be controlled by sight?

OR...do we by FAITH, continue prevailing in prayer, coming boldly before the throne, pouring our heart, and our need out to a God who hears...and who cares?

Which report will we believe...the report that sight produces, which is often nothing...or the continued prodding that faith produces...to not give up...to continue on no matter what? May we all be people who live by faith. No matter what your needs are today child of God, DO NOT give up! Continue in faith and watch as God pours into your life!

You Already Have God's Approval

Colossians 3:3 *"For you died to this world, and your new life is hidden with Christ in God."*

So often, as born-again believers, we find it difficult to understand our identity, as a child of God. Our focus tends to land on what we believe about our worth...or what we believe to be deficient thereof. This lack of true understanding can lead to feelings of oppression, feeling powerless, having no sense of direction or purpose, difficulty making decisions, and even loss in the ability to dream, or to have hope in your life. We may feel condemned after making even the slightest mistake...and then fall into the pattern of trying repeatedly to earn God's approval.

What so many don't understand is that you already have God's approval! At salvation, you were transformed in your spirit...and you were made righteous in the eyes of God. How did that happen? It's because now you are IN Christ! Your righteousness doesn't depend on you! It is totally based on the finished work of Jesus at the cross! This is good news!

Something else happened at salvation that I want to explain. You died to this world. When Jesus died on the cross, we died with Him. We are His seed. And any issue of sin in our lives was settled at this point. We were eternally redeemed. We were bought with a price...the precious blood of Christ. Because the Lord Jesus died, we who are His seed died also. Christ's finished work in the past, is what has given us a future. Jesus was raised from the dead...and we are in union with His life, forever hidden in Him. We possess eternal life because when the Lord was raised, we who are in Him, and are His seed, were raised with Him, into newness of life!

You can Not out-sin the grace of God! When you are His child, you have been made new! You have a new identity. The Bible says if any man is in Christ, he is a new creature...a new creation! You are not just reformed or rehabilitated. You have been made completely new and you are living in union with Christ! Your righteousness is a free and beautiful gift. Accept it! Live in it!

Learn To Let Go Of Your Own Plans - And Trust His

1Kings 17:6 *"and the ravens brought him bread and flesh in the morning, and bread and flesh in the evening, and he drank of the brook..."*

The Old Testament prophet Elijah had just confronted the King who worshiped Baal...and now The Lord had spoken to Elijah to hide himself by a brook called Cherith. There, God had commanded the ravens to bring him food, morning and evening....and he was able to drink water from the brook. God's provision is amazing to me. In a nation that was required by law to care for its prophets, it's interesting that God used ravens (unclean animals) to care for Elijah...but God has help where and when we least expect it. He can provide for us in ways that we would never be able to imagine!

It happened that eventually, the brook dried up, because there had been no rain in the land. When that happened, The Lord spoke to Elijah to arise, and to leave that place. God had something else in mind for Elijah...a new plan...and He sent him to a widow woman who cared for him. I have wondered a couple of times...what would have happened if Elijah hadn't listened to God? What if he had simply decided that his own plan was better...or that God's plan didn't make sense so he would go his own way? What if he had stayed where he was? Having sat next to a dry brook or two in my life, I know how difficult change can be.

Most change really isn't bad. It's just that we become accustomed to our life the way it is...and to shake things up a bit, just isn't in our plan. Some of the most difficult times we experience can be in some of the simplest things...moving from one house to another...changing jobs...meeting new people...but these can also be some of the most rewarding things!

Years ago, my husband and I began to know that it was time for us to move forward in our lives, and to leave some of the people we loved most in the world. We knew that The Lord was calling us out from where we were. We knew that He wanted us to sit at His feet. We knew that He wanted a deeper relationship with us...and we knew that these things wouldn't happen if we stayed where we were.

Some folks ridiculed us. Some tried to persuade us to stay. All thought we were crazy...but we knew that we were hearing from The Lord.

Beloved, God has a beautiful plan for your life...as well as a purpose. Sometimes however, the plan of God doesn't seem to make sense. Sometimes it isn't the popular thing among friends. Sometimes it doesn't unfold in such a way that you can see every step...but if you'll trust Him...you will begin to see that His purpose for you is much greater than you might have imagined. When Elijah was sitting by the brook, being fed by the ravens, I wonder if he could have imagined that God was going to use him to provide food for a widow woman...or that he would have the privilege to pray for a young man who had died, and to see that man come back to life.

Much of the time, we cannot see what lies ahead, and it just seems easier to stay in our comfort zones.

I encourage you today...if you have begun to sense the nudge in your heart from the Holy Spirit, that it's time for something to change...pay attention. Is there an area in your life that has simply "dried up"? Is God speaking to you that it's time to move on? Is there something that used to hold a great deal of joy for you, that has now become only what is expected? I know change can be difficult...but when you get to the other side of whatever it is that God is speaking to you about...you will begin to know and understand what the purpose was in the change...and you will enjoy getting to know The Lord in an even deeper way. Your trust in God will grow, as you realize you are letting go of your own ideas, and are trusting His. You will be less affected by the opinions of others, as you learn that God can fully speak to YOU about your life. Wherever it is that He is taking you...do not fear. He is going with you! Ask Him to prepare your heart for the journey...and remember Psalm 16..."thou wilt show me the path of life...in thy presence is fullness of joy...at thy right hand, there are pleasures forevermore."

God's Love Never Gives Up On Us

1 Corinthians 13:4-8 *"Love suffers long and is kind; love does not envy; love does not boast or parade itself, it is not puffed up. It does not behave rudely, does not seek its own, is not provoked, thinks no evil; does not rejoice in iniquity, but rejoices in the truth; bears all things, believes all things, hopes all things, endures all things. Love never fails."*

The Apostle John told us that God IS love. We could insert His beautiful name into this verse and see that GOD suffers long and is kind. GOD does not envy. GOD does not boast and is not puffed up. GOD does not behave rudely; GOD does not seek His own, is not provoked, thinks no evil. GOD does not rejoice in iniquity but rejoices in truth. GOD bears all things, believes all things, hopes all things, endures all things. GOD never fails.

Now that is pretty eye opening. The word "love" in these passages is the Greek word *agape*, It is a love that surpasses the type of worldly love that we have seen demonstrated in Hollywood. A lot of that is not love. It's lust. The love that God demonstrates never gives up on someone. It lays down its' own life. It's longsuffering, or patience, holds firmly through great difficulty. Love is slow to anger. It endures personal wrongs without retaliation. It bears up under the imperfections, faults and differences of others.

Kindness is patience, in action. Someone who is kind seeks out and looks for opportunities to meet the needs of others, without repayment. Someone who is kind, is also tender and forgiving. It is the kindness of God that leads men to repentance. Kindness motivates others toward positive change.
Selfless love is not jealous. It doesn't brag and is not arrogant. Someone who is jealous might want what others have. He might not applaud the success of others. He might like to have all the attention. But a selfless love is one that wants to see someone else succeed. It's a love that encourages and builds up those around us. It's a love that is not rude and does not needlessly offend others. It is sensitive to the feelings and needs of people. It is tactful and courteous. Selfless love does not seek its' own. It does not demand its' own way. I heard someone say once that if we cured selfishness, we could plant a garden of Eden. Selfishness (or self-centeredness) is probably the root problem of the human race. But laying down our need to be right is what could change marriages, breathe new life into relationships, and bring hope to the world.

Selfless love is not provoked. It isn't touchy. It doesn't hold people hostage. It is a love that lets go of a wrong suffered. It is used of God, not imputing guilt to us, but instead imputing righteousness to our account. Selfless love doesn't keep a tally of wrongs done until every one is paid for. It doesn't remind the other person of past wrongs. Love is never glad when others do wrong. Love rejoices in truth. It gets excited over the victories of others. It expresses joy over the growth of the people around it.

Love doesn't broadcast the problems of others. It defends their character whenever possible. It will not lie about weaknesses. Love will always protect. It is not pessimistic. It refuses to take any kind of failure as final. It rests on the promises of God. Love is wholly directed to the other person. This is the way that God loves...and if we want to love one another, we must focus on His love for us. It will change our lives forever.

Are You Convinced Yet?

Song of Solomon 1:4B *"We will rejoice and be glad in you; We will remember and extol your love more than wine."*

The Song of Solomon is a beautiful story in the Word of God. It's a story of overcoming. It's a story of a deep, overwhelming, nearly indescribable love...an agape love that is perfect, it is fearless, and it opens the heart of men to understand the love of God in a much more intimate way. It's a story that involves us, because every one of us is represented by the Shulamite woman in the story. Inspired by the Holy Spirit, it was written to bring change to us, to remind us of the truth that we are deeply cherished, and to bring transformation to the heart of the believer.

Jesus Christ is revealed as the heavenly bride groom. He is the LOVE of God, made man. We are the greatly loved by Jesus in this story. Learning to walk in true intimacy and tenderness with Him is so greatly gratifying. We are the Shulamite and Jesus is the King. He is OUR King. The Hebrew word for Solomon and the Hebrew root word for Shulamite are one and the same word. One is masculine while the other is feminine. When you believe and follow Christ, according to John 17:21, you are one with Him.

We are the bride of Christ. And Jesus prepares His bride by convincing her of His love for her, even in her weakness. You will not find any angry expectations here, and no disappointment at her failures. Jesus does not shame us into maturity. He loves us into the fullness of our destiny. I've heard it described that He puts a crown upon our head, and then watches as we grow up to fit into that crown.

The love of our Lord engulfs us and meets us at each step of our own journey. We may go through trials, but His strong arms of love carry us. It's as if we are deeply immersed...in the safety of His love! His desire to see us perfected in His love brings strength in the most trying situation. In the story of the Song of Solomon, the Shulamite fails Him...and we do too sometimes, but nothing can diminish the love of our groom for us. Even when we have fallen short in some way, the love of Jesus passionately pursues us. It's a love that sustains us. It's the story of ages...the greatest love story ever told. And it will change our concept of Who God is, and how much He loves us.

As our love for our groom develops and the intimacy with Him matures, we learn that any walls that we've built, that might have brought separation from the One Who loves us, must come down.

We can no longer hide behind a wall of wrong feelings about ourselves, or about Him. Jesus is our companion and His love for us will flood our hearts with overwhelming joy for all eternity. We need to fill our minds with the truth of how God sees us. People may judge us by our greatest weaknesses. God sees the glory of His Son shining in and through us.

You may look in the mirror and see the imperfections. You may go through your day and wish you were braver, stronger, more beautiful. But remember, that He sees you as perfect. Hide that truth in your heart today and go forward believing that you are completely flawless...perfect in His eyes!

You Are Rooted In Christ - And He Has Blessed You With Life Giving Strength

Colossians 2:10 *"and ye are complete in Him, which is the head of all principality and power."*

From the moment you were born again, reborn into the kingdom of God...your life changed. The Bible says that you became new...a new creation. You became complete. You are whole. You have everything you need to live and walk in victory in this life. There is no lack!
If you look up that word "complete" in the Greek, it means to be full, to cause to abound, to be liberally supplied, or to fill to the top so that nothing can be added. You are literally overflowing in the goodness and the blessings of God! You lack nothing that you need for life. Oh, you may FEEL as though you are missing something, but the word of God states emphatically that you have been made complete. In Christ dwells all the fullness of God...and you are in Christ! Amazing!
In Christ, you have been made free. You are not under the law, but you are IN Him! All of the promises of God in Christ are ALREADY yes and amen! You have been forgiven. You stand before Him... faultless. You've been redeemed by His blood, and you are accepted. You have been adopted. You were chosen by Him. You are His child, His beloved. He has blessed you with wisdom and with understanding. Your hope is fully in Him, and it is an anchor that keeps you steady in times of trial. You have received an inheritance...and you were sealed with the Holy Spirit...
Paul's prayer for you was powerful. He prayed that the Father would give to you the spirit of wisdom and revelation in the knowledge of Him. He prayed that the eyes of your understanding would be enlightened...and that you would know the hope of His calling and the riches of the glory of this inheritance. He prayed that you would know the power given to you...the same power that raised Christ from the dead! This was indeed a power filled prayer!
If you are in a battle of any kind, remember who He has made you to be. You are not weak. You are not without strength. You don't have to live in depression or discouragement. The promises of God are yours.
You can walk in peace and joy. You can be at rest, not because of anything you do...but because of what Jesus has done. He is the Head over all principality and power. As a plant draws nourishment from the soil through its roots, we are rooted in Christ...and we draw life giving strength...from Him.
Knowing Christ...and who you have been made to be IN Him...is what you stand on when dealing with any kind of battle. He is your unique Source of wisdom and power...and you are complete...in Him!

Look Past What You May Be Going Through - And See Into Your Situation With Spiritual Eyes

2 Corinthians 4:18 *"what is seen is temporary, but what is unseen is eternal."*

Wow! That is powerful. Think about it! The things that we can see with our physical eyes are all temporary. They won't always be here...but the things that we can't physically see...are eternal. They are never ending...timeless.

It may seem right now to you that the season you are in will never end. It may look from where you sit, like this is an ongoing situation that could last forever...but it WILL pass. It IS temporary. Your life is NOT defined by whatever circumstance you are facing. It is defined by God. It is defined by Who He says you are.

Have you ever been to a corn maze in the fall? It's a lot of fun, with the rows and paths that seem to stretch out endlessly, and seem to be taking you closer to the end. But those paths can be misleading. Finding the way through is both fun and frustrating. Sometimes life can feel that way. You're looking for the right way – the way that will take you to the goal. You believe you've figured this out. You jump up and down to try to see over the top of all the high rows of corn. You're sure the next turn is the one that will get you to the exit – but when you take it, you realize you're right back where you started. There are more paths, more twists and turns, and more decisions! Whew! The idea of enduring something without there being an end could overwhelm anyone...but the optimum perspective is the one taken from above. God sees the beginning as well as the end. He knows every twist and turn. Wisdom speaks through His word...and His word stresses emphatically that when you trust Him with all of your heart...when you don't lean on your own understanding or what you might think you know...when you acknowledge Him...He WILL direct your path. You don't have to rely on what you see to direct you through life. You can rely on the Eternal One Who will never fail you.

Don't give in to weakness by dwelling on what you see today. Look through it. Look past it...and see into your situation with spiritual eyesight. What a beautiful vision!

73

Let's Learn To Honor The Ancient Boundaries God Set In Our Midst

Proverbs 22:28 *"Do not move an ancient boundary stone set up by your forefathers"*

The context of this Proverb is also found in Deuteronomy 19:14, as well as Proverbs 23:10. The concern is the infringement on another's land that would be unjust, especially that of the fatherless. Injustice is something that God hates, the oppression of the helpless and weak by the strong. Sadly, it's not only the world that is guilty of this, but the church as well.

Boundary stones were used to mark out land and fields. When they entered the land, they placed boundary stones to mark the lands each would possess. Their forefathers established these boundaries, and they were not to be changed, especially when they were changed to take advantage of someone unable to defend their rights or land.

When we as the church fail to see the hurting and needy among us, we are crossing into what Solomon warns of here. When we want more personal visibility and prominence at the cost of someone else being pushed further "back" we are overstepping and actually moving a boundary. When we are only impressed with the prominent and strong, and fail to see the vulnerable and weak, we should be conscience stricken of what Solomon is talking about. When we are "super star" and "super ministry" driven, when we run here and there seeking the next great "move of God", and fail to appreciate and honor those who labor faithfully among us without any fanfare, we are in danger of not discerning the ancient boundaries.

Paul encourages the Corinthians to give "greater honor" to the "less seemly" members. When the church functions as a business or as a worldly enterprise rather than as a community and spiritual family, we run the risk of moving ancient boundaries. Paul says, "The parts that we think are less honorable, we treat with special honor. And the parts that are not presentable are treated with special modesty, while our presentable parts need no special treatment. But God has combined the members of the body and has given greater honor to the parts that lacked it..."

Living a life for ourselves is contrary to the heart of God. We truly need one another. We are an integral part of something incredible. We have all been given an inheritance, the Holy Spirit being the deposit.

We honor Him when we honor one another. Let that be our heart and desire in this day. Let's break away from the world's values and pattern that have been so embraced by the church in the western world, and let's pray that a genuine honor for each member will in fact be more and more evident in our churches. Let's learn to love the ancient boundaries that God by His Holy Spirit has set in our midst.

First and Last

Genesis 26:33 "And Jacob said to Esau (his brother), 'Swear to me this day...and Esau swore to him...and sold his birthright unto Jacob.'"

Just this week, I heard someone teach on this verse, and for me, it was life changing! I have read this passage many times and did not fully understand the significance of it. Jacob and Esau were twins. Esau was born first and the custom in that day was for the oldest male child to receive a double portion of the inheritance. One day, Esau came in from the field hungry, as Jacob had been in the kitchen, cooking a pot of soup. Esau commented that his birthright was really of no profit to him, and he sold it that day to Jacob...for a bowl of soup. This was no small thing! Esau's birthright included the future possession of the land of Canaan by his children's children, and the covenant made with Abraham. Believing Jacob valued these things. But unbelieving Esau despised them.

As born-again children of God who are in Christ, we have also received an inheritance...a birthright. We have been made righteous. We are not under the law, but under Christ, who IS grace. Nothing can separate us from the love of God. We've been given love, joy and peace. We've been given strength, and healing belongs to us. We were chosen, and we've been adopted into the family of God. He sees us as holy and without blame. We are His workmanship, brought near to Him by the blood of Christ. This is only a small part of our inheritance.

This week as I was thinking about this verse and what it means to sell or give away your birthright, I had an opportunity arise to worry about how a situation in my life might turn out. The minute I started to think about all of the what ifs...the Lord spoke to me. He reminded me that peace is part of my inheritance...but that it's up to me to choose it. And I realized that I would never want to exchange my birthright for worry. That was it for me. I was free. And I chose not to worry again about the circumstance.

Saints, worry is NOT part of your inheritance! Peace is! Fear and doubt are not part of your inheritance. Do not allow temptation to knock at the door of your heart and then persuade you to give away what Jesus died for you to have!

Esau was the firstborn but gave away his birthright for a bowl of soup. There was another firstborn Son. This Son came for all of us…to give us back our birthright. He came that we would have life in abundance. He is the First and the Last, and I want to walk fully in what He died for me to have. Who's with me?

Where The Word Of The King Is, There Is Power

Matthew 8:3 *"Jesus reached out His hand and touched him, saying 'I am willing; be cleansed.' Immediately his leprosy was cleansed."*

Most of us are familiar with the healing of the leper in Matthew 8. It is a beautiful account of God's willingness to touch and heal the sick, no matter how unclean they may be. Whenever we doubt God's willingness to heal us, we should listen to the words of Jesus again: "I am willing; be cleansed." He is the same yesterday, today, and forever!

Since the Bible is clear about God's willingness to heal, why do we still have problems with our health? Why do we still experience symptoms in our bodies?
I believe that the answer is found in what Jesus told the leper to do next. He told him to go and show himself to the priest. (Matthew 8:4) This was the law then for lepers who were healed. (Leviticus 14:2-3) And he was to hear the priest pronounce the word clean over him. (Leviticus 14:7)

You see, as believers, when we received Jesus, His blood cleansed us from sin as well as sickness. (Isaiah 53:4-5) But we keep hearing people pronounce sin, sickness, poverty and death over us. We keep hearing people tell us that we are unclean, undeserving, poor, weak, and that it is only natural that we grow old and sickly, and then die. God is waiting for a priesthood that will rise up and pronounce His people clean!
Where can we find such a priest?

Who are the priests today? You and I! In fact, we have more authority to pronounce good things than the Levitical priests of the Old Testament. They were just priests. But we are king-priests by the blood of Jesus! (Revelation 1:5-6) Where the word of the king is, there is power. (Ecclesiastes 8:4) And by the word of a priest, every controversy and every assault shall be settled. (Deuteronomy 21:5)

Beloved, God has cleansed you, so pronounce yourself clean! Right now, put your hand on your heart and pronounce good things over yourself. Say, "I pronounce myself clean, righteous, healed, whole and abundantly supplied by the blood of Jesus!" By your word as a king-priest, every assault against you shall be settled!

Step Out In Faith And Believe God

Proverbs 29:25 *"The fear of man bringeth a snare; but whoso putteth his trust in The Lord shall be made safe."*

Every verse in the Bible is alive with power and hope...but this one in particular really speaks to me. I believe it is because I have struggled in this area. I grew up shy and wanting people to like me. I still don't like to disappoint anyone or let them down. This at times has been to my own detriment.

Several times over the years, when I believed that God was speaking to me about a direction for my life, I would go to speak with someone I trusted to confirm what I was hearing. On several occasions, I was talked out of taking the path that I believed I should take. On most of these occasions, the person I'd gone to would cast a new vision for me...and I would follow it, not trusting that I had heard from God. I am not saying that we shouldn't get advice or confirmation from someone we trust. What I am saying is that God speaks to each of us. And He may not be speaking to the people in our lives about His purpose for you or for me.

I've had a few broken hearts over the years, as the Lord attempted to lead me, but I didn't trust that I could hear from Him. What I was really dealing with was a fear of man...not wanting to let anyone down...as well as a trust issue. I'm so thankful that He has taught me that those who put their trust in Him will be made safe. And I Praise God that He is the Restorer of dreams, once lost!

Several years ago, I met someone who shared his dream with me. He had stepped out in faith, in what seemed to me to be a nearly impossible endeavor...but he was convinced that he had heard from The Lord. He shared with me that he had come to a point in his life where he simply had to do what He believed God had laid on his heart, even when it didn't make sense to anyone, even if he had to stand alone, even if it meant leaving some behind...even if it meant laying down his life.

I was so struck by what he said to me that day...and then...as sweetly as one can imagine...the Lord spoke to me. He simply reminded me that His sheep hear His voice. He didn't relate to me that certain sheep hear His voice, or that only pastors hear His voice, or that only those in ministry hear His voice. He said, "My sheep hear My voice."

I cannot tell you how life changing that was! I knew that I was one of His sheep. And I recognized the precious voice of my Shepherd.

We cannot choose to follow man, believing that every way that a man leads will be the right way. We must follow Christ. Period.

Much of the time, I don't think we even realize what we are doing...and I'm certainly not against getting some wise counsel. But I want every one of you to know...that God DOES speak to you. If you read the book of Acts, you will see how the Holy Spirit led people, and even stopped them at times if the situation warranted. This is how it should be in the life of a believer.

The fear of man brings a snare, beloved. A snare is like a trap...and it can hold you to where you feel unable to move in any direction...and worse...you can't see your way out.

Is there something that God has been speaking to you about? Is there a longing in your heart in a certain direction that you have a real passion for? And are you making decisions based on His leading or on what might be favorable with man? My encouragement to you is simply, "whoso putteth his trust in The Lord shall be made safe." The voice of our Shepherd is the One that we want to heed and follow. And when we do, even when things seem impossible...even when they don't make sense...even when we can't see the outcome...even when we must go alone...we can trust in His leading, and in His promise. Follow Christ beloved. You will never regret it.

God Has Dealt To Each One The Measure Of Faith

Romans 12:3 *"God has dealt to each one the measure of faith"*

As children of God, we should never believe for a moment that we don't have any faith, or that our faith is lacking in some way, or that someone else has been given more than we have been given. To think this would be to think God a liar...because His Word tells us that God has dealt to each one of us the measure of faith. This verse is pretty clear. We have all received the same measure. Why then, do some people seem to have so much faith, while others seem to have very little?

Faith is like a muscle. All of us are born with a measure of muscles. Some of us develop them better than others. Some exercise and their muscles become stronger. Others are more sedentary and their muscles atrophy. Likewise, our faith grows stronger when we use it. It also grows stronger when we feed it. Any time that we read or hear God's word, we are feeding our faith. When we begin to confess His Word out of our mouths, and believe it as being true, our faith grows deeper.

Beloved, you have been given faith. God gave it to each of us. God does not play favorites. He doesn't give out a large measure to one person, and then cheat someone else. That would just not be in the character or nature of God.   Start using your faith, believing that it is this measure of faith that causes you to draw from the inexhaustible power of a faithFULL and loving God!

A Cord Of Three Strands Is Not Easily Broken

Ecclesiastes 4:12 *"Though one may be overpowered, two can defend themselves. A cord of three stands is not quickly broken."*

When you have been in a good relationship, you realize the deep importance of intimacy. We were created to need each other.

The actual Hebrew doesn't say "three strands", but simply *three*. The meaning is that three smaller cords twisted together bring greater strength. Three smaller cords are stronger than two cords twisted together by themselves. The picture is powerful. We need each other. We need God,

Everything we achieve in life, every blessing that God pours out, we want to share with the people closest to us. When or if a relationship were to fail, we would definitely sense the loss of that relationship.

This verse offers the key to maintaining successful relationships In any friendship, or marriage, when we have Jesus as the center, when He lives in both our hearts, we have a cord of three strands. We need to be more intentional about inviting Jesus into our time spent with friends, and ultimately, we need Him as a permanent part of our marriages. He is the strand in the three-cord strand that cannot be quickly broken. We need that third strand. We need Him to bridge any communication gaps, to break any ties that are at an impasse, and even to help us in ways that we feel are falling short in regards to our relationships. He is the One who takes our meager offerings in a relationship and works His loaves and fishes miracle to make sure that everyone is nourished and satisfied.

From my perspective, I can't really see how any relationship can survive without that third strand. Invite Him today into your marriage, your friendships, and become aware of the fact that He is there. You will have a new sense in your relationships of the strength that comes with a three-cord strand, that cannot easily be broken.

Our Hope Is In The God Of Quiet Strength

2 Corinthians 4:8 *"We are troubled on every side, but not crushed; perplexed but not driven to despair, hunted down and persecuted, but not deserted; struck down but not destroyed"*

And we are never without hope. If you look up the word "hope" in the Hebrew, it means a "quiet strength". In this world that is so full of hopelessness, we as believers not only worship and trust a God of "quiet strength", but He has filled US with it as well.

You can't turn on the news right now without hearing about all of the bad reports. I won't even give credit to any of it by naming it. We have to ask ourselves daily whose report will we believe? God's report reminds us that we can trust Him in ALL things. He tells us to trust Him with all our heart, and not to lean on our own understanding. He says that we are MORE than conquerors through Him. And as the above verse reminds us, we might be troubled on every side, but we are NOT crushed.

One of the most rewarding things I ever got to be part of was a Purity Seminar years ago. The coordinator of this event was a dear friend of mine, and she said one of the wisest, yet simplest things to this young group of women that she was ministering to. She told them to make the decision NOW to honor God with their lives. That way, when they were tempted in any way, their decision was already made. These precious young women began to consider all of the things they were facing in life, and nearly all of them that day decided to believe God, to trust Him, to take Him at His word. When they were troubled on every side in the future, when they were perplexed, persecuted, or pressured, they would already KNOW that they didn't have to make decisions at a point of weakness. Their decision was already made. They would follow Christ!

Beloved, we should never give ourselves the freedom to doubt God. We should never give ourselves the ability in any way to waver. We can make a decision NOW that in the most difficult trial, we will choose to believe God. Decision made!

It is easy to fall into the habit of doubt, worry, and even fear. Let us refuse to give in... AHEAD of time! We do not ever need to experience confusion. We are women who have decided to believe God. Our hope is in the God of "quiet strength". And as we trust Him, the scriptures remind us that He will be with us, He will fight our battles, and we will be victorious!

We Have Been Declared Righteous!

John 16:8 *"And He, when He comes, will convict the world about sin, and about righteousness, and about judgment."* 2 Corinthians 5:21 *"For He made Him who knew no sin to be sin for us, that we might become the righteousness of God, in Him."*

The Holy Spirit is not condemning us, or convicting us of sin. He is actually doing quite the opposite. He is convicting the world of sin...but He has said that as believers, we have been made righteous! This righteousness is not something that we have earned or worked to obtain. It is an inheritance. Because we are in Christ, we have been declared righteous. I John 5:18 says "we know that whosoever is born of God sinneth not..." Are you born of God? Then you are kept, held, stayed...by faith in righteousness, both HIS, and YOURS!

This is based on our faith in Jesus finished work, not our own works...not the things we attempt to do to make ourselves right with God. Because of Jesus, we are already right with God! When we are working to obtain the blessings of God and increase His favor on our lives, we are actually trusting more in our own works than we do the finished work of Jesus. It is a tiring daily effort to attempt to manage an endless inventory of moral uprightness, in order to please God...when in fact, God is already pleased with us...and we are complete in Him.

It is the job of the Holy Spirit to bring out the treasure that you are and were made to be...to reveal to you the love of God for you, to show you that you are perfect in His eyes, to reveal your amazing gifts, and to allow you to see that there isn't another "you" anywhere in the world. You are unique and amazing!

Don't listen to those who would try to persuade you to believe differently. No matter how sincere a person's intention may be, anyone seeking righteousness by works is actually rejecting the righteousness of Christ. When you trust in His righteousness, you will begin to believe in, and live out the amazing plan that God has for you.

It Is Our Faith That Overcomes The World

1 John 5:4 *"For everyone born of God is victorious and overcomes the world; and this is the victory that has conquered and overcome the world - our (continuing, persistent) faith (in Jesus, the Son of God)."*

John explains so well what it means to overcome the world. It is our *faith* that overcomes the world. But faith must have an object. There must be something (or someone) that we have faith IN. The object of our faith is Jesus Christ. It is our faith in the Person and even the work of the Lord Jesus that gains victory over the world, and the things of the world. It is trusting in the death, burial and resurrection of Christ as our Savior, not only for the forgiveness of sins, but also to bring life in abundance. It is an everlasting life that overcomes the world.

It's our identification with Jesus and His finished work by faith, that causes us to be overcomers. Remember that Jesus Himself told us, "these things I have spoken unto you, that in Me, ye might have peace. In the world, ye shall have tribulation; but be of good cheer... I have overcome the world." Hallelujah! Jesus overcame the world! And we are in Christ! We are overcomers as well! As members of Christ's body, by faith, we are loved and accepted by the Father. And we have overcome the ungodly world system that is saturated with the unthinkable and seeks to entrap us in its many temptations and enticements.

The life of a believer can be a bit like an immigrant living in a foreign land. As believers, we live here on earth, but our citizenship is in heaven. The believer will appear different, act differently, and have a different mindset than the culture he/she is living in, because this is not our permanent home. We are anticipating a glorious reunion in our homeland with our family. But once the truth is enthroned in our hearts, and completely believed, that Jesus truly is the Son of God, our attitudes toward this world begin to change. We see the world as He sees it. We see the need for a lost and dying people to know the truth, and to be set free and delivered from the kingdom of darkness. We begin to know the genuine love of Christ for the unbeliever, and we want to be the arms and legs and mouthpiece and heart of God to those who don't yet know Christ, so that they too will have life everlasting.

God has given us all we need to live an overcoming life in Christ. Our faith overcomes the enslaving power of the world to try to rule in our lives. It breaks the spell of the world's allurement. And it leads us into obedience with freedom and joy. The blinders have fallen off beloved, and we see things for what they truly are. Let us live for His honor and glory always. For He alone is Worthy.

Peace Is Not The Absence of Problems. It Is The Presence Of God

Philippians 4:7 *"The peace of God, which transcends all understanding, will guard your hearts and minds in Christ Jesus"*

Several years ago, I found myself in the hospital after having experienced a very serious, life threatening illness. I remember sitting up in my bed as they came and shared the news with me that I would need to have surgery the next day. Everyone around me seemed to be in a panic. The news that had been revealed to me wasn't good. And yet, in the midst of it all, I was experiencing the peace that passes all understanding. By the world's standards, there would be no reason for the calm that I was experiencing...but as a child of God, we do not live by the world's standards. We choose to believe God. We stand on what we know to be truth...and we know that we are in His very capable hands.

The unlimited, indefinable peace of God does not come to us via our own effort. We cannot relax or meditate ourselves into the depths of this peace. We cannot mandate it by managing our own circumstances. We cannot "will it" by virtue of sheer desire. We cannot think our way into it with our intellect. We cannot orchestrate it with our vast skills. We cannot obtain it with our finances. We cannot steal it from anyone's possession...but it can be ours...simply by believing.

I've heard it said that it isn't the water that surrounds a boat that can sink it. It is the water that gets inside that can take a huge vessel and with an unthinkable force, bring the ship to the bottom of the ocean. In the same way, the situations that are going on around you cannot take you down, if what is IN you is the presence, and the power of God.

This peace is so evident when everything is falling around you, and yet you have a sure and steady stillness at your core. In the chaos you have more clarity than in so-called ordinary times. When everything is moving, it becomes easy to focus on the one thing that remains unshakable. I've learned that peace is not the absence of problems. It is the presence of God.

When you finally recognize peace as the presence of Christ, you will never want anything else.

Come Into Agreement With God And See Your Life Change

Mark 4:16-17 *"And some are like the seed that lands in the gravel. When they first hear the Word, they respond with great enthusiasm. But there is such a shallow soil of character that when the emotions wear off and some difficulty arrives, there is nothing to show for it."*

It is meditating in the word of God that will transform your life. Think about that caterpillar that gets transformed into a butterfly. It is similar when we soak in the scriptures. They will change our life by changing us, from the inside out. We can be surrounded with difficult circumstances, but when we are completely convinced about Who Jesus is, as well as who we have become in Him, it changes our hearts. It changes our walk with Him. It changes the way we see others. It changes our future.

So often, we get excited about new things, especially new spiritual undertakings. However, sometimes when the going gets tough, we can become discouraged and give up. And often as a new believer, people will find themselves in a clash of culture, as the values of the Kingdom conflict with the values of the world around them. At times, the world around a new believer tends to push back. At times, it is ridicule. At times, rejection. Often, it is blatant persecution, especially from those who have known us for a long time.

Renewing our minds to understand and come into agreement with God's word is the answer. Moving into a new place in our hearts, where we cannot be moved from what, and WHO we have come to believe is essential. So often, I've seen some precious new believer placed into ministry, when they are sincerely seeking the Lord, but simply haven't grown strong enough yet in their belief system to be able to handle all of the possible situations that can easily arise. This can and does result in fruitlessness.

If you took a seed and planted it in shallow ground, it would indeed germinate, and it would probably grow rather quickly. In fact, it would grow faster than a seed planted in deeper soil. A seed that has been planted in deeper soil will take all its energy and direct it toward the root first. The seed planted in the shallower ground doesn't have a choice. It directs its best effort into the growth of the plant that you can see above the ground.

It works the same way in the lives of people who are born into the kingdom of God.

The plant that has grown in the shallow soil will seem to far outgrow the plant that is growing in deeper soil. But here's the difference. The plant growing in the shallow soil will not last. It will quickly begin to whither and eventually will die. The seed planted in the deeper soil will sustain life, grow to maturity and bear fruit!

Some believers simply make the mistake of not getting firmly planted in the truth of God's word before jumping in with both feet. Then, the person's faith wanes when troubles arise. We must grow and live from personal depth in the Word of God. We've got to have our own root system. Then, we begin to act on what we know, and on Who we believe in!

He Is The Seal Upon Your Heart

Song of Solomon 8:6 *"Fasten me upon Your heart as a seal of fire forever more. This living, consuming flame will seal you as My prisoner of love."*

The seal spoken of is one of promise. It protects and upholds. It carries favor and acceptance. We belong to the King of kings. This seal is a royal emblem that cannot be broken. Breaking a royal seal meant certain death in the days of Solomon. This was not a seal made of wax, but a supernatural seal, made of love. Jesus invites us to place Him as that Seal of love upon our hearts. As Christ becomes the fiery seal over our lives, we know we have been brought into the Lordship of Jesus Christ. He occupies and possesses our hearts, our souls, our spirit, and our life. His divine love is the Seal.

The love of God holds us fast and will never let us go. You could run from His love, but it would seek you out. Relentless love is a love that pursues and doesn't quit. There is a power in the love of Jesus that claims everything in us as being completely His. Jesus gave His life for us on the cross. As He did so, His thoughts were of us. They were of you. He was looking to the time when you would take Him as a Seal upon your heart. For Him, the grave was **the means to find you**! How incredible is that?

Jesus final words as He offered Himself up were "it is finished." The language that Jesus spoke was Aramaic, and the word He actually spoke was "kalah". This word is incredible. It has two meanings. The first is to be finished or accomplished. But secondly, the word also means "to be a bride". A bride is what completes a man. The very last word of your King as He died for you was a sigh for His bride! He was thinking of you.

Love never fails. The love of Jesus will not let you down in any way. His love is as strong as death. It is indestructible. It is a banner over our lives. Its' holy flame burns forever. No deluge of water can quench Christ's love for us. No flood can drown it. This love enables us to live victoriously, triumph over temptations and to be MORE than conquerors! We have a fixed, abiding place in His heart...and He in ours. We are constantly and continuously loved, on His mind, and supported by Him. In a world that is filled with anger, it is a great comfort to know that we are Sealed by the Love of our Savior. We are prisoners of love. I wouldn't have it any other way.

89

You Have Been Made New

2 Corinthians 5:17 *"Therefore, if any man be in Christ, he is a new creature. Old things are passed away, all things are become new."*

This verse really encourages me! When we are in Christ, we have become new. We are given new life and we are not the same anymore. We are not reformed. We are not rehabilitated. We aren't even reinvented! We aren't turning over a new leaf. We have died with Christ, and no longer live for ourselves. Jesus Christ now lives in us, and He didn't just clean us up. We have been made to be a new creation.

As a new creation, we begin to look to Jesus, instead of self. We may not "feel" any change at first, but the Holy Spirit now resides in us. We have become His temple, or dwelling place. We begin to notice that we simply delight in the things of God. Our purpose, desires, direction and understanding are different. We have a new outlook. We begin to see people with a greater kind of love and compassion than we have ever experienced before. We are no longer slaves to sin. We are sons and we are daughters of the Most High, and we have been empowered and made righteous by the blood of Jesus.

We have been delivered from the power of darkness, and translated into the kingdom of God. There we have authority to speak to the mountains in our lives. We are secure in the love of our Heavenly Father, and as He is in this world...so are we!

All of this provision was made for us at the cross...and it is here that we stand. It is here that the promises of God are yes and amen. It is here where old things, the old way of life has passed away. We no longer see ourselves through the lens of this world. We see ourselves through the lens of God...whole...healed...prosperous...righteous...clean...secure..adopted ...and loved! Beloved... YOU are a new creation in Christ!

May We Never Operate On The Basis Of Doubt

Romans 14:17 *"For the kingdom of God is not eating and drinking, but is righteousness, peace and joy in the Holy Spirit."*

The kingdom of God is that heavenly sphere of life, where His children are willingly governed by the Holy Spirit, in which righteousness reigns. Man does not live by bread alone, but by the whole truth of God's Word, which stretches far beyond the temporal and the necessities of this world. The substance of God's kingdom does not consist of external things, but of spiritual matters, which are also eternal and give birth to righteousness, peace and joy.

Father, how wonderful that Your kingdom, and Your role in people's lives, is
not a matter of food and drink. It is a kingdom that operates in righteousness, in holiness, and integrity in the Holy Spirit. Thank you Lord that You have made us a part of that kingdom, and that we have been delivered from the kingdom of darkness. We are now a part of the kingdom of Your precious Son. Thank you that you have made us acceptable to you, as well as a blessing to others.

Let all of us, the members of Your family, pursue what makes for peace and for mutual uplifting. Let none of us, for the sake of personal rights, work against Your labor of love in someone else. Help us to appreciate who you have made us to be, in Christ, but help each of us to understand that even though we are all different, we are all made in Your image. Guide us to see that it is right not to act in a way that would make a brother or sister stumble

We are called, not to judge one another, but to love one another. When we lose focus, we choose to look to You, Lord. Remember that you are completely acceptable to God. So is your brother.

May we never allow our liberty in Christ (which is a good thing) to be the cause of a brother to fall in any way. May we never do anything from the basis of doubt, but only out of our increase of trust in You.

YOU Are One Of The Most Brilliant Facets Of Our God

Psalm 45:11 *"The King is enthralled by your beauty"*

Are you talking about me? The one with the frizzy hair, slightly overweight, a few bottles of hair dye under my belt, and a handful of grandkids in the rear view mirror... Me...beautiful?

Yes, you! Every one of you! We are all lovely in the eyes of God. Always. He created us and loves us just as we are...the daughters of the King that He intended from the time we were little girls.

You are beautiful in the eyes of your Creator. You are desired by Him. And He has called the one and only you to be His bride! He has betrothed you to Himself, and He has given Himself to you...completely. The beauty that he sees in you goes way beyond what you are going to see of yourself in the mirror. His love for you is perfect. It is with His whole heart that His commitment to you stands. And it is forever.

If you look up the word *enthralled*, it means to be completely captivated, fascinated, and even enchanted by someone or something. The King is absolutely enthralled by you. True beauty is what He sees. And it isn't just what is on the outside. It's what's on the inside. He knows your heart. He knows what motivates you. You are the pinnacle, the finishing touch on creation. And we all are representative of one of the most brilliant facets of our God.

If you aren't feeling particularly beautiful, ask God to help you to see yourself through His eyes. Ask Him to show you the beauty that He sees that is on the inside. Ask Him to show you the peace He has given you, which will radiate out to others as nothing less than pure magnetism...alluring others to come to know Jesus, if for no other reason than to discover what it is that makes you shine.

Smile and be at rest. The King is indeed enthralled by your beauty.

You Are Now The Resident Of A New Kingdom

Colossians 1:13 *"For He has rescued us and has drawn us to Himself from the dominion of darkness, and has transferred us to the kingdom of His beloved Son"*

Saints of God, this passage thrills me! Think about it. We, as children of God, have been drawn to Jesus, and then drawn away and removed from the dominion of darkness. I looked up the meaning of the word "dominion". It means the territory of a government or its control. Until we were born again into the kingdom of God, that is the kingdom where we lived. It's the world's kingdom, and Jesus instructed us to have no friendship with the world and its ways. The world's kingdom is dark. The people in it are lost and confused. They are seeking answers that cannot be found without stepping outside of that kingdom. Truth for some is nonexistent. Hope is no longer alive. Sadly, there are many who live in this kingdom.
But Jesus has drawn you beloved. His desire was not only that you be rescued from that kingdom, but that you were completely delivered. He wants you to be free from the darkness, the control, the hopelessness. And His desire is that you never look back, because you don't live there any longer. You have been transferred. You've been brought into the kingdom of God's dear Son. This, my friend, is a kingdom of light. He IS light.
His is the kingdom of rest, where we cast our burdens upon the Lord and no longer carry them ourselves. It's the kingdom where hope is regained and rebuilt in our lives. It's the kingdom where we walk in His Spirit, and where the fruit of that kingdom, the love, joy, peace, patience, kindness, goodness, faithfulness, gentleness and self control are very evident. These things permeate our hearts and help direct our steps. We now pursue peace. We are able to love, because God is in us, and He IS love. It's the kingdom of righteousness, forgiveness, and healing. It's the kingdom where we become the dwelling place of God, and where His presence in us builds the confidence we need to know that we are never alone in what we may be facing. It is a kingdom where we worship and where we begin to look at what we have instead of what we do not have. We begin to see Jesus in every situation. We begin to see others through His eyes. We offer thanksgiving because we are truly grateful.
This kingdom is our true home, our dwelling place. It is where we were always meant to be...and for that, we are most satisfied.

Are You Recognizing Jesus?

Luke 24:15-16 *"While they were talking and discussing it, Jesus Himself came up and began walking with them. But their eyes were prevented from recognizing Him."*

This story took place after the crucifixion and resurrection of the Lord Jesus. Two of His followers were walking on the road to Emmaus, talking with each other about all of the events of the last few days. Jesus walked up to them as they were having this conversation. And a very strange thing happened. They didn't know Who He was. How was this possible? The crucifixion had happened only days before, and the people in the township were very aware of Who Jesus was, especially those who had been His followers. The Bible actually gives us a clue here. One of the men was Cleopas. If you check out John 19:25, Cleopas' wife was standing at the cross with Mary Magdalene during the crucifixion. Now, these two men who were speaking about these recent events had the Lord Himself standing with them, speaking with them, walking with them...and they did not recognize Him.

If you look into other sightings of the Lord after His resurrection, you'll find that no one immediately recognized Jesus. This seemed vaguely familiar to me. You see, at times, it has been difficult for me to recognize Jesus in my life. It has been challenging to see His hand as I have faced tough situations. But I think even more strangely, it has been a bit of a stretch to see Him in day to day life, in those simple moments, the quiet moments, the normal moments.

This is curious, considering He lives in me. He lives in you too, if you have invited Him into your heart, and life. Yet, we can go through our day and barely recognize His presence. In Mark 16:12 it says that when He walked up to these two men on the road to Emmaus, He appeared in a different form. What was this different form? Eventually, people did recognize Him. So, what was it that caused them to not immediately know Him?

I believe the answer is found in 1 Corinthians 2:14, which says, "But the natural man does not receive the things of the Spirit of God, for they are foolishness to him; nor can he know them, because they are spiritually discerned." Wow. We are so often looking through our natural eyes, seeking something natural. But God is Spirit. I believe that these two men on the road to Emmaus, as well as a host of others, did not immediately recognize Jesus because He had a new body. He still looked the same, but somehow He had changed.

They would have recognized Him had He been in His natural body, but this verse tells us that the natural man (that's us) doesn't accept or even believe the things of the Spirit, for they are foolishness to him. They are spiritually discerned.

How can we as believers, rectify this? We can look into the Word of God, and believe what it tells us, rather than believing what we see naturally. The Bible tells us that God would never leave us. It specifically says in Ephesians 1 that He would never leave His children as orphans. We are not alone, beloved. I strongly encourage you today to begin to look for Jesus in the scriptures. Look for His promises, see how they apply in your life. Then look at what He says about you. It will certainly change your life.

Our Mission Statement For Life - That We May Know Him

Philippians 3:10 *"That I may know Him, and the power of His resurrection, and the fellowship of His sufferings, being made conformable unto His death."*

The word 'know' in the Greek is actually speaking of a very intimate relationship, a deeply personal one. Paul states the purpose for his life...to KNOW Him. Paul was looking for that very deep and cherished bond. Knowing Him isn't just "knowing about" Him. It's about experiencing an intense, familiar, trusting, intimacy. This is the kind of relationship that Paul says he is pressing toward with the Living God.

The power of His resurrection is the life that overcame death. It brings triumph, bliss, and delight...even in the midst of the most difficult of life's challenges. The power of His resurrection is a living hope for a beautiful future...with Jesus, it's the enabling grace that sustains me. It's the kingdom come now...here...on earth as it is in heaven.

The fellowship of His sufferings may be a little harder to comprehend...but to have fellowship is to share something in common. Believe me, there is a joy unspeakable in this fellowship that is not a depressing, miserable existence. It is an uncommon life and attitude...one that sets us apart as believers...with less of "self" life...and more of His life. His heart becomes your heart. His desires become your desires.

Paul says that this is his purpose. It is quite a mission statement for life. May we experience and walk in that power daily...the power of the resurrection of Jesus! And may we all grasp and embrace that same heart.

He Is The Master Of Every Wave

John 14:27 *"Peace I leave with you...My peace give I unto you...not as the world giveth, give I unto you. Let not your heart be troubled, neither let it be afraid."*

God's heart is big enough to hold anything you may be carrying. He holds your joy as well as your pain. He is with you in tears as well as in laughter. He has not forgotten you...no matter what you might be tempted to believe. He doesn't love you less when circumstances change, or things aren't going well. His love for you is from everlasting to everlasting. His love for you is perfect. His love for you is powerful. His love for you is unchanging. His love for you can be trusted.

The result of this incredulous love relationship with The Lord...IS peace. Jesus specified that it is not the same kind of peace that the world gives, which is often described as the absence of conflict. It is a confident assurance of the love that holds us, and the arms that carry us. It is a place without fear.

Peace, by definition, means contentment, a quiet rest, a state of tranquility. It is a place without rage or havoc from war. Have you ever felt like there was a war going on around you...or in you? Whether it was a situation that came into your life that crept in unexpectedly, or just the wrestling of combative thoughts that try to permeate your soul, you have been given a gift. Jesus left you an inheritance. He has instructed us to let not our hearts be troubled, neither let them be afraid. This means that we have some say in how our life goes. We have some say about the emotional things that try to penetrate our thinking. We don't have to live in that place of havoc. We have been called to live in a place of calm. Peace is your inheritance. It can't be taken from you by your circumstances.

Jesus has given peace...right smack dab in the middle of your situation...your heartache...your pressure. And He hasn't given it in the way that the world gives, because it is He who stills the storm and quiets the waves. We can rest in the boat...content...knowing that our Anchor holds firm. No amount of water can swallow up our ship, because He is the Master of every wave. That is peace.

The King Of Kings Is Holding Out His Scepter To You

Esther 5:2 *"And it was so that when the king saw Esther the queen standing in the court, that she obtained favor in his sight; and the king held out to Esther the golden scepter that was in his hand. So Esther drew near, and touched the top of the scepter"*

There isn't a story anywhere is scripture that stirs my spirit more than the story of Esther. If I were going to choose a woman from the Bible to pattern my life after, it would be her. I admire her courage, her wisdom, her timing, her discernment, and her strength.

When Esther addressed the king, she had no way of knowing if he would welcome her by extending the scepter to her. During this time in history, if the king held out the scepter to you, it meant that you were allowed to approach the throne and speak with him. If he did not hold out the scepter, not only were you not allowed to approach him, but it was a possibility that you would be put to death. Esther hadn't been summoned by the king in 30 days. She had no way of knowing what the outcome would be to her act of bravery.

Today, we may approach the throne of God boldly. The scepter of the King is extended to us. And it is never withdrawn. The Lord invites us to come to Him at all times, often, and to openly and boldly share our thoughts and our hearts with Him. We have nothing to fear. The King of kings and Lord of lords is beckoning you. Come!

Today, I want you to do something. I am asking all of you to spend some time reminding yourself of Who Christ is to you...this wonderful King. I would love for you to spend some time encouraging yourself in the Lord. We all seem to find time to strengthen our bodies with the right foods and exercise. Today, I want you to strengthen your Soul. I have done this the last few days by getting into the scriptures and reminding myself of some things...

The Lord IS my strength. He is my rock and my fortress. He is my deliverer, my God. He IS my strength when I am weak. He IS the One in Whom I trust. He is my Shield, my Salvation, my High Tower that I can run into. When I call upon His name, He hears me. He saves me from my enemies. He has drawn me out of many waters that could have drowned me. He has delivered me from those who have hated me and from those who were too strong for me. He IS my stay. He is what I stand on. All other ground is sinking sand.

He is my Deliverer. He is merciful and will enlighten my darkness when I am surrounded. By Him, I can run through a troop and leap over a wall. His ways are perfect. He makes my feet like hinds feet and sets me upon high places. He has given me the shield of salvation, and His right hand holds me up. His gentleness has made me great. He has made my feet not to slip. He has delivered me from the strivings of people. He is my rock and my salvation. Whom shall I fear? The Lord is the strength of my life. Though a host should camp against me, I will be confident in My God. He encamps around them that fear Him. They who seek Him will not lack any good thing. He is near to those who have a broken heart. While we were yet sinners, He died for us. We have been justified by His blood. He is the God of peace that passes all understanding. He will keep my heart and my mind through Jesus Christ.

I could go on and on...but today I ask you to search the scriptures and find a word that is just for you. Let it be something that simply reminds you how much you mean to God, and how deep His love is for you. Like the king in the book of Esther, the King of kings holds out His hand and His scepter to you today. He simply says, "Come to Me". Today, will you simply touch the top of His scepter? He accepts you. He loves you...and you have His favor.

Plant Yourself Firmly In Him, and Don't Look Back

Philippians 3:13-14 *"Brethren, I count not myself to have apprehended; but this one thing I do...forgetting those things which are behind, and reaching forth unto those things which are before...I press toward the mark for the prize of the high calling of God in Christ Jesus"*

Forgetting those things which were behind him...and reaching forth to the things which were ahead. That was the life of Paul.

Paul had reason to look back and feel sorrow, shame, and even guilt. Acts 8:1 says that he was consenting (or giving his approval) to the stoning of Stephen. Stephen was a man of God, full of faith and power, according to Acts 6:8. In the very next chapter of the book of Acts, Saul is journeying toward Damascus when suddenly a light shines round about him from heaven, and the Lord Himself begins to speak to Saul. I have focused so often over the years on those words..."Saul, why persecutest thou me? I am Jesus whom thou persecutest. It is hard for thee to kick against the pricks." That particular phrase means simply that Saul (who later became Paul) was only hurting himself in his actions of rebellion against God...but the most revealing statement from Christ Himself comes next, when He simply tells Saul to "Arise". The Lord gives Saul specific instructions where to go, and Saul arises and follows the Lord's instructions.

From that time on, Paul was a changed man. He was no longer Saul, the one who persecuted God's people, the one who had been so proud of his heritage, the one who gave his approval in the stoning death of Stephen. He was now Paul, the one who was God's chosen vessel (Acts 9:15), the one who would bring the message of the gospel to the gentiles, the one who, despite many trials and much suffering for Christ's name's sake, arose, went forward, and followed Christ.

I wonder if it was difficult for him to not look back, and dwell on what he had been part of with Stephen, and countless others. If he had not arisen, as Christ instructed him, if he had not gone forward, the New Testament as we know it, would not exist...at least, it's writer wouldn't have been Paul. We might not see some of the incredible writings that we have come to know, love and hide in our hearts over the years of our walk with God.

I think sometimes about Lot's wife, looking back to the city of Sodom, and turning into a pillar of salt. I believe that there is some significance to this. The area where Lot lived was covered in salt. I discovered that one day while reading Genesis 13. Lot's wife looked back at the old life, and where she had been, and what she had come from...and she became what was in her past. If you have time, read that passage in Genesis 19. Earlier in the same passage, the angel of the Lord had spoken the same thing to Lot that he spoke to Paul...Arise!

Beloved, there is a message of hope in this. We need to see it for our own lives today. I have seen with my own eyes, the precious people of God, literally "stuck"...in the past...unable to go forward...when in fact, God is saying, "Arise". When you are His child, you do not have to live in the past. Jesus has already carried your guilt, and your shame. You do not need to carry that heavy load any longer. God not only loves you, but He has a purpose for you. He has a plan for your life. He wants you to go forward. He has need of you. Imagine once again, if Paul had stayed stuck in the past. The entire future of millions of people over hundreds of years would be different. Then imagine for a moment what the future might be for you, if you could simply let go of the past. Not one of us can walk forward and backward at the same time. It just can't be done. Paul knew this. He knew that in order to fulfill the call of God on his life, he would have to forget those things which were behind him, and he would have to press forward, toward the mark of the high calling of God in his life.

Beloved, there is a high calling on your life as well. The Lord loves you, just as He loved Paul. He wants you to be free of the things that may have held you captive. Today, I believe that He would say to you, as He said to Paul...Arise! Stop right now. Drop the heavy load that you have been carrying. Give it to Jesus...and then begin to walk forward, no looking back at your past failures. Keeping your eyes on the things you feel you have failed at will be like tying a chain around your soul. It will hold you prisoner, when in fact, you have been set free. Keep your eyes on God, beloved...that you may know Him, as Paul said. Arise! Go forward. Press in to Jesus. Trust Him. Plant yourself firmly in Him, and do not look back. You go girl!

The Lord Will Certainly Help You

Isaiah 41:13 *"For I the Lord thy God will hold thy right hand, saying unto thee, 'Fear not; I will help thee'".*

These powerful words that the Lord spoke to His people in Israel, probably about 2700 years ago, still apply to God's people today, to you, and to me The Lord has not forgotten you, beloved. He sees your struggles. He knows the situation that you are in...and He has not changed. His words to you today are "Fear Not. I will help you." He will literally hold you and walk through with you, whatever you are dealing with.

I've often wondered why the Lord mentioned holding our right hand specifically. I found out while studying this that the right hand is mentioned 132 times in the scriptures. The right hand is considered to be a synonym for goodness. In Hebrews 12:2, Jesus sat down at the right hand of the throne of God. This was a location of honor. In Psalm 18:35, it mentions that "your right hand has held me up." This is referring to help and/or strength being given when needed. The right hand has been thought to be a powerful hand for using weaponry, and so it also signifies protection, This declaration from the Lord has an even greater depth than what we might see on the surface.

You can stick this promise directly in the face of adversity...and stand on it. Your God would never leave you. People may leave your side, but God will not abandon you. This verse is the antidote to any fear you may be facing or any lack of trust that you might be dealing with. Meditate on it. Believe it. Stand on it.

We do not have to fear anything that we may be going through if we know that God will never leave us. Yes, we may not always "feel" His presence, but we can't go by what we feel. We go by the truth that is in His Word. And His Word says we have nothing to fear. He promises His presence always, even to the end of the age.

Coming To Jesus Is An Unveiling

2 Corinthians 3:18 *"We, who with unveiled faces all reflect the Lord's glory, are being transformed into His likeness"*

A veil is not merely an old-fashioned face covering, or a beautiful white lacy cloth reserved for a bride...or even something black on a widow's hat. A veil can be anything that we hide behind.... which then breaks our direct eye contact with God.

The Jews were not able to look upon the face of Moses. The mere afterglow of God's glory was something that the people couldn't behold. Therefore, he was obliged to veil it. But we, as believers, with faces uncovered, look closely... As clearly as we can see our natural face in a mirror, the glorious promises and privileges of the gospel of Christ are observed. We contemplate them. We desire them. We hope in them. And we apprehend them by faith as we are changed from glory to glory.

What do you hide behind? That's a question that can really make you think. Some hide behind their reputation, or their children, their friends, their money or lack of it, their perceived unworthiness, their past, their mistakes, their definition of themselves, pride, family, job title...or even self-image. Even religion can be a veil.

Coming to Jesus is an unveiling. We have a chance to understand and expose the veil...to come out from behind the curtain of shame. Turn your unveiled face to the Son and let Him shine on you, transforming you into the radiant beauty that He sees in you.

He RISES To Show You Compassion

Isaiah 30:18 *"Yet the Lord longs to be gracious to you...He rises to show you compassion. For the Lord is a God of justice. Blessed are all who wait for Him"*

The ongoing stubbornness and rebellion of the children of Israel is a bit shocking, when you consider all that the Lord did for His chosen nation. Despite the covenant He made with them, and in spite of the many promises He made to them, they seemed intent on defying their Lord. They continuously turned their back on the grace He showered on them.

Over and over, they relied on their own strength instead of trusting Him. Many times, they made alliances with their heathen neighbors, rather than turning to the Lord for protection or help. God reminded them often that their resistance to Him would cause them pain. Their insistence on turning to the world for help, and for seeking alliance with the heathen nations even brought disgrace on them as a nation.

Isaiah reminded them that their salvation would be in repentance and in rest. He reminded them that their strength would be found in quiet confidence in God. They rejected all of His gracious messages, and messengers. They continued to defy the Lord. And yet...the LORD desired to be gracious to His people. In His longsuffering, mercy was prepared to wait patiently, and to have compassion on them. He is a God of justice. How blessed are all who wait for Him.

It's easy for us to be critical of Israel's ongoing rebellion. But we can also find ourselves trusting in the world's answers, straying from the path of peace, depending on our own resources, or even leaving our first Love - Who bought us, with His own precious blood.

May we learn from Israel's failure so that we will not make the same mistakes. May we not harden our own hearts to His gentle voice and gracious promptings. His grace toward us will continue - until Jesus comes to set up His eternal kingdom on the earth...because He longs to be gracious to all of His children, and He waits to have compassion on us all.

The longing of your heavenly Father is to be gracious to you. Pretty astounding!

Jesus Came To Be Our Shield

Ephesians 6:16 *"Above all, taking the shield of faith, wherewith ye shall be able to quench all the fiery darts of the wicked"*

The Bible tells us that as believers, we will battle against principalities and powers. This is a powerful passage. It relays to us that we must depend on God's strength. It tells us that He has provided us with spiritual armor that we need to "put on" daily.

In ancient warfare, it was common for armies to use a storm of arrows to terrify the enemy. The Roman army had a piece of armor that provided a solid defense against this kind of attack. It was the battle shield. This shield wasn't like the round metal disks that you see in movies. It was a large rectangular defense of metal that covered the entire length of a man's body. Soldiers would link up shoulder to shoulder with their shields held in front of them, and then move across the battlefield like an armored tank.

When the apostle Paul thought about our struggles, he realized that God has given us a weapon like the one the ancient Romans used. God has given us a shield of faith! Paul's description of that shield uses the word "thureos", which means "a door shaped shield". The Greek word for door is "thura". The "thureos" was a large rectangular shield about 5 feet high and 3 feet wide. It was also called a castle shield. In other words, it was a portable fortress.

Because the "thureos" was large, if it had been made of wood or metal, it would have been difficult to carry. To construct it, the Romans began with a wooden framework. Over it, they fastened seven layers of tough leather from the skin of a bull or calf, until the shield was about 4 - 5 inches thick, and then they nailed them securely in place. As the soldiers got ready to go into battle, they dipped the shield in a nearby river to saturate it with water, so it would not only stop an arrow, but it would also quench the fire of an arrow that was burning.

Think with me for a moment about how this shield was constructed. The skin of a calf or bull was stretched out over a wooden frame. In the Old Testament, the animal required for a sin offering was a bull of a calf. That skin was a symbol of a sacrifice for sin. This sacrifice was stretched out and nailed to a wooden framework. Its' purpose was to take upon itself all of the arrows intended for the soldier.

The shield represents what God has provided in Christ for us...a perfect sacrifice. This sacrifice was stretched out and nailed to a wooden cross. His purpose was to receive upon Himself all the sin that you and I have ever committed, past, present and future. God has given us a shield, and His name is Jesus! He came to take upon Himself every arrow that Satan intended for us. We need to realize that when an arrow of the enemy strikes, Jesus has come to be our Shield. How do we activate our shield of faith? We trigger it by standing on His word. As we do this, we will see that when battle comes, we are ready to hold our Shield high. We are ready to stand on what we believe and know to be true. Beloved, Jesus hung on the cross as your Shield. Because of this, you can claim His promise that "My God will meet ALL your needs, according to his riches in glory, in Christ Jesus". Take your stand in faith. Declare victory! Declare that every arrow is being quenched! Thank the Lord Jesus.

The cross of Christ has become a door for you. It has opened the way for eternal life. Thank Him that His death on the cross has formed a shield on your behalf.

In The Twinkling Of An Eye, At The Last Trump, We Will Be Changed

1 Corinthians 15:52 *"In a moment, in the twinkling of an eye, at the last trumpet; for the trumpet will sound, and the dead will be raised imperishable, and we will be changed."*

As a child, I had a recurring dream about Jesus' return. In the dream, I was standing on the front porch of the old house that we lived in. It was a dark and stormy night, and I would hear the sound of a trumpet blowing. Of course, being about 7 years old, I didn't realize that it was a trumpet. But I did sense that it was somehow calling to me. Then I would look up in my dream, and the clouds would split open. And there, in all His glory, was Jesus.

Paul described so well what will take place when the dead in Christ rise from their graves, and the fact that we will all be completely changed and wondrously transformed. When Jesus returns for His church, it will be a glorious day! We'll discover that the laws of God's universe, where the spiritual follow the natural, are maintained at the resurrection of the dead. Just as a physical being comes before a spiritual being, and a natural birth precedes a spiritual birth, so it will be when our bodily resurrection takes place before our spiritual resurrection.

The first Adam was a terrestrial man who came from the physical dust of the ground. The last Adam (Jesus) is the spiritual Lord, who came from heaven. Jesus was the first-fruit from the dead. He was the very first member of a new race of people Who would rise to life immortal. Paul explains that the dead in Christ are returned to life in a split-second, in a moment of time, in the twinkling of an eye. At that moment, Christians who have died will be raised, and given incorruptible bodies, which will be like the resurrected body of the Lord Jesus.

Christ was raised with a body of flesh and bone because his blood was shed to pay for our sin. In like manner, we will also be raised with bodies of flesh and bone - and when we see Him, we will be like Him. But instead of blood pulsing through our bodies to bring life, it is the Spirit of God Who will enliven our resurrected bodies with His eternal life breath.

107

God has designated that those in their graves will be raised first into life immortal, and immediately thereafter the living saints will also be changed into eternal beings. Together, both living and resurrected saints will be taken into the heavens.

The dream I had as a child was so real to me. There was a reason for that. It IS real. And I hope it happens in my lifetime. How about you?

Cast Away That Old Garment. Come To Jesus And Be Made Whole

Mark 10:50 *"And he, casting away his garment, rose, and came to Jesus"*

The story of blind Bartimaeus has always intrigued and encouraged me. It touches my heart. Here we have a man who is blind, who sits by the highway, begging. Those who had to resort to asking for money or panhandling, as we would call it today, were considered by the general public to be outcasts. Bartimaeus heard that Jesus was coming, and as He approached, Bartimaeus began to cry out to Him...but as He did so, the crowds tried to silence him.

I remember a time of doing some of my own "crying out". Someone tried to silence me. It became one of those times when I had to make a decision...do I push ahead with what I believe God spoke to me...or do I allow the voice of the naysayer to stop me right in my tracks? I love what Bartimaeus did. He cried out the more! As he cried, Jesus heard him.

Beloved, Jesus hears you. He hears your prayers. He hears it when you cry out. Don't give up!!! Push through! Press on! There was a great crowd surrounding Jesus that day...and therefore Bartimaeus as well...but whatever the crowd may be saying to you...stand on what you believe...and cry out the more!

Jesus stopped what He was doing. He stood still and called for Bartimaeus. At this point the crowd changed their tune. Now they spoke kindly to Bartimaeus and told him to be of good comfort, that the Master was calling him. Sometimes others don't see right away that God is doing something in your life...they haven't heard what you've heard in your heart when He has spoken to you. Again, this is the time to plant yourself firmly on what you believe and Who you are believing! Jesus is living IN you, and when you call on Him, He hears. He stops. He cares.

During the time that this story took place, it was customary for people to wear garments that identified who they were in life. If you were a blind beggar, people would know you by your garment. I love what Bartimaeus did with his garment when Jesus called him. He cast it away! Then he rose and came to Jesus! This is so significant. This was a step of faith...this was a man acting on what he believed...and WHO he believed in.

This was a man thinking that he may be blind now...but he had just come in contact with the One who heals. This was a man casting off that old identity and coming to Christ to be made whole!

Beloved, when we have come to Christ, the Bible tells us that we have been made new! The old man is dead. All things have become new. The garment that a believer wears is a garment of righteousness! Jesus has become your identity! We can throw aside every hindrance. We can lay aside every weight. We can cast away the garment of our own sufficiency! And we come to Jesus...where we receive wholeness, strength, peace, eternal life, pardon. Today, cast off whatever hindrances may have held you back. Rise up! Run to Jesus! He will hear you...and He delights in answering!

Which war are you fighting?

2 Chronicles 20:3 *"And Jehoshaphat feared, and set himself to seek the Lord, and proclaimed a fast throughout all Judah."*

There is a story in the Old Testament in which Jehoshaphat, the king of the kingdom of Judah, was getting ready to go to war against the Moabites and Ammonites. We are told in 2 Chronicles 20:3 that Jehoshaphat was afraid...and so he set himself determinedly to seek the Lord. This is such a beautiful story of courage, even in the face of wickedness.

Jehoshaphat states in verse 9, that even if evil were to come upon them, or sword, or plague...they would stand before God, they would cry out to Him, and they WOULD hear His voice. Further down in verse 15, we see that God...the One Who is always faithful, spoke to Jehoshaphat, and told him..."Be not afraid or dismayed by reason of this great multitude...for the battle is not yours, but God's."

How often do we feel like we have to fight our own battles? And even more astoundingly, how often have we felt alone...when God has told us that He will NEVER leave us or forsake us. How often have we, like Jehoshaphat, felt afraid? God knew of the fear that Jehoshaphat was dealing with...and He addressed it by telling him not to be afraid or dismayed...because He would fight this battle for Him.

You may be thinking...'well, that was Jehoshaphat...what about my situation?' We can see from verse 16 that God did give Jehoshaphat some instructions. He told him to go down against the enemy the next day, to take his position, to stand still, and to watch, as the Lord, Who is with him... fights for him.

Beloved, God has not changed. He fought for Jehoshaphat, and He will fight for you. He may give you some instructions along the way, but He is with you, and will defend you, with as much might and strength, as He did for Jehoshaphat.
Verse 18 says that Jehoshaphat bowed with his face to the ground, and simply began to worship the Lord. Can you imagine the kind of change that could come about for every one of us if we simply began to trust God in every situation...if we got our eyes off of the situation we were in, and if we simply began to worship the king. In doing so, we are actually fighting a different kind of battle...the ONLY battle, as far as I know...that God tells us to fight...and that is the fight of faith.

1 Timothy 6:12 tells us to "Fight the good fight of faith...in the conflict with evil." When we are faced with difficult situations, people, insurmountable problems, our stance every time should be to fight the good fight of faith...to cast our cares upon Jesus, to fix our gaze upon Him, and not the problem at hand, to meditate in His word that is alive, to allow it to bring life to our situation, to worship, and to remind ourselves that He will ALWAYS fight for us.

Today as you pray, remember to cast your cares upon Jesus. He is equipped to carry you. Fight the good fight of faith to which you can then take hold of the amazing eternal life you've been given, and to which you were called. Multiplied blessings to you!

There Is Unimaginable Joy For All Who Believe

John 14:1 *"Do not let your heart be troubled. You believe in God and trust Him. Have faith, hold onto it, rely on it, keep going...and believe also in Me."*

This verse says something significant to me. It was spoken by the Lord not long before He was crucified. In a time that must have been extremely difficult, He reminded His disciples NOT to allow their hearts to be troubled! This is astounding!
First of all, He was letting them know that they had some say over how they would react and subsequently respond to the events that were going on around them. They could choose to not allow their hearts to be troubled. And secondly, they could choose to not allow their hearts to be troubled, even when the events of that time were about to change their lives...even when things seemed heartbreaking.

Let not your heart be troubled. It's as if He is speaking to me personally...to all of us. And the words are comforting. They remind us that neither the things of the world that darken our lives, nor the imaginations of our hearts that can also cloud our minds and thoughts, must shift our trust from the Word of God. These heartfelt words came from Him, the God of ALL comfort.

The words were spoken immediately after Peter was to discover that he would deny the Lord three times. They were uttered to the confused disciples as they approached their greatest time of trial...as the One they loved and trusted was taken from them, and all hope of the coming kingdom of Jesus seemed to have evaporated. They were spoken by the One, Who was facing rejection, betrayal, false accusation, an unjust trial, and the weight of the sin of the world. He was facing the cross. He was facing death. He was facing hell. He was facing His own darkest hour as the face of His Father would be turned away from Him.

In the midst of all this, Jesus spoke these amazing words of comfort and encouragement to their troubled hearts. They were caring words that have traveled down the corridor of time...to us. Because these words apply to you and me, just as they did to the disciples. "Let NOT your heart be troubled." Little did the disciples know that following that terrible night of sorrow and pain, they would experience incredible joy on that glorious resurrection morning that was to follow. And there is unimaginable joy for all who believe God and trust Christ, our Lord, Savior, and kinsman Redeemer.

113

He gave them tools to keep them from worry and fear...and we have the same tools. He has given us the gift of faith. And He has proven Himself to be trustworthy. We know that because He overcame the world, the flesh and the devil...that we too are overcomers...because we are IN Him! This is the victory that overcomes the world!
We may be facing challenging times, but there will be joy for us as well, on that glorious day when Jesus comes in the clouds to take us to be with Himself...so...Let NOT your heart be troubled!

Lean On God, And You Will Not Fall

Proverbs 3:5 *"Trust in the Lord with all thine heart and lean not unto thine own understanding"*

This is one of my favorite verses in all of scripture. Trust God. Pretty simple, right? Or is it? The verse also reminds us not to lean on our own understanding. How often as we go through our day, along with its ups and downs, do we lean on what we THINK we know? How often do we reason out WHY someone said what they said, or WHEN this trial is going to be over, or HOW it's going to end? How often do we write our own version of the ending to the story, that has not yet even been fully told?

A friend of mine shared something that was pretty insightful with me, just recently. She told me that reasoning is an act of the flesh. The need to understand everything is actually a desire that comes from the soulish realm...and God is Spirit. That makes this verse so much clearer to me. God, in my opinion, is actually trying to protect us, by reminding us that our trust should always be in Him, even if we don't yet understand or see clearly into whatever the situation might be.

The Bible encourages us to receive Godly counsel when we need help, but how often have we gone to someone, poured out our heart to that person, and realized that they know even less than we do about the situation? Even more incredibly, how often, in desperation, have we taken that counsel and run with it, when all along God was quietly speaking over us..."Just trust Me."

Don't think that you have to have everything in your life figured out before you can move forward. When we only have enough light on the path we are walking to see the next step, that's okay. We don't need to reason out our lives and have every answer. We put our trust in Him. Period.

I heard someone very wise say recently that you will only fall if you choose to lean on something. When we are leaning on God, we will never fall, never fail, and never be confused. Beloved, no matter what dark cloud may be hanging over your life today, trust God. Don't lean on anything else. No matter what people may be saying, don't prop yourself up on their words, thinking they will hold you up. Trust God. Don't put faith in anything but Him. He IS the Light that will bring glorious understanding into your circumstance.

Salvation Is A Gift

Romans 4:5 *"But to him that worketh not, but believeth on him that justified the ungodly, his faith is counted for righteousness"*

Some folks, when they realize that we are saved by God through faith, start to worry if they have enough. They wonder if their faith is strong enough or deep enough. When we are thinking along those lines, we are missing the point. It was Jesus Christ who saved us. It is He who has justified the ungodly, not we ourselves. Salvation is not based on feelings or even actions. Jesus is strong enough to save us, no matter how weak we may see ourselves. Salvation is a gift...simply because He loves us...not because we have earned it.

God also says that we can come boldly before His throne when we bring our needs to Him. I personally do not believe that He wants us to come to Him afraid or feeling unworthy.

When we are "IN Christ", we can have the assurance that His death, burial and resurrection have justified us, and qualified us to not only come to Him boldly, but to receive from Him.

This was the kind of boldness that the woman with the issue of blood had when she touched Jesus. By touching Him, she knew that she was breaking a Levitical law which states that anyone with a bodily discharge is unclean and should not even appear in public...let alone touch another person. But she refused to feel condemned by the law. She believed what she had heard about Jesus and she was confident that there would be only love and compassion from Him. She boldly pressed her way through the crowd to touch Jesus, who in turn spoke to her..."daughter, your faith has made you whole".

Romans 4:5 talks about faith that believes that God justifies even the ungodly when they simply come to Him. When you believe this, it gives you boldness to come to God, even when you are feeling "unclean" because you've somehow blown it.

When you have failed in some way, don't run away from God. Run TO Him boldly...knowing that you are justified by the blood of Christ and not by your good behavior. Remember today that you are not only His child...but that you are deeply loved and very highly favored.

Look At God, and Remind Yourself Of How Big He Is!

Jonah 2:8 *"They that observe lying vanities forsake their own mercy"*

The second chapter of the book of Jonah fascinates me. Jesus referred to the story of Jonah in Matthew 12:40 when He spoke prophetically about being in the heart of the earth for three days and three nights. Now Jonah was in a desperate situation, having been swallowed by a large fish, and having lived in the belly of it with no foreseeable way out. I can only imagine what it must have been like in there. The first thing I think of is darkness...an inability to see even your hand in front of your face. Then I think of odor. Let's just say that it couldn't have been pleasant amid whatever the contents were in that fish's belly. Then there was probably no real room to move about or breathe....and lastly, as I said...only two ways out...one at each end of the fish...umm...I can only imagine that Jonah didn't want to go either way.

In the midst of this seemingly impossible situation, and out of the belly of what the Bible actually calls hell, Jonah begins to cry out to the living God...and God hears his voice! Have you ever been there? Obviously, I'm not talking about a giant fish...but difficult situations can seem giant too. Sometimes we feel like we are in a true fight for our life...and we can't see the way out. It's just too dark from where we are sitting. It's too overwhelming. There don't seem to be any answers....but God!

Jonah's description of his situation demonstrates that without God, he would have been completely helpless...but Jonah wasn't without God...and neither are you. When Jonah's soul fainted within him...when he felt as though he didn't have another ounce of strength, he remembered The Lord his God...and he cried out to Him. God heard Jonah's cries.

Beloved, we are never without God. We are never left alone in the darkness. Jesus, the Light of the world...lives in us! His Word says that not only will He never leave us...but He will never fail us. There may be times when people fail us. There may be times when we fail ourselves...but there will never be a time when God will fail you. You can trust Him...even when the storm clouds seem to be surrounding you.

Jonah made an incredible statement when he said, "they that observe lying vanities forsake their own mercy." He was saying that those who are busy looking at their circumstances..(observing lying vanities)...those who are diligently watching what is going on around them...who give attention to problems...are actually lifting the problems higher than they are lifting Jesus in their lives. In the Old Testament, they referred to this as idol worship. An idol is anything that is held in reverence above God. It can become something that you literally begin to put your trust in. Some observe idols of ambition...some idols of the flesh...some idols of intellect...while still others observe idols of self will. But these "idols"...these things that we give attention to and even become consumed with...are lying vanities. They seem to demand to be in the highest place in our lives...the place where only Jesus should sit. They bring worry, anxiety, incredible angst....while a life with Jesus at the Head of every situation, brings peace, hope and strength.

The mercies of God are new every morning. When our focus is on trouble...instead of on Jesus...we can actually end up unknowingly forsaking our own mercy, because we aren't steadfastly beholding and trusting the One Who will never leave us.

Beloved, Jesus IS truth. When everything around you tries to persuade you how bad your problem is...recognize as Jonah did, the lying vanity...and realize your full dependence on God...and His faithfulness to you. We don't need to look at our problems and remind ourselves of how big they are. We need to look at our God, and remind ourselves of how big He is! That is the truth that will carry you through any situation!

Jesus' Finished Work Is Sufficient

Galatians 3:3 *"Are you so foolish? Having begun by the Spirit, are you now being perfected by the flesh?"*

In each of his letters, Paul emphasized the importance of understanding that salvation is a free gift of God's grace, which is received by faith alone in Christ. There are three distinct parts to salvation. 1. Justification. 2. Sanctification. 3. Glorification.

Justification takes place in a moment of time. The moment one hears and believes the gospel, that Christ has died as the sacrifice for their sin, and is risen from the dead. By faith in Christ, a lost sinner becomes a saved saint. He is now justified in the sight of God and is declared as being righteous.

Sanctification is the life-long process, carried out by grace through faith...where we are enabled by the Holy Spirit within, to progress from spiritual infancy to spiritual maturity. This happens as we submit to His leading and guiding...by His gracious empowering and not by fleshly works.

Glorification takes place only after the death, or rapture, of the child of God.

Certain people had entered the church at Galatia, and were teaching a mixture of Judaism and Christianity, which Paul identified as a false gospel, that would stunt the growth of believers. These false teachers were legalists, who were trying to incorporate components from the Law of Moses with elements of the Church-age doctrine. The Law of Moses was given as a schoolmaster to point people to Christ for Salvation. The Judaizers were teaching that salvation depended on doing good works and keeping the Law, as well as by faith in Jesus.

They believed that good works had to be added to Jesus' finished work on the cross-otherwise they might not be saved, or could even lose their salvation. But the Law could never save. It could only expose sin and reveal the need for a Savior.

No one is able to be justified by works of the Law, so how can we expect to be sanctified by the works of the law? How can we grow in grace, mature in the faith, and become spiritual believers through man's ungodly works of the flesh?

If the power of the Holy Spirit was needed for us to be justified, how could we become sanctified through our own fleshly works? Sadly, today there are those that still hold fast to this false, works oriented teaching.

We need to remember that if any works of the flesh are added to Christ's finished work on the cross...His life was given in vain. We weren't saved by what we have done. We were saved by what Christ has already done on our account. His work on the cross is sufficient to justify, sanctify and glorify All.

There Is Beautiful Growth Happening In The Ground Of Your Heart

Mark 4:26-29 *"Jesus also said, "This is what the kingdom of God is like. A man scatters seed on the ground. Night and day, whether he sleeps or gets up, the seed sprouts and grows, though he does not know how. All by itself, the soil produces grain...first the stalk, then the head, then the full kernel in the head. As soon as the grain is ripe, he puts the sickle to it, because the harvest has come."*

I have gone through seasons of questioning why I wasn't seeing spiritual growth in my life. Ever been there? Ever felt like you've been "stuck" for a while? This verse is such a powerful verse! And it's such an encouragement when we have given in to the "feeling" that we're going nowhere.

This parable is very revealing. It shows us that spiritual growth is a continual thing. It's a process that is accomplished over time, and ends in a beautiful harvest of growth, freedom, and newfound trust. This verse carries a promise to each of us who are seeking The Lord, who are scattering the seed of His word on the ground of our hearts. It promises that the seed will sprout. It will grow...even though we may not see it happening.

There is a big difference between fact and truth. The fact may be that you aren't "feeling" like you're going anywhere...but the truth is that you are. The truth is that when you are feeding the ground of your heart with the seed...the Word of God (the Gospel of Christ), when the seed is being nourished by the soil...and by the sun, (or should I say Son), that seed does sprout and grow, it does bring life...whether you see it happening or not.

I had a vegetable garden many years ago. I planted seeds in the soil, and watered them daily. And daily I would watch for any sign of life to begin to peek up through the soil. It took a long time. It was a process. What I didn't know at the time was that the seed actually was growing underneath the surface where I couldn't yet see it!
Seed has transforming power. It takes the land that was once barren and produces a fruitful field from it. There is a beautiful growth happening in the soil of your heart, beloved. Nurture it. Protect it! Wait for it! There is a harvest coming!

Remember Jesus!

"You brought my life up from the pit, oh Lord my God...when my life was ebbing away, I remembered you Lord, and my prayer rose to you"
Jonah 2:6-7

Probably many of us feel as though we could have penned this scripture ourselves. In my own life, I credit God alone for lifting my life out of the pit. When life as we know it, has seemed to "ebb away", we remember and acknowledge the incredible and merciful God who hears our prayers and knows our hearts. Even when we have forgotten Him...forgotten what He has done in our lives...forgotten the finished work of Christ on the cross...forgotten that by His blood, we are saved, forgiven, and redeemed, He has not forgotten us. The fact that He hears our prayers, and has forgiven our iniquities is proof that He is truly shepherding our lives. Even if we, as the sheep of His pasture tend to stray from the path, He is there, and celebrates our return to His fold. Never do I want to be wrapped up in the cares of this life so that I forget the wonder of my God.

I don't want to remember Him at the last minute. I don't want to forget to thank Him. I don't want to come to Him as a last resort. I want Him! I want Him front and center in my life...as the first person I talk to...as the first arms I run to.

A dear friend of mine was going to a prayer meeting one night. She had received some difficult news earlier that day. Her mind was cluttered with the day's events. She thought about not attending the prayer meeting as she didn't feel that she would be in the right frame of mind to receive anything spiritually that evening. Then it dawned on her. She could give. She could forget about herself and go, with Jesus in mind. She could go and minister to Him! Now, that is an astounding idea! She remembered Jesus!

Lord, may we never forget our redemption from the pit. May we never forget the wonder of YOU! May it keep us humble and draw us ever closer.

You Are Not Ordinary, Beloved. You Are EXTRAORDINARY!

"When they saw the courage of Peter and John and realized that they were unschooled, ordinary men, they were astonished and they took note that these men had been with Jesus." Acts 4:13

Unschooled, ordinary men were the men who turned the Roman Empire and the world upside down. They were unschooled in regards to the religious jargon and tradition of the day, and they were ordinary in that there was nothing about them that stood out and made you take notice. They were blue collar, hardworking men who didn't have degrees, fame, visibility or stature. But there was something very distinctive about them, something that resulted in astonishment among the lawyers, political leaders, and professional religious leaders of their day.

First, the Holy Spirit records that they were witnessed to be "courageous". They were courageous because they had no fear of man, which is rare. When questioned harshly about healing a man crippled from birth, they testified of the resurrection power of the Lord Jesus to the very men who had crucified Him. They were unafraid of speaking the truth, and unafraid of the consequences. When threatened, their response was, "Judge for yourselves whether it is right in God's sight to obey you rather than God. For we cannot help speaking about what we have seen and heard." Where there is a holy fear of God, there is no fear of man.

God takes very ordinary people, men and women who are the "least" in the eyes of the world, and makes them extra ordinary. When a man is born again, he is marked with the mark of God on his life. God writes His name on our foreheads, and fills us with His Spirit. He takes the fearful and gives them great boldness, the insecure and gives them great confidence, and makes lowly uneducated fisherman strong and gifted leaders. He uses our human weakness to manifest the great strength of His grace, and confounds the world's wisdom with the apparent "foolishness" of the message of the cross. Yes, the follower of Jesus is anything but ordinary.

The verse also says, "They took note that these men had been with Jesus." No greater compliment can be given to a man or a woman. To have it be evident that we have been "with Him" is the goal of our being sent to the world.

Had He wanted to remove us from this world when we first believed, He could have easily just "snatched" us up right then. But He didn't; He left us to testify and reveal the Kingdom of God to a lost and dying world.

God isn't looking for "super" Christians in this day. He is looking for ordinary men and women who will walk with Him, whom He can cause to become courageous ambassadors of reconciliation as they live out their lives as His new creation in this dying world. You are those who will confound the wise and shame the strong. You are the extra-ordinary, courageous ones He now sends out; you and I, extraordinary people.

Personalize This Verse And Truly See How Much You Are Loved

Ephesians 1:3-4 *"Blessed be the God and Father of our Lord, Jesus Christ who hath blessed us with all spiritual blessings in heavenly places in Christ; according as He hath chosen us in Him before the foundation of the world, that we should be holy and without blame before Him in Love"*

Beloved, I am asking you today, to indulge me for just a moment. The verse above speaks volumes to me, and I'd like for you to personalize it. In every spot where you can, I want you to insert your name...so it would read like this: "Blessed be the God and Father of our Lord, Jesus Christ, who hath blessed, me, Judy, with all spiritual blessings in heavenly places in Christ...according as He hath chosen me, Judy, in Him before the foundation of the world, that I Judy, should be holy and without blame before Him in love" Wow!

Precious child of God...if each of us only KNEW how MUCH God loves us! If we took every Scripture and made it personal, it would change the way we think about how much we are loved. It would help us to see ourselves differently. It would help us to see ourselves through the eyes of God...to know that we are valuable to Him.

Beloved, He CHOSE you...before the foundation of the world! Before He thought of anything else, He thought of YOU! He knew YOU! And, because you are in Him, you are seen by Your God as being Holy! You are blameless! Just let that sink for a minute. I know that we all fail at times. But God has blessed us with ALL spiritual blessings In Christ...our salvation...the power to live daily in Him...the hope of eternal life...the joy, and the peace that come in having a relationship with Him. Because we have an intimate relationship with Him, we can enjoy those blessings now!

Dear one...today, I am asking you to REMEMBER and personalize this passage. You have been chosen by the Creator of the Universe to be HIS. You are in Christ. You will find strength to face whatever your day brings...in simply Remembering!

125

The Layers Of The Love Of God Will Only Grow Deeper

Hosea 2:19-20 *"And I will betroth thee unto me forever; yea, I will betroth thee unto me in righteousness, and in judgement, and in lovingkindness, and in mercies. I will even betroth thee unto me in faithfulness; and thou shalt know the Lord"*

I cannot begin to comprehend the love of God. It seems to me that there are so many layers to the depth of that love, that if we were to peel away each layer one at a time, there would be just as many layers remaining...because His love is endless. I have read the incredible story of Hosea and Gomer, and cried...because it speaks so loudly to me that although Gomer was unfaithful...although Israel was unfaithful...although we are unfaithful...God's love is unchanging. He continually offers forgiveness, and a renewed relationship with Himself.

God asks Hosea to do the unthinkable...to buy back his adulterous, and unrepentant wife, and then to continue to love her, and to forgive her. Hosea could have divorced her, but he didn't. Hosea even had to pay to get her back, although the amount required was small, because at that point, Gomer was not considered to be worth much to anyone. But to Hosea, she was priceless. He loved her just as God loved Israel, and just as He loves us. No matter how low any of us have ever sunk...God has already "bought us back", redeemed us. He has done so in the death and resurrection of His Son. The price that He paid to be our Redeemer was great. He paid with His life.

I recently watched an excellent movie that told the story of a woman during WWII who was pregnant out of wedlock. Her father arranged a marriage with a man that she had never met, and throughout the rest of the movie, that man began to demonstrate the love of God to her. He pursued her with that love. He continually reached out to her, and her heart began to change. As she started to see the love of Christ, demonstrated to her by her husband, her heart softened and she repented of her former life. Then she and her husband began a beautiful and deeply loving relationship.

God's wedding gift to His people, both in Hosea's day, and in our own, is His Son. Through no merit of our own, He forgives us and makes us right with Him. There is no way by our own efforts to reach God's high standard for moral and spiritual life, but He graciously accepts us, forgives us, and draws us into a relationship with Him. In that relationship, we have personal and intimate communion with Him.

God's love for you is unchanging...and it is everlasting...and He wants you to know Him as you never have before. I challenge each of us today to take some time with our Beloved. There is no higher honor than to sit at His feet. There is no greater joy than knowing Him...and then realizing that as you sink deeper into the layers of that love, that those layers will only grow and sustain you throughout your life.

Our Lives Are Hidden With God In Christ

Romans 7:4 *"Therefore, my brethren, you too died to the Law through the crucified body of Christ, so that you may belong to another, to Him who was raised from the dead, in order that we may bear fruit for God."*

This verse is unreal! As believers, we are not only NOT under the Law, we are dead to it! When Jesus was crucified, died and then rose from the dead, we died to the Law so that we might belong to Him! Now, as His bride, we are able to bear fruit for God!
If you read the previous verses, you find that the Law had jurisdiction over a person as long as he or she lived. Just as a married woman is bound to her husband as long as he is alive but is released from that marriage if the husband dies, those who were under the Law, were similarly "married" to it. Verse three says that a woman would be considered to be an adulteress if she united herself to another man while her husband was alive. Jesus wanted intimacy with His followers. And intimacy required a marriage. Somehow, a death had to be involved. And that death occurred when through the crucified body of Christ, we died to the Law.
Verse six goes on to say that we have been released from the Law and its penalty, having died through Christ to that by which we were held captive. Those under the Law were literally held captive by it. But now, we serve God in the newness of the Spirit...His Spirit...and not in the oldness of the letter of the Law. We learned from previous verses that we died with Christ and were risen with Him. We died to SELF and the old sin nature, so that by faith we are born again, into God's family and our life is hidden with Christ in God. Because we are in Christ, we are also dead to the Law. Jesus paid the price for every sin we have ever committed, and He took the punishment for every broken Law through His sacrificial death and glorious resurrection.

Jesus died to pay the penalty for our sin, but He also died to break the power of sin, the bondage to Satan, and the curse of the Law, and He did all of this on OUR account. As members of His body, we died to the Law because we are in Christ and part of His body. We are positioned in Him and clothed in His righteousness. We have His everlasting life living in us, and are able to bear good fruit, to the glory of God.
We praise God that we have been made one with the Lord Jesus, and because of that union with Him we have died to sin and to the curse of the Law. As we abide in Him and He in us, we can bring forth the fruit of righteousness - to His praise and glory!

In Him, You Are Complete

Jeremiah 31:14 *"And my people shall be satisfied with my goodness, saith the Lord"*

Have you looked for satisfaction in other places, when it is Jesus alone who will satisfy you? Have you given yourself to endeavors, projects, labors and relationships, and yet have never experienced the feeling of satisfaction that you long for and desire?

His intention is for His children to be satisfied...in Him. The child of God deserves to know His Father, and to be well acquainted with His words..."Well done, good and faithful servant". You are His child, and He desires that you be content and satisfied, in whatever state you find yourself.

He gave His life so that satisfaction could be yours. He conquered discontentment and dissatisfaction. He did it so that you might no longer hold on to those "things", but that you would hold on to Him. He began a work in you that He promises to complete.

He gives you a new sense of purpose NOW. Be confident that He is with you. He is faithful and does establish you. In Christ, you are perfectly accepted, cherished, and chosen. The secret of living a satisfied life is to know His love, which passes human knowledge.

He loves, forgives, strengthens, and renews you. He not only brings hope...He IS Hope! To know His love is to know His mercy as well. It is His joy to give you His satisfaction.

Today, hear His loving words to you. " In Me, you are complete". See yourself as having died with Him to the hunger for material things. You have escaped from the world's vain desires, and His desires for you have become yours.

Do not live as if you still belong to the world. Know how much He enjoys your love; therefore, enjoy His goodness and His love toward you...and be satisfied.

Even If We Are Faithless, He Remains FaithFULL

"For this reason I am sending to you Timothy, my son whom I love, who is faithful in the Lord. He will remind you of my way of life in Christ Jesus, which agrees with what I teach everywhere in every church." 1 Corinthians 4:17

Faithfulness is one of the fruits of the Holy Spirit's activity in the life of a believer. It is a godly quality that has great benefit in the church of the Lord Jesus.

The essence of faithfulness is reliability, consistency, and trustworthiness. Sadly, these are becoming harder and harder to find in our day. The problem with a materialistic, consumer-oriented society is that it caters to the individual's needs and wants. The spirit of the age has promoted a mindset that says, "I am the center of my universe." This is the lie that Satan duped Eve with in the garden. It led to death then, and it still leads to death today.

Faithfulness is *otherly* in every sense and every way. That's a word you don't often hear. To be found faithful implies that someone else's expectation, desire, or need has been met. Of course, not only are we called to be faithful in our service of one another, we are first to be faithful to the Lord, He whose name is Faithful and True. Faithfulness is the essence of the character of God. If we are faithless, He remains faithful because He cannot deny Himself.

We are also to be found faithful to the truth by walking in the truth. Faithfulness as a believer encompasses every area of my life as I walk with God, love the community of the redeemed, and live as His new creation, faithful to the truth and testimony of Jesus Christ. I live a faithful life because it is the character of God, and the life of God indwells me by His Spirit. It is a primary characteristic of His new humanity on the earth.

Jesus said that the saints would need patient endurance and faithfulness in the last days. We are living in those days. May you be found to have been faithful by the Lord; faithful first to Him, and to the Good News that testifies so clearly of His faithfulness.

Jesus looked to God And His Unlimited Resources

Mark 6:41 *" And when He had taken the five loaves and two fishes, He looked up to heaven, and blessed and broke the loaves, and gave them to His disciples to set before them. "*

This tiny little passage speaks volumes to me. Jesus, as He was preparing to feed more than 5000 people, was faced with only having two small fish, and five loaves of bread. From what I understand, a loaf at that time was not like a loaf that we might see today in the grocery store. It didn't come sliced, and ready to feed a large crowd. It was usually a small, almost bite-sized piece of bread, meant for one person. I've often wondered what passed through the mind of Jesus as He "looked up to heaven" before blessing and breaking the bread.

That phrase "looked up to heaven" is really telling. We might picture the Savior simply looking upwards, giving thanks, and then breaking the bread. But when you study the meaning of the phrase, it actually means that He looked up...and recovered sight. Jesus could have looked to the limited resource of the bread and the fish...but instead He looked to God....and His unlimited resources!

According to Webster, the word "recovered" means to regain strength, or to retrieve or rescue something. What Jesus recovered was His ability to see into the provision of God, the ability to trust that with God, all things are possible, and the confidence to firmly believe and stand in those truths. He looked up to God. He was no longer looking at the limited resources He held in His hands. He was looking at God's inexhaustible and limitless provision.

I don't know what you may be looking at in the natural right now, that may seem limited in some way. But I know that just as Jesus did, we can pause, and look up to heaven...look up and regain our spiritual eyesight and vision...and we will see that for us, just as for The Lord, God's provision is perfect...and it is even greater than we might think.

Even In Affliction, You Will Grow Stronger!

Your God will not leave you...no, Not EVER! Exodus 1:12 *"but the more they afflicted them, the more they multiplied and grew"*.

This passage is from the story of the children of Israel, while they were still in Egypt. A new king had taken the throne over Egypt. His concern was that the Israelites had grown to be stronger and greater in number than the Egyptians. So...he set taskmasters over them, to afflict them with many burdens. But...what was the outcome? The Israelites got STRONGER and they GREW in number! The king of Egypt must have been left scratching his head over this...because he clearly didn't know or understand the God of Israel.

Beloved, I do not know what you might be facing today...but I do know Jesus. When affliction has come into your life, in any form...you too can GROW. You can gather strength and get stronger as you rest in the arms of your Savior. Your level of trust will also grow as you cast your cares on Jesus, believing that He will not leave you...no, Not EVER!

Your peace will increase, your joy will flow, and your strength will multiply...as you look to Jesus...the Author and Finisher of your faith...in full assurance that the Author is also the Originator, Creator, Master, and Founder of that faith.

As you come through any affliction in your life, you will be able to look back...and see that as great as that affliction was...even greater were the hands that carried you...even deeper your trust and assurance in Him became...and in a more substantial way, your awareness of His presence in your life grew and developed. Looking unto Him, eyes and heart fully fixed – will increase your trust...causing you to live in the purpose and plan that was heavenly designed for you!

His Scepter Is Always Extended To You

Hebrews 4:16 *" Let us therefore come boldly to the throne of grace, that we may obtain mercy and find grace to help in time of need"*

God's love and His forgiveness seem to go hand in hand...as do His love and grace. When you accept Him into your life and heart, His love, mercy, and grace come also. You begin to notice that He is not a distant God, before Whom we are to shrink or grovel. It is because of the merit, the worthiness, the excellence, and the virtue of Christ's amazing sacrificial offering of Himself upon the cross, on our behalf, that we have this astounding entitlement. We are called to enter the throne room confidently and with the assurance of a child approaching his or her beloved father.

This Throne of Grace is the eternal seat of the Lord of heaven and earth. It was by His grace that the veil of the temple, which separated man from God, was torn in two from top to bottom, providing access into the presence of our heavenly Father. And through His Son, we have received the gracious invitation to come boldly to God's Throne of Grace, in time of need.

We can come to Him at any time. His is a scepter that is always extended to His beloved family. He never rescinds it. When we are in need, He is very willing that we should come to Him, and sit on His lap, so to speak...to pour out our hearts to the One who will be merciful, and who will sustain us in time of need. We never cower anxiously before His magnificent presence. There is nothing greater than knowing Him. There is nothing on this earth that draws us in the way that He has..."therefore, let us draw near with confidence to the Throne of Grace."

Such is a life of great meaning and purpose.

The Truth Must Be Settled In Our Hearts

John 20:27 *"Put your finger here; see my hands. Reach out your hand and put it into my side. Stop doubting and believe".*

Even though we know what's true, at times it is hard to believe. Doubt creeps in when every circumstance appears to contradict what we know to be true. This is part of the walk of faith, part of our learning to trust God and His Word and not our own emotions, our flesh, or our own conclusions. Our emotions and conclusions aren't evil or bad, but they must be held up to the light of the Word of God and its truth, and not believed on their own.

Thomas was having a hard time believing the other disciples' claim that they had seen the Lord, now risen from the dead. Of course that would be hard to believe. It went against everything he knew to be true. Dead people don't rise from the dead. Dead people don't talk, walk or appear suddenly in locked rooms. It simply wasn't believable. But as is always the case, the issue wasn't what Thomas felt, or sensed, or held on to as truth, but what was actually true. And, it was true; Jesus had risen from the dead. He was alive!

The resurrection of Jesus Christ is the key to the hope we have as Christians. Because He is raised, because He lives right now, we have hope for our future. Because He is risen, our hope extends, not just to the future we can see in this life, but to the future we cannot yet see, in the life to come. We are going to spend eternity with Jesus! This is the most essential of all truths to believe and to understand. Its implications release the power for living the life we are now called to live on the earth.

This truth must be settled in our hearts. The truth of the resurrection must be an anchor of our souls, a place we can always return to regain our bearings, to remind our hearts that this life is worth the price. Paul said in 1 Corinthians 15 that if Christ is not raised from the dead, we are of all men most to be pitied. Because he understood it was the primary truth that guaranteed our future. And if it wasn't true, our hope was a pipe dream.

Do you live your life from a place of confidence in your future, or are you still uncertain what lies ahead. Beloved, settle your heart into the revelation of the Son of God, that He is risen, and lives evermore.

He was the "firstborn among many brethren", first born from among the dead, and because He lives and now has become my life, I too live in Him. This I believe to be true, in spite of what I see or feel...or even don't yet see!

Uncertainty isn't sin unless we turn away from the truth. But the more I walk with God and come to know His heart and character, the more convinced I am of the truth of His Word. There is no greater truth that affects my life on earth than the truth that He has risen and overcome death. Set your heart and mind upon that truth. Settle it in your heart, not just casually, but deeply. It will set you free.

He Is There...Because He Promised To Be

Numbers 21:17 *"Then Israel began singing this song...Spring up O well; sing ye unto it"*

This was a strange song and a strange well. The children of Israel had been traveling over the desert's barren sands, and they were thirsty for water, but there was none in sight. Then God spoke to Moses and said, "Gather the people together and I will give them water" (vs. 16)

The people then gathered around with their rods. As they began to dig deeply into the burning sand, they sang, "Spring up, o well! Sing about it"...Soon, a gurgling sound was heard, and suddenly a rush of water appeared, filling the well and running along the ground. As they had dug the well in the desert, they had tapped the stream that ran below that was unseen but had been there for a very long time.

What a beautiful picture this is! And it describes for us the river of blessings that flows through our lives. When we begin to respond with faith and even praise, we begin to see God, the river of living water, even in the most barren desert. If each of us were to begin to really look at our lives, we wouldn't have to dig very deep to know the presence of our God in every situation. We would be able to see how He has carried us through, each and every time. When we looked at our own strength and realized that it was actually HIS, and knew that we have come through those situations, those needs, and every dark time...because of Him, the chorus of praise that would raise up from the very depth of our soul would sound like an entire choir singing a resounding "Hallelujah". Underneath all of the emotions, there lies the strength of Jesus, quietly waiting to be tapped into...almost unseen except that we know He is there...because He promises to be.

And to that I say...Hallelujah...to the Lamb of God.

May We Be Faithful, Unstoppable Servants Of The One Who Saved Us

Romans 8:18 *"For I reckon that the sufferings of this present time are not worthy to be compared with the glory which shall be revealed in us"*

I have seen a side to the life of Paul that I had never really seen before. What is it that could change a man, from one who persecuted Christians, to one who loved the people of God, who was willing literally to risk life and limb to preach a message of hope to the gentile?. What was it that drove him? How did he withstand imprisonment, shipwreck, being bitten by a deadly snake and surviving, being abandoned by those who were with him, and on top of all that, knowing that it was time for his departure? Paul had surrendered his life to God's perfect will. He knew that the Romans could not lay a hand on him without God's permission. God's glory was the issue in every situation that Paul encountered. His thought in everything he did was "to live is Christ".

Each night in the dark dungeon in Rome, Paul knew he was one day closer to certain execution. The only reason he had been spared so long was the problem of his Roman citizenship. Many Christians had been fed to the lions in the amphitheater, packed with spectators. Emperor Nero could not legally sentence Paul to this type of death...hence, Paul's expression in 2 Timothy 4:17 "I was delivered from the lion's mouth"...not by Nero but by God.

Paul's words in 2 Timothy 4:6-8 were "For I am now ready to be offered, and the time of my departure is at hand. I have fought a good fight. I have finished my course, I have kept the faith. Henceforth, there is laid up for me a crown of righteousness which the Lord, the righteous judge, shall give me at that day; and not to me only, but to all them also that love His appearing". Paul wasn't just pulling a word picture out of a hat. Anyone in the Roman empire would have known exactly what he was referring to. In the year A.D. 67, the year of Paul's death, Nero had the audacity to enter himself in the Olympic games. The Olympic athletes had literally spent their lives training for the event...but the 30 year old overweight emperor used medications to induce vomiting rather than to exercise to get into shape. He was literally in a pitiful physical condition and very ill-prepared, but who would be the one to tell him so?

No one at that time would have had the nerve to approach him and tell him that he could not compete. So, he cast himself on a chariot at the Olympic games and drove a ten horse team.
He fell from this chariot and had to at some point, be helped back into it...and though he failed to stay the course, and he ended up quitting before the race was finished, the judges nevertheless awarded him the prize. A wreath was placed on his head and he was hailed victorious.

Needless to say, word of this humiliating victory spread quickly and soon after Nero returned to Rome, the apostle Paul wrote his stirring final testimony..."I have fought the good fight. I have finished the race. I have kept the faith. Now there is in store for me a crown of righteousness, which the Lord, the RIGHTEOUS Judge, will award to me". Amazing! I had never put all of this together before.

Paul's life has become such an inspiration to me. Traditional teaching down through the years teaches us that two soldiers brought Paul word of his death. They approached him and asked for his prayers that they might also believe in Christ. Then they led Paul out of the city to his death.

"For I reckon that the sufferings of this present time are not worthy to be compared with the glory which shall be revealed in us"...the RIGHTEOUS Judge now raised a wreath of righteousness and placed it on the head of his faithful servant. He had finished the race. He had kept the faith.

The knowledge of Christ that Paul had acquired in his lifetime was worth every loss, every trial. Dear brothers and sisters...if that partial knowledge of our precious Lord and Savior is worth everything, and we know it is, then what will full knowledge be like when we one day see HIM face to face? "Oh, the depth of the riches of the wisdom and knowledge of God". One day, we all will "grasp how wide, and how long and how high and how deep is the love of God"

Until then, may we be faithful, unstoppable servants of the One who saved us.

When You Feed, You Fight!

Deuteronomy 8:3 *"....so He fed you with manna which you did not know, nor did your fathers know, that He might make you know that man does not live by bread alone; but man lives by every word that proceeds from the mouth of the Lord."*

It is the Word of God that we live by! The Word is life sustaining. EVERY word that proceeds from the mouth of the Lord strengthens and nourishes. Just as our physical bodies need food, our spirit man needs food. We do not live by bread (physical food) alone. It is the Word of God that brings nourishment to our spirits, and sustains us.

Amazingly, the word *bread* in the verse above is from the Greek letter "Lahem", which does mean *bread*...but it also means "to fight". Why did God give this letter two meanings? Because when you feed, you fight! Feeding is fighting the enemy. Feeding on the Word of God, feeding our spirit, is how we fight. We don't fight or stand against the enemy in our life by actually fighting, as with our fists. We fight by feeding! We consume the Word, and the enemy is defeated. When God feeds you through His Word, He is fighting for you!

Psalm 23 reminds us that we shall not be in lack, and that God prepares a table for us in the presence of our enemies. While the symptoms are still in the body, feed! While addiction is there, consume the Word! When you are receiving a negative report of some kind, don't give up. Continue to ingest the Word. It is how we fight. While the problem is still there, remember that feeding is fighting.

1 Timothy 6:12 reminds us to fight the good fight of faith. When going through any kind of battle, your part in that battle is to stay in faith. How do we fight to stay in faith? We feed! And we thank God that He has given us the means to win this battle. Thank Him for the "bread" that He has given us. Thank Him for His overcoming power that lives in us! The devil tries to tell you that you can still see the problem, but you can remind him that your eyes are on the Lord! You aren't looking at the problem. You are consuming the Word!

In Luke 5, the disciples had been out fishing all night, but had caught nothing. Jesus instructed them to lower their nets and try again. At His word, they did so...and they caught a net breaking load of fish! So often, I think, we give up too quickly. We throw in the towel, when Jesus is reminding us to keep going! He went on to make breakfast for His disciples. He FED His sheep! To eat is to fight! When you continue to feed, God continues to fight. Never give up, beloved!

End The War With Yourself

I John 3:21 *"Beloved, if our heart condemn us not, then have we confidence toward God"*

Your Savior continually calls to you with love and with kindness. He has sung over you in the night when sleep was your only purpose. In the day, He has rejoiced over you when you were completely unaware. Despite this, He has heard you, beloved one, when the words that you have spoken over yourself have been harsh, even cruel.

Why? How is it that you see yourself as a failure? Do you not know that what He sees is amazingly perfect? He has heard your private battle cry and He longs for you to walk in truth. Has He ever waged war against His own...His beloved?

No...Never!

He called you. He has brought you into His glorious kingdom, where peace and righteousness reign. He has given you new life, made you a new creation, and has gently reminded you that you are no longer a part of the kingdom that is filled with hatred. Would He actually send you back to the hopelessness that He freed you from?

When you came to Him, you gave Him your heart. You held it out to Him, like a gift, to be received. And He did receive it...and then lifted you up into His heart. You became a gem to Him...rare, precious, and fitting well into the Father's resplendent heavenly crown. You realize how brightly the light of Jesus shines into your life...but do you remind yourself of the fact that the light shines from you, as well as in you?

You, dear one, are a bright and beautiful reflection of Him. You are a perfect jewel in the heart of God. Please do not devalue the gem of God.

He has given you peace, chosen one. He has called you to it. You are free to enjoy it, to walk in it, and to be who you were created to be. To be kind to yourself is to hold Him in the highest regard.

Because you love Jesus, and because you know that He loves you...end the war with yourself.

May We Rest In His Transforming Power

Colossians 3:8, 10 *"But now ye also put off all these; anger, wrath, malice, blasphemy, filthy communication out of your mouth...and put on the new man, which is renewed in knowledge after the image of Him that created him"*

These passages give us an incredible promise. We have been made new. There is a new man inside the heart of each and every believer. The Bible says that the old man is dead. Now, you may wonder, if the old man is dead, why do I continue to struggle with anger, malice, filthy communication, etc?

It's because we haven't "put on" the new man! The new man is renewed in knowledge after the image of his Creator. The moment that we are born again, we are made a new creation in Christ. We are given a new nature, the resurrected life of Jesus within. The Holy Spirit comes to indwell our bodies, to teach us, guard us and guide us. He is not teaching the old sin nature. It is dead and cannot be reformed or trained into Godly righteousness.

When the old man tries to carry out the law through self-effort, this is self- righteousness, and it is unacceptable to God. It is the new, born again life we received at salvation that begins to grow in grace and knowledge of Jesus. We are clothed in His righteousness, and should not seek to cover ourselves in self-righteousness. Our growth comes in yielding ourselves to the Holy Spirit. As Christians, we are a reflection of the new life and not the old. This happens as we come to know the Lord Jesus more and more.

If we as believers, want our lives to be different...if we want others to see Christ in us...then may we simply rest in God's transforming power. May we walk in the strength to lay down and put aside our need to be right, or to have the control, and may our greatest desire not only be to be like Him, but for others to see Him in our lives. Growing in Him, and knowing Him is the greatest treasure that any of us could ever have.

May He help each of us today to simply get our eyes and our minds off ourselves. May we put off the old way of life, and may we simply put on the new way of life...given by Christ Jesus, and guided by the Holy Spirit. May we continue to see as He changes us, from glory to glory, into His image.

He Came Once, For All, To Bring Abundant Life

John 10:10 *"the thief cometh not but for to steal, and to kill, and to destroy. I am come that they might have life, and that they might have it more abundantly."*

These are the words of Jesus...the One who laid down His life for us...and He is telling us here that His purpose in coming, was to make sure that we would have abundant life! If you look up that word "life" in the original language, it is talking about life overflowing...life that is completely full of all the goodness of God! This is what your Savior came to give you! The objective in His coming was the exact opposite of the thief. He came once, for all, that in Him...the sheep would have life.

And yet, some of us have believed and even been taught, that sickness comes from God...that He is trying to teach us and make us more Christlike through it. Beloved, this could not be further from the truth. Although it is certainly possible, when we have been afflicted with some type of illness, for The Lord to speak to us, and for us to gather strength from Him, but He is NOT the One who sends it. Jesus Himself was not taught through sickness or disease.

God called sickness a curse in Deuteronomy 28:59-61. Jesus called it bondage in Luke 13:16. Peter referred to it as satanic oppression in Acts 10:38. God is not fond of sickness. He doesn't send it. He is completely against it. He has done everything in His power to make sure that His children walk in healing and good health.

It is the devil who steals, kills and destroys. Sickness steals quality of life. It kills and aborts vision in one's life, and destroys hope. Jesus said that He has come so that we could experience life, in abundance! Was God ever sick? No!! And Jesus didn't come to bind us in ropes of bondage! He came to set us free!

Godly Conception Will Bring About New Vision For Your Life

1 Samuel 12:24 *"Only fear the Lord, (with awe and profound reverence) and serve Him faithfully with all your heart; for consider what great things He has done for you."*

Consider what God has done for you. Think on those things. Ponder them. Meditate. When you are considering the things that God has done, you are creating an intimacy and a oneness with Him.

Let's think for a moment about what you are thinking about. What is it that you are considering, pondering and meditating on? There is a reason that the Lord instructs us on the matter of thought. It's because of conception. You heard me right. We conceive thoughts in our minds. And we all know what happens after conception takes place. We give birth!

Think about this, beloved. If you are pondering and thinking about the great things He has done for you, the conception that will take place in your mind will be one of trust. What will begin to grow in the womb of your heart will be hope, and what will eventually be birthed, will be faith. You will begin to realize that time and again, God has been with you. He has been the One to bring you through whatever situation you were facing. He has been faithful. He has fought for you, carried you, and has always loved you! Now the realization has become hope, and hope has given birth to faith! What a beautiful delivery!

1 Peter 1:23 says "for you have been born again, not of seed which is perishable, but is imperishable and immortal, that is, through the living and everlasting word of God."

When something is born, it's because that something was first conceived. Whether we're talking of the seed of God's word, or the seed of a man united with a woman, we're speaking of life being contained within these systems of delivery. Once something is conceived, there is a divine, pre-planned trajectory of growth and eventual birth or fulfillment.

So, with this in mind, what happens when we are allowing ourselves to think the worst, to dwell on what "might" happen, to give permission for our imaginations to run wild?

143

I've heard people say that in their thought life, they've gone from having a headache to believing they have a brain tumor, or seeing themselves sick, even dying. This should never happen as a child of God. We don't want to risk conception. We don't want to give birth to the "child" of unbelief, or of doubt, or even hopelessness.

Beloved, think about what you're thinking about. Don't allow any negative thoughts that might conceive in your heart, eventually giving birth. Stop those thoughts quickly. Godly conception will bring about new vision for your life. In all situations, consider the great things that God has done for you.

Apply Yourself To A Life Of Faith

Hebrews 6:11-12 *"We want each of you to show this same diligence to the very end, in order to make your hope sure. We do not want you to become lazy, but to imitate those who through faith and patience inherit what has been promised".*

For many recently, there has been a rediscovery of the message of grace, and there is a returning to the centrality of the Good News of God's gracious provision through His Son. But in re-emphasizing grace as foundational, much confusion theologically has entered the church. Most of us have heard the term, "sloppy agape", which is to say that some understand grace to be a "free ticket" to now live however they want, believing that grace will always be available regardless of how they live.

This is a dangerous and unbiblical understanding of the grace of God that has been provided in the Lord Jesus Christ. When grace is understood in a true Biblical sense, and is active in the life of a believer, Paul says it "teaches us to say 'No' to ungodliness." In other words, grace is not only provision for sin, it is an enabling power to keep us from sinning! This is the spirit in which the text in Hebrews was written. It is an admonishment to apply diligence in our faith and it assumes a proper understanding of the work of grace in the life of the believer.

The writer to the Hebrews says that diligence is needed to the very end. Some translations use the word "earnestness". In other words there has to be a seriousness and an effort in our faith. He warns of people becoming lazy in their faith and running the risk of missing their full inheritance. That doesn't mean "losing their salvation', it means not living life to the fullest, and missing the full blessing of God in this life. That would be tragic because we also know that how we live this life as believers has great reward in the life to come. "Don't forfeit any of your inheritance!" he warns.

What is needed the writer says, is diligence in our faith; earnestness, seriousness, and our full participation "to the very end". Imitate others, he also says, who live this way. Imitate their faith and their patience as they live for God. Apply yourself to a life of faith, always dependent on the enabling grace and power of the Life that is at work in you, but also fully aware that our participation in this life is the outworking of our faith. True faith will always lead to good works. Godly works come from resting in God's grace. Rest and grace, works and diligence; they are two sides of the same wonderful coin. The rest and the grace is His part, that which is finished in Christ. Our part is to be diligent in believing, diligent in resting, and earnest in living out of His grace. This is not a time for casual Christianity. In fact, there is no such thing.

We Are Strong In the Lord, and In The Power Of His Might

Ephesians 6:10 *"Be strong in the Lord and in the power of His might"*

What a beautiful passage to memorize and hide in your heart. This verse is not only an encouragement, it's an instruction. When we start to falter, our first reaction can tend to be one of panic, and wondering...what do I do? But the word of God is alive with power! And it is alive in US! We can be strong in any situation because of that living Word! We do not have to rely on our own power. We lean on His! We trust His Word. We dig in our heels and BELIEVE!

There isn't one situation, one temptation, or one question that cannot be answered with the response "Be strong in the Lord and in the power of His might". On a multiple-choice test, this is answer "d": All of the above. Use this verse to steady yourself in shaky moments until you regain your stability on the solid Rock of your salvation.

As children of the family of God, we can stand firm in the power of HIS might - and not take courage in our own strength. We have enormous blessings that are ours, in Christ, but we also realize that we are living in a world in which we are engaged in a war - one that is not fought with fleshly weapons. This is a conflict that is fought in the spiritual realm, and requires a heavenly power from above. It is strength that is outside of our human capacity. It is power that comes from God. We can, and are, strong in the Lord and in the power of His might.

God is not telling you to be tough on your own, or to come up with the right thing to do. He is saying to rely on His power, His strength, and to allow Him to do for you what He knows best.

Put Your Foot On The Neck Of Unbelief

Joshua 10:5 "Therefore, the five kings of the Amorites...the King of Jerusalem, the King of Hebron, the King of Jarmuth, and King of Lachish, and the King of Eglon gathered themselves together and went up...they and all their hosts...and encamped before Gibeon and made war against it."

Years ago, I heard someone teach on this passage. These five kings were uniting to make war on the Gibeonites, who turned to Joshua and the Israelites for help. As this teacher had studied this passage, he made an observation. The Lord quickened to his heart that the five kings represented in this story are also represented in our lives today...by our five senses. We enjoy our sense of sight, of hearing, of taste, of smell...and of touch. We trust in the sense of what each one brings. We love to see a beautiful sunset. We enjoy listening to and hearing good music. We love to smell and then taste delicious food. It's amazing to hold someone's hand that we love, or touch the skin of a newborn baby. Our five senses are pretty awesome! At the same time, these five senses can also be good evangelists for unbelief. With all that is going on in the world these days, in the news, and life in general, we may have opportunities to choose doubt...to begin to question what we believe...and WHO we believe. The facts that we deal with daily in the news and the world around us may not be good. But the TRUTH is that God has not changed. His word is still true. His promises are still going to be carried out. His heart FOR you remains committed TO you! He still knows the end from the beginning, and we CAN trust Him...no matter what we may be seeing or hearing. God is faithful. Trust placed in Him is better than facts placed in our five senses, that will only bring confusion to our hearts. In the story, five of Joshua's captains put their foot on the necks of the five kings. Then Joshua told the captains..."Fear not, nor be dismayed. Be strong and of a good courage...for thus shall the Lord do to ALL your enemies against whom you fight." Beloved, when you are in a battle...no matter what kind of battle it is...remember that you can put your foot on the neck of unbelief. You can quickly crush out doubt by putting your foot on it! You can wipe out the fear you've been dealing with, by putting your foot on the neck of fear. Cut off its air supply! Stop it in its tracks! You can put your foot on the neck of confusion...because you have a God Who is faithful, and in Whom you can trust. There is nothing that can come into our lives that can ever change the goodness of God! And He is willing and able to stand with us in every battle!

Jesus Passionately Pursues Us

Luke 15:32 *"But it was fitting to celebrate and rejoice, for this brother of yours was as good as dead, and has begun to live again. He was lost and has been found."*

Have you ever thought about the fact that the way in which we portray God to the people around us really does paint a picture in their minds and hearts of the nature of God? The way that people see Jesus in us is likely to change the direction they take in their own lives. Years ago, a dear friend of mine led me to Jesus. This friend had been through some unbelievably difficult circumstances in her life. I was going through some of the same situations in my own life, and was paying attention to how she handled things. It was literally because of the love and grace that she demonstrated toward the person who was hurting her that I could see Christ in her. I wanted what she had. There was nothing phony about this woman. She was as genuine as they came. The decision I made that day to receive Christ, as we sat talking in her back yard, was the best decision I've ever made. And, it was the most important decision I've ever made. It was a decision that was eternal. As the song says, "When we've been there 10,000 years (in heaven) bright, shining as the sun, we've no less days to sing His praise than when we first begun."

The way people see us matters. One of the best examples from the Bible that I can think of is the story of the Prodigal son. I have wondered at times what might have happened to him if he had come across his older brother when he returned home, before he ran into his father. Because he saw his father first, he was met with love, with joy, with acceptance. His father was so happy to embrace his son. The older brother was, on the other hand, angry, jealous and unforgiving. If he had gotten ahold of his brother first, he might have represented the heart of their father being the same as his own. It could have completely changed the direction of the Prodigal because of the rejection and hopelessness he may have represented.

We never really know what a hug can mean to someone. And think about this. Jesus loved us while we were yet in sin. Jesus has passionately pursued us, and would never reject us. It is His desire for all to come to Him. This son, who had been lost, was now found. He had been the emblem of one who refused to depend on or be governed by anyone. But now, in the heart of the father, he was received, welcomed and celebrated. Not one of us is worthless to God. May we have eyes to see the priceless value of every living soul.

Do You Need To See To Believe?

Psalm 106:12-15 *"Then they believed His promises and sang His praise. But they soon forgot what He had done, and did not wait for His counsel. In the desert, they gave in to their craving; in the wasteland, they put God to the test."*

In Hebrews 11:27 we read that Moses "persevered because he saw Him who is invisible". Yet in the above passage, exactly the opposite was true of the children of Israel. They persevered only when their circumstances were favorable, because they were primarily influenced by whatever appealed to their senses, instead of trusting in the invisible and eternal God.

Even today, there are those who live inconsistent lives because they have become preoccupied with things that are external. Some focus on their circumstances rather than focusing on God. It is so easy to get our minds on the problem, and off God. Beloved, God desires that we grow in our ability to see Him in everything, and to exercise faith, even when we have we have not yet seen what the outcome will be.

We read of the children of Israel that "*THEN* they believed His promises"...They did not believe until *AFTER* they saw...once they saw Him work..."THEN they believed." They doubted God when they came to the Red Sea, but when He opened the way and led them across, and they *SAW* Pharaoh and his army drowned, "*THEN* they believed". The Israelites continued to live this kind of up and down existence, because their faith was dependent upon their circumstances...but dear child of God...this is *NOT* the kind of faith that God wants us to have.

The world says that "seeing is believing", but God wants us to believe in order to see. The psalmist said "I would have despaired unless I had *believed that I would see* the goodness of the Lord in the land of the living".

Do you believe God only when your circumstances are favorable, or do you believe no matter what your circumstances might be? Faith is believing what we do not see, and the reward for this kind of faith is to see what we believe.

We Have Everything We Need For Life and Godliness - In Him

Colossians 2:17 " *These are a shadow of the things that were to come; but the body is found in Christ.* "

Amazing! God's intent from the beginning was for all things to be summed up in Christ. All of God's eternal purpose is found in His Son. In Jesus is all that God has provided for mankind for now...and for eternity.

The Old Covenant dealt with types and shadows. I believe that types were a picture of the fullness that Jesus would bring. Shadows were veiled glimpses into His glory. They are intangible images of something that is real. The purpose of the laws, feasts and holidays in the Old Testament were to point us toward Christ. They were shadows of what was real...Jesus!

Old Testament types and shadows become a New Testament reality - which are all bound in the Person and work of the Lord Jesus. They are shadows of the things to come. But the physical, tangible, and eternal reality belongs to Jesus alone - Who is the Messiah and Savior of the world.

The blood of bulls and goats never could cleanse the heart or conscience of an individual. It was a foreshadowing of the cross and of the power that would come through the blood of Christ to cleanse...and to deliver. The Sabbath was a mere hint at the incredible abiding rest that God would provide through Jesus!

May we live in the reality of who we are in Christ, and rejoice in the freedom that He has brought. May we rejoice in the perfect freedom that Jesus purchased for us. May we not look backward to our former way of living, but live our lives under the new covenant of grace, which was cut at Calvary and is fulfilled in the Lord Jesus. He is the completeness of God. He is the truth of God. He is the reality of God...and we have everything we need for life and godliness...in Him.

Jesus Came To Seek and Save That Which Was Lost

Luke 19:8 *"And Zacchaeus stood, and said unto The Lord, 'behold, Lord, the half of my goods I give to the poor; and if I have taken anything from any man by false accusation, I restore him fourfold.'"*

Zacchaeus was a publican...a tax collector. Tax collectors were among the most unpopular and even despised people in Israel. It was common knowledge that they made themselves rich by gouging their fellow Jews unfairly.

One day, Jesus visited Zacchaeus. The Bible makes no mention of Jesus rebuking him for living a dishonest lifestyle. Instead, Jesus showed him love by spending time with him. Before long, Zacchaeus stood up and declared to Jesus that he would restore fourfold to anyone he had taken from illegally. He also stated that he would give half of his goods to the poor.

Time spent with Jesus can change anyone's heart. Moments spent in His presence can change us as well. Without any kind of criticism, accusation or judgment, Jesus helped bring about an inward transformation in the heart of this man...and it seemed to have happened in a brief period of time. Then Zacchaeus began to outwardly respond to that inward transformation.

Verse 10 goes on to say that the Son of Man came to seek and to save that which was lost. The crowds of Jesus day were displeased that Jesus had gone home with the tax collector. The crowds today might respond in a much similar manner. But Jesus loved Zacchaeus, and Zacchaeus responded to that love.

In every society, certain groups are considered to be "unapproachable". I remember ministering to a certain group one time, and being chided for spending time with them. But even now, Jesus wants to seek and to save those who are lost...and He isn't looking backward. He isn't looking at where they came from, or what they came out of. He longs to bring the lost into His kingdom.

We should never give in to pressure from people who are regarding someone's past, or the kind of life they've lived up until now...Jesus died for us ALL...and by Him...we are forgiven and made new!

Hallelujah! Remember that Jesus invited HIMSELF to Zacchaeus house, and because of that outpouring of love...shown to a man that many considered "untouchable", Jesus was able to emphatically say, "this day is salvation come to this house" Amen!

God (Immanuel) is With Us

Isaiah 8:11-14a *"For the Lord spoke thus to me with a strong hand, and instructed me that I should not walk in the way of this people, saying: '"Do not say, "A Conspiracy", concerning all that this people call a conspiracy. Nor be afraid of their threats, nor be troubled. The Lord of hosts, Him you shall follow. Let Him be your fear. Let Him be your dread. For He will be a sanctuary for those who fear and trust Him."*

The Israelites were once again dealing with war from the surrounding nations. But in the midst of what was happening, God spoke the above to the prophet Isaiah. He was reminding him once again to not take on the ways of the people in those nations, and especially not to see things the way they saw things. The Lord was very intentional when He said, "Do Not Say, 'A Conspiracy'".

There is so much going on in our own world right now. By the time you are reading this, my hope is that much of it will have been resolved.. I believe that the same words He spoke to Isaiah, He would remind us of at this time. I woke up this morning, opened my Bible, and these words literally jumped off the page and into my own heart, the same way I'm guessing they did with the prophet.

Beloved, when we are looking at the people around us, the news (which is often not true), and those in authority for answers, we are only going to end up with more questions. Often we will end up confused. I feel surrounded some days and almost engulfed by all of the conspiracy theories, and the actual harmful plots and secret plans that people have related to me as truth. I don't watch news, but I get plenty of news, just from answering my phone. I occasionally get on social media, and have wondered where the believers are, who might put out a word of encouragement, instead of another conspiracy theory or more news that only drives people to hopelessness.

It is time that we as believers rise up. God gave us a recipe here to follow. We are not to fear what the world fears. We are to look to Him, and to regard His holiness. When the verse speaks of Him being our source of fear, it means, He is the one we are to reverence, and to run to with our needs. He shall be a sanctuary (a sacred, indestructible shelter for those who fear and trust in Him). What a beautiful promise in the midst of chaos. Verse 10, it reminds us that "God (Immanuel) is with us".

Saints of God, no matter what we are seeing, hearing or thinking, God is with us now. He has not left us. We need not be afraid of any kind of threat that we may hear. We need not be troubled. He is not only with us, but He is IN us. When we have received Christ, we are His. He is a very present help, Who never leaves us, no matter what we are going through. THAT...is what we can put our trust in, hang on to, and stand on!

The Lord Blesses You Out Of Zion

2 Corinthians 3:5-6 *"Not that we are sufficient of ourselves to think anything as of ourselves; but our sufficiency is of God; Who also hath made us able ministers of the new testament; not of the letter, but of the spirit; for the letter killeth, but the spirit giveth life"*

According to the notes regarding these verses in my Bible, "The letter killeth, but the spirit giveth life" means that trying to be saved by keeping the Old Testament laws ends in death. Only by trusting in God can a person receive eternal life through Christ. No one but Jesus has ever fulfilled the Law perfectly. The Law makes people realize their sin, but it cannot give life. Eternal life comes through Christ...and a new life is given to all who put their trust in Him.

I read something interesting recently. To the Jews, the feast of Pentecost is a celebration of the giving of God's law. It takes place 50 days after the Passover feast. When God gave the Israelites the Ten Commandments at Mount Sinai, it was 50 days after they had celebrated their first Passover, and come out of slavery in Egypt.

But what happened after God gave them the law on the first Pentecost? Three thousand people died. (Exodus 32:28) Contrast this with another Pentecost in the New Testament. In the book of Acts, it says that when Pentecost had fully come, God gave the Holy Spirit, and three thousand people got saved! (Acts 2:41), which goes to show that the letter (the law) kills, but the Spirit gives life!

The law, which was "written and engraved on stones" ministered death. This is why the Apostle Paul called it the "ministry of death" (2 Cor. 3:7-9). On the other hand, the Spirit ministers life.

When we come under the law by trying to keep God's commandments in order to be blessed, it leads to death, lack of joy, discouragement, condemnation, depression, frustration, hopelessness. But when we rely on the Spirit, it brings life into every situation. We have a sense of hope, courage in the midst of adversity, a deep sense of joy, breakthroughs and new ideas, and a sense of being led...peace and wonder, and manifestation of the fruit of the Spirit (Gal. 3:5)

The law was given on Mount Sinai...but the Spirit on Mount Zion. This is why the Bible says that "you have not come to the mountain (Sinai) that may be touched and that burned with fire, and to blackness and darkness and tempest.

But you have come to Mount Zion, and to the city of the living God, the heavenly Jerusalem, to an innumerable company of angels" (Heb.12:18,22). The Lord blesses you out of Zion (Psalm 128:5).

Beloved, He has given you His Spirit. He has made you a new creation. Today, thank Him for all that He has done. You are truly blessed.

Cultivate and Nurture Your Heart Daily

Song of Solomon 1:6 *"I have not guarded my vineyard within"*

The vineyard that this verse is speaking about is the heart. The Shulamite was saying that she had not guarded hers. Guarding, protecting and nourishing our heart is vitally important. We want to pursue Christ with an undistracted love. We are called to a daily cultivating of our hearts. One time several years ago, I was in a situation with someone that was quite difficult and had been going on for some time. I decided to talk to my pastor about it. I wasn't sure how to handle things, or how to move forward, and I was a bit surprised at my pastor's advice. He told me that it was time to guard my heart. He said that nurturing my own personal communion and commitment with God was important. That advice was life changing for me. Our life in the Spirit is a vineyard, a garden for the Lord. Don't ever make the choice to neglect it. Cultivating the heart daily is a responsibility that should be taken seriously.

If we move on down to verse 8, it says "Listen My radiant one. If you ever lose sight of Me, just follow in my footsteps. Come with your cares and burdens. Come to the sanctuary of my shepherds. There you will find me." Jesus sees us as His radiant one! And He cares enough about us to instruct us not to lose sight of Him. If we do somehow lose sight, we can easily find our way by simply following His footsteps, getting into the Word. Jesus is aware when our garden (our heart) isn't being kept. We are radiant to Him despite this. Jesus does not define us by the unkept vineyard. He never sees us as unlovely, even though it is often the way in which we see ourselves. He doesn't define us by our actions, or lack of them. He's not looking at the unkept heart. He sees us by the virtues that have been planted in us... that grow into their fullness as they are nourished and fed.

It's imperative that we know and understand that we are perfect in His sight. When we are free to allow this to sink in, hope is born and released into our hearts. Doubt, fear and accusation cannot take root in us. When we are tempted to quit, it is this revelation that redeems us from a pattern of self disgust and condemnation. Knowing how God sees you is the true healing balm of the wounded heart. Anything else is just a Band-Aid. The love of God heals. It casts out fear and brings in confidence. God's deep affection removes loneliness and rejection from our hearts. His overwhelming love overcomes our insecurities and makes us whole again. Praise God!

The Lord Is Your Master. He Is Your Guide.

Revelation 2:7 *"To him who overcomes I will grant to eat of the fruit of the tree of life, which is in the paradise of God"*

God knows our afflictions, distresses and pressing troubles...and He is with us. He wants us to understand that He is our shelter and strong tower that we can not only run to, but feel safe in, no matter what the circumstances.

It is easy to become discouraged when we are in the midst of a difficult set of circumstances, or when our body is in pain, or when the trial that we have endured seems endless, or when we don't know what the future holds. We do know that HE holds the future! So, we must do one thing. This is such a key to freedom. We must keep our eyes and our hearts FIXED on the Lord. He says that where our treasure is, there our heart will be also...and He lives in our hearts.

We have been made one with Him, and as we trust in, and lean on Him, our circumstances begin to seem smaller. He has said in the Bible that the one who overcomes will receive from Him hidden manna to eat...and a white stone with his or her name written on it. Do not be afraid to overcome, beloved. Do not be afraid to face the storms around you. Do not shrink back in the face of danger. Your God is with you...and He has already overcome the world and its sorrows. It is because of Him that you are an overcomer. The problems in this life will not defeat you...and you will not be consumed, when your heart is fixed on God.

The Lord is your Master. There isn't anything that can exalt itself over your life as master or guide...no affliction, no pain or trouble of any kind. These things do not have any power over you. Jesus does. The Lord is your Master.

The Possibilities Are Endless

Matthew 7:20 *"Nothing will be impossible for you"*

It is possible for believers who are completely willing to trust in the power of the Lord for their safekeeping and victory, to lead a life of continually receiving His promises... exactly as they are, and finding them to be true.

It is possible to daily "cast all your care (anxiety) upon Him" and experience deep peace in the process.

It is possible, having done all to stand, that you continue to hold firm and believe.

It is possible to have the tenacity to have a "don't quit" attitude, and to NEVER give up.

It is possible to trust in the Lord, and lean NOT onto our own understanding.

It is possible to see God in our circumstances and to walk in His love and deep care for us.

It is possible to go through difficult situations, trusting fully in Him for the outcome.

It is possible to have our thoughts and the desires of our hearts purified in the deepest sense of the word.

It is possible to become strong in the power of His might, and to take refuge in the power of God.

It is possible to "Let not your heart be troubled"

It is possible to KNOW and BELIEVE that you are MORE than a conqueror through Him who loves you.

It is possible to not be conformed to this world, but to be transformed and changed as you mature spiritually.

It is possible to fully believe that as a child of God, NOTHING is impossible for you!

Smother Me With Kisses

Song of Solomon 1:2 *"Smother me with kisses"*

The love of our King stepped out of eternity. It was not a momentary thought that Jesus came to lay down His life for His bride. He is eternally ours...and we are His. It is His love that endures forever. There are places in our hearts that will be healed by this beautiful love. This is a romance that is real, and passionate. And this kiss from the King is a metaphor of intimacy with Jesus, a heavenly kiss that awakens our spirit to His affection toward us. Jesus does not wait until we are perfect before He enjoys us. He loves the weak, the immature, the rejected by others, and those who feel incomplete. And it's because Jesus sees us as courageous and heroic, before we ever begin to see ourselves that way. He smiles at the thought of us. He is the lover of our soul. A kiss is one of the most tender expressions of love known to man. It's ok to run into His arms and abandon yourself completely to Him.

Often, when someone blesses my life in some way, I see it as a kiss from God. Recently, we spent the weekend with friends, who absolutely pampered us for the entire weekend. They cooked for us, took us to lunch, listened to our hearts, prayed for us, washed our car, and even filled it up with gas. As if all that wasn't enough, when we got ready to leave, our friend came up to hand me something. It was money for another tank of gas. I explained to him that his wife had already filled our tank. He then told me..."She heard from Jesus...but so did I." Wow! I had such a sense of having been kissed by the Lord. My husband and I drove for several miles, in complete silence. We were simply basking in His presence...and in the knowledge that we were on His mind. We had just been kissed!

God loves you in the same way that He loves His Son. The measure of the Father's love and affection for Jesus is the same measure of His love for us. This is and should be the ultimate statement of our worth to Him. Jesus left everything to make us His own. He has loved us freely, without requiring anything of us to attract such love. He saw us. He knew us. He bought us. And He brought us back to Himself.

The cry of the Shulamite was "Smother me with kisses". May it be our cry too. He is certainly very willing to oblige.

One Day Every Eye Will See Him

John 20:-7 *"Then cometh Simon Peter following Him, and went into the sepulcher, and seeth the linen clothes lie, and the napkin that was about his head, not lying with the linen clothes, but wrapped together in a place by itself"*

This week I learned something new. I found out that it was a Jewish tradition, when you visited someone's home for a meal, to fold up your napkin and leave it placed on the table when you left. This simple gesture actually made a statement to the host, that you wanted to come back. It meant that the guest had enjoyed the meal, as well as the company, and that he or she very much wanted to be invited back.

There are so many little things that happened during the life of Christ that mean so much. Nothing that happened was insignificant in any way. Everything points back to Him.

After Jesus was crucified and buried in the tomb, Mary Magdalene came early in the morning on the first day of the week, and found the large stone rolled away from the grave. She ran to get Peter and John, who came back to the sepulcher...and Peter, upon entering, saw that the grave clothes were left, as if Jesus had passed right through them...but the head piece...the napkin.. was wrapped in a place by itself. The napkin was left in such a way that it made a statement, especially at that time in history. Jesus was simply saying that He is coming back.

After learning that this week, I have to tell you that I don't know if I will ever look at a napkin the same way again! I have thought about making the folded napkin my own way of telling friends and loved ones that I want to be invited back...but I think more than anything, I am reminded that our beloved Lord and Savior IS coming back. The napkin was just another reminder of that promise. One day, every eye will see Him...and every knee will bow. One day, He will break through the clouds.

Tonight when you are having dinner, may you simply be reminded of His return. May you be confident that He will accomplish all that He has promised. May you know that He is the living Christ...and that you can be certain of your own resurrection because of Him. The divine power that brought Jesus back to life, lives in us as well. I will never look at my napkin in the same way again! Praise the Lord!

You Are Under The King's Favor And Love

Proverbs 19:12 *"The King's wrath is as the roaring of a lion; but His favor is as the dew upon the grass"*

The Bible also tells us that the devil walks about like a roaring lion, seeking whom he may devour. Have you ever wondered why he acts like a roaring lion?

It may have something to do with that lion's roar. In the Bible, the roaring of a lion speaks of the king's wrath. "The King's wrath is as the roaring of a lion". So, when the devil walks about like a roaring lion, he may deceive us, giving us the impression that the King is angry with us. When we believe that God is angry with us, we can begin to lose hope. When we think that God is displeased, we won't be confident of His love toward us. Instead, we may expect punishment from Him. For some, this has driven them away from a relationship with the very King who loves them and wants to bless them!

Child of God, even when you fail, or you've blown it in some way, God is not angry with you. Galatians 3:13 says "Christ has redeemed us from the curse of the law, having been made a curse for us". As this sinks into your heart, and you realize what Christ has truly done for you, I believe you will fall even more deeply in love with your King! Your sin was taken away, and the Lamb of God became your burnt offering.

There is a law called the law of double jeopardy. It states that the same crime cannot be tried twice. Today, as a believer, you will not have to serve a sentence that has already been served for you. This should make you leap in your spirit with joy, and thanksgiving! You are loved, and you are not under the King's wrath, but under His favor and love.

161

You Are Hidden with Christ

Colossians 3:2 *"Set your affections on things above, not on things on the earth"*

To set your affection on things above means to look at life from God's perspective and seek Him. Then watch as His desires become yours. This can totally change your life. When your focus changes from the things of this earth to things eternal, you will begin to notice some differences . The fear that once tried to cling to you will be a thing of the past. The depression that tore at your heart will become a joy that bursts open from deep within. And that broken heart will be made whole again. Your desires will change. Your future will look bright again.

There is a reason that Paul has called on us to keep our hearts and minds focused on heavenly things and not earthly pursuits. It's because we have been raised to a new life in Christ! We are His spiritual seed, and have become a new creation! We exchanged our earthly residency for a beautiful new citizenship in heaven, and there is no going back.

Since we have been raised to a new life in Jesus, and we've been clothed in the righteousness of Christ, as well as the fact that we have been given an amazing gift, that of eternal life, showered with every spiritual blessing, and have received a heavenly inheritance as well as having been seated with Christ in the heavenlies, why would we focus on things of this earth? We live by trusting in Jesus, where we find our sufficiency, knowing that in this world, we will have tribulation...but Christ has overcome the world, and we are in Him.

Look up beloved. Drink in the warmth of God's presence. This may be your temporary home, but your mind, your focus, each and every thought can be changed by simply seeing life through God's eyes. By shifting that spiritual focus, and looking less at the world around you, you gain peace, you gain direction, and you gain clarity.

We truly can make great strides toward understanding how temporary all of this is. We just need to remember that there is much more going on than what appears to be. When we cannot change our circumstances, we can change our vision.

Today, hide yourself with Christ in God.

Refuse To Be A "Slinger"

II Kings 3:25 "And they beat down the cities, and on every good piece of land cast every man his stone, and filled it; and they stopped all the wells of water and felled all the good trees: howbeit the slingers went about it, and smote it"

There were people in the Bible who were referred to as "slingers". They defeated their enemies by slinging stones and throwing dirt into their wells...thereby contaminating their life source of water.

Today, things happen a bit differently. Most people don't own a well or have one on their property. But we have all known people who sling accusation, judgement, criticism and who find fault with others. Unfortunately, we have done it ourselves. We judge others for their actions, when we ourselves are equally guilty, simply by finding fault. We run to someone in the church under the guise of "praying for that person". By the time the story makes its way through many conversations, much of the truth has been lost. It's dirty business, for sure. That is certainly the way that Jesus saw it. He said that it isn't what goes in to a man's body that defiles him, it is what comes out of his mouth that defiles.

We defile people with our words. We stop up the wells of friends, of family, of those we love...these are the very wells of living water that run through the Spirit of every believer.

As a child, I remember when my grandmother died on my dad's side. He and his sister were planning her funeral. Somehow they got into an argument about who was going to pay for the flowers for their mother...they didn't speak again for 35 years! What a terrible waste of time, and of a wonderful relationship. Words are containers for power, and when used incorrectly, they can do so much damage.

We have all known people who simply want to be right...whatever the cost. Recently, I had to take a step back from a friendship because of the angry words that continually came at me from this person. It wasn't always directed right at me...sometimes it was directed at others...but I still heard it. It still went into my spirit, and at times stopped up my well. I would often come away from spending time with this person, feeling ill. The truth was, I was ill. I had been defiled.

Friends, how many of us could honestly say that some of the greatest hurt we have experienced in our lives has been started by words. Some of the biggest wars the world has ever known were started by words...and unfortunately, much of this is going on in the church.

Beloved, none of us want "slingers" in our lives...people who are constantly negative, critical, and judgmental...people who throw dirt on the very dreams that God has given us, people who hurl insults at others...and we certainly don't want to become "slingers" ourselves. Refuse to be a "slinger" who contaminates your very own faith and walk with God by your words, as well as the faith of those around you. Begin to pay attention to what you are saying, and to what is being said around you. Ask for God's help in this endeavor. Spending time with Him will fill you with fresh "living water". You will be edified, and will become a source of encouragement not only for those around you, but in your own walk as well.

Overcoming Rejection - Part 1

Genesis 29:30 *"Then Jacob also went in to Rachel, and he also loved Rachel more than Leah..."*

The story of Leah and Rachel can be seen as one of heartache and rejection. Jacob loved Rachel. He worked 7 years for her, but at the end of those years, Rachel's father gave Leah to Jacob. She was Rachel's sister. Then he told Jacob that in order for him to give Rachel to him, he would have to work another 7 years. Jacob worked the next 7 years for Rachel because he loved her so much. This was now 14 years that he had worked for her. In those days, it was not uncommon for a man to have more than one wife. Jacob married both Leah and Rachel. It was also very common in those days to have large families. A woman was somewhat defined by how many children she could give her husband. She was considered to be especially blessed when she could give her husband a son.

So, imagine the pain that both of these women endured...Leah was able to give Jacob many sons. But Leah also knew that she wasn't loved. Rachel, on the other hand, was loved but had a hard time getting pregnant, and had to watch as her sister kept giving Jacob son after son. Both women were feeling the pain of rejection in one way or another.

God saw that pain. And God sees unloved people. He knew that Jacob didn't love Leah. But God often selects what man rejects. He knew the heart of Leah, that she wanted so much to be loved. And so, God gave her many sons.

For all of you who have dealt with some type of rejection...an unloving or abusive spouse, a parent who simply didn't care, a friend who has betrayed you, the hurt of not being included...I want you to know that God accepts and loves what people reject. He saw that Leah was rejected, and He took her up (Psalm 27:10). He took up her cause. He is the God of the widow and the orphan, those who have been left alone. He selects the rejected. He chooses the unchosen. For every unloved Leah who has been overlooked, God sees you. Beloved, never look at rejection as the end. See it as a redirection.

When you have been rejected in some way by someone, I believe it's a sign that you're not in their altitude. God wants to take you higher. He wants to take them too, but they are free to choose, just as you are. You've been approved by God. He loves you.

165

He has declared His love over you, like a banner over your life. He chose you, adopted you as His, and now you are part of His family. This is important to remember and stay focused on. Nothing and no one can remove you from the hand, or the heart of God. You are His, and will remain so, forever!

Look to Him, beloved. The next time you start to feel the sting of rejection, or betrayal. Remind yourself that you were created on purpose! And your Creator sees. He will be everything that you need.

Overcoming Rejection - Part 2

Genesis 29:32 *"So Leah conceived and bore a son, and she called his name Reuben, for she said, 'The Lord has surely looked on my affliction. Now, therefore, my husband will love me.'"*

Leah had found herself in a painful situation. She was married to a man who didn't love her. So, Leah decided to take the matter into her own hands. She had come up with a plan. Perhaps if she could produce a son for Jacob, he might love her. Leah put her plan into motion, and tried over and over to win the love of her husband. She was to become pregnant several times, and delivered many sons to Jacob. But Leah lived day after day in the same heartache. Her husband simply did not love her. In fact, it was her sister that he deeply cared for.

Leah is a picture of so many lives who are "doing" to win approval. We want to be loved. We were created to be loved. We are at times willing to jump through any hoop, just to receive a simple pat of approval on the back, or an "attaboy".

A friend of mine years ago had been deeply wounded by her parents as a child. She never told me what had happened, only that she wasn't loved. This precious sister was convinced that she was unlovable. If you were her friend, she would do things on purpose to sabotage the friendship, so that she could reject you before you could reject her. It was deeply painful to both people involved. But in each case, if only we could have seen the truth...Jesus was enough. It is His love that bears all things, believes all things, hopes all things, endures all things. It is His love that suffers long and is kind. It is His love that does not seek its own. It seeks US. It is His love that never fails.

Leah had many children. She purposed to try to please Jacob. In the friendship that I had with this person, I jumped through many hoops. I also purposed to try to please her. However, there comes a time beloved, when we need to realize that Jesus is enough. His love has been enough to carry me through great loss in my life, to strengthen me when I didn't know how I would or even could face another day. His love has been my confidence when I needed to press through something that seemed impossible. His love is what will accept me and protect me in the days to come, and His love is what the Bible says will guide me, even unto death.

The world's definition of love involves leaving someone's side or letting go if things get too difficult. God's love NEVER lets you go. There IS nothing that is too difficult for Him. YOU are not too difficult for Him. He came that you might have and experience LIFE. He IS love, and He will continue to love you, guide you, and sustain you...no matter what state you may be in. He will draw you to Himself and engulf you in a love that you can trust in, a love that will never let you go. Believe it. Rest in it. Jump in with both feet, and hang on. Let the love of God keep you afloat. He will certainly not fail you.

Overcoming Rejection - Part 3

Genesis 30:1 "Now when Rachel saw that she bore Jacob no children, she envied her sister, and said to Jacob, "Give me children or else I die!"

Rachel is a picture of someone who has it going on - on the outside. But on the inside, she was depressed, unhappy, and filled with hopelessness. She was loved and wanted by her husband. But she was unable to give him a child. She was jealous of her sister, Leah, who had given Jacob many children. Both women were miserable. Have you ever been jealous of anyone? Have you wished your life was more like theirs? Have you been envious of their relationships, their money, their accomplishments? Do you know that some of the people that we thought had it all together, and that we've been jealous of, aren't as happy as we think? Some of the most popular people cry themselves to sleep at night...and we are totally unaware of what they might be dealing with. Some lives look great on the outside, but can be empty on the inside. Beloved, I implore you...don't spend your life wanting what other people have...or what you THINK they have. Rachel was loved, but couldn't have children. Leah was not loved, but had many sons. Both lived lives that were unfulfilling, and I'm sure the thought of "if only" entered their minds from time to time. One sister was unloved. One sister was unfruitful. Both felt rejected. Today, I am speaking to those with a sense of being unloved. I want you to understand that you ARE loved! God's plan for your life is so much greater than you could ever imagine...and He wants to turn the rejection you may be facing, into a BLESSING! Out of the things that you may see as flaws, failures, or insecurity, God's view is from a higher place. And He sees that you are worthy, chosen, loved, redeemed. Those thoughts that you may be having about yourself sometimes come from a place deep within, that has been so familiar with doubt and insecurity about yourself that you've become convinced. Those thoughts also can be hurled at you by the great deceiver, the father of lies, the one in whom no truth is even possible...the devil. So, here's what you do the next time those thoughts come. When he tries to remind you of your past...you remind him of his future! And if he tries to frighten you about your future, you describe his to him. He only has a short time left on this earth, and he knows it. He will eventually be thrown into the lake of fire! YOU, on the other hand, will spend eternity with Jesus! Your future is so bright, so glorious, so hope filled, and so BLESSED, that your imagination can barely picture how amazing it's going to be! You, beautiful daughter of the Most High God, are deeply loved, and most highly favored. Don't ever believe anything less!

Overcoming Rejection - Part 4

Matthew 1:2 *"Abraham begat Isaac. Isaac begat Jacob. Jacob begat Judah and his brethren."*

We've focused for several days now on the story of Leah and Rachel. They were sisters, and both were married to Jacob. One sister, Leah, was unloved by Jacob. The other sister, Rachel, was unfruitful. She couldn't bare children for a long time. Both felt rejected. As the story progresses, Leah decided to take matters into her own hands. She sent her oldest son into the field to bring her mandrakes. Mandrakes were a narcotic plant, thought by ancient people to be an aphrodisiac, or cure for infertility. When Rachel saw that Leah had mandrakes, she asked Leah to give her some of the ones she had. Leah was upset and answered, "It's no small thing that you've taken my husband, but now you want my son's mandrakes also?" Rachel then told Leah that she could have Jacob that night, if she would just give her some of the mandrakes.

These two sisters were obviously frustrated with life, frustrated with each other, frustrated with Jacob, and most likely frustrated at God. They both decided to take things into their own hands, kind of like Abraham and Sarah had done so many years before. What they failed to think about is that one action by God is better than a lifetime of mandrakes, or of trying to MAKE things happen on your own. Rachel did eventually conceive. Genesis 30:22 says that God remembered the prayers of Rachel and opened her womb. She gave birth to a son and named him Joseph.

Now, I'd like to share something amazing with you! We have the Bible, the rest of the story and the lineage of this family, that they didn't yet see. In Matthew 1:2, we see the beginning of the genealogy of Jesus, the Christ. We see in verse 2 that Judah was Jacob and Leah's son! Then, many generations later, in verse 16, we see that "Jacob (A different Jacob), was the father of Joseph, the husband of Mary (Jesus' mother), by whom Jesus was born, Who is called "the Messiah". The Savior of the world was born out of the rejection of the woman who was unloved!

Child of God, if you have ever felt rejected or unloved, God's plan is bigger. He can and He wants to turn the rejection you're facing into a blessing. Out of whatever rejection you may be facing, you are still chosen, loved, and worthy! Continue to trust Him, beloved. Continue to praise Him, and to believe that he is a GOOD FATHER, Who wants to see you walk in the blessings that He has provided for you!

As if that weren't enough, Rachel's son, Joseph, went on to save Egypt as well as his entire family! Saints, if you are feeling rejected, I strongly encourage you to look past your situation. God is not done with you. He is working on your behalf. Rachel, who couldn't produce, produced a child who saved a nation. The line of Leah's son produced the Savior! If we could move past the pain in our lives, we would see that God has not forsaken us! Just like He promised He would never do!

There is LIFE after rejection! There is hope when we don't see hope. And there is a deep abiding love that permeates your life. It is a love that will bring with it a greater blessing than you could have ever imagined!

Secure because we know Him

Psalm 91:1 *"He who dwells in the shelter of the Most High will remain secure, and rest in the shadow of the Almighty (Whose power no enemy can withstand.)"*

Our amazing God is good. That is the truth about His nature...and Who He is. Knowing Who God is lends to our security in Him. We are secure because we know His character. We know that He will not act outside of that character. We know that the very nature of God is good. We know that He is a loving Father, who cares deeply for His children. Having this knowledge is what will sustain us when we are facing life's challenges.

We don't have to fear or worry about how things will turn out. We can rest in Who He is! We dwell in a place of peace...simply because we have a beautiful relationship with the One Who gives life. When we are more aware of His goodness than we are of our own situation...when we can trust in His nature...when we can rely on who we KNOW Him to be...we will find ourselves abiding in that secret place of the Most High...that place where trouble, fear, doubt may be trying to find us...but it can't...because we are in resting His presence.

When we trust and believe that God is truly for us, and that He is working behind the scenes on our behalf, we can rely on His unfailing faithfulness. We can live in a place of expectation! We expect His favor. We expect His goodness to go before us. We expect that He can and will work through even the situations that we might deem to be impossible...because we know that He is the God of impossible things...and we trust in that truth. We are confident in His nature. Beloved...you are outrageously loved by this incredible God. He can't help but love you...that's who He is!

See Yourself The Way God Sees You

James 1:23-24 *"For if anyone only listens to the word without obeying it, he is like a man who looks carefully at his natural face in a mirror; for once he has looked at himself and gone away, he immediately forgets what he looked like."*

Do you realize that you've never really seen yourself? Of course, you can look at your hands, and legs and feet, but you have never seen yourself as you truly are, face to face. You have seen a reflection of who you are. This verse is a great reminder that God wants us to see ourselves as we truly are. But He is reminding us that we don't need to run into the dressing room and grab a mirror. We will see ourselves quite clearly by simply picking up the Bible, and looking into it. One of the fundamental purposes of the Word of God is to give us true self knowledge, and when we look into it, we see ourselves as God wants us to see ourselves.

Jesus said He would lead us into all truth. I believe the truth in this passage is simple. It is easy to forget what we look like. It is easy to forget who we are in Christ, and who we have been made to be. If you read 2 Samuel 9, Mephibosheth was the son of Jonathan and grandson of Saul. After Jonathan's death, David went forth to show kindness to Saul's house. Mephibosheth had become lame at a young age and had lived his life as a cripple. When David called him forth, his response was, "What is thy servant, that thou shouldest look upon such a dead dog as I am?" His identity was based on his disability, when in fact he was the grandson of a king. He had forgotten his royal lineage, but David looked beyond his disability and offered him a place at the King's table.

How often do we also forget that we are children of the King of Kings? The enemy would like nothing better than for us to focus on what we see as our disabilities so that we are distracted from the call of God on our lives. When you look in the mirror, who do you see? Hopefully, you see a child of God who is being transformed from glory to glory!

We are the glory of the Lord! In Christ, we are a chosen generation. We are part of a royal priesthood, and the King has offered us a place at His table. We are heirs of His great throne. We don't ever have to see ourselves with a victim mentality. We are victors...overcomers!

173

As in a mirror, we should allow God's word to reflect an image of who we truly are. When it shows us our gifts, we should use them. When it shows us how we could treat someone better, we should pay attention, recognize what is true, and change the way we move forward. When it shows how we can live in the power of God, we should begin to walk in that power, believing what the mirror says, above what our circumstances say.

Let your time of daily devotion be an opportunity to see yourself the way that God sees you. Let it be a time of response. And let the Word of God richly dwell in your life, as well as being a reflection to those around you.

Are You Moving, But Going Nowhere? Who Are You Following?

Matthew 15:14 *"If a blind man leads a blind man, both will fall into the pit."*

I recently read a story about a group of genuine lovers of God. Their hearts were fully committed to the Lord Jesus. The desire and dedication they shared was admirable... but they had something else in common. They looked to the approval of others in their group. In order to uphold tradition, they ended up simply following one another. They were men and women...who followed Christ, but walked in a circle...each person following the person in front of them. They moved. They had the desire to truly know Jesus...but they went nowhere. Hebrews 6:12 says that we should "follow those who by faith and patience inherit the promises."

Some of us unfortunately, have followed that same path. We have followed the person in front of us. It may have been a friend, or possibly a leader...and now we find ourselves confused and uncertain. We want to trust and believe that The Lord can lead us personally, but we seem to be clinging tightly to that person we've followed for so long. We have become very familiar with the way they operate. Somehow we don't know how to move forward on our own any more. We want to try. But we are afraid we will fail. We don't think we can make it without them. We may have seen that following them isn't the best path for our lives. We've seen the mistakes that they've made. We've been hurt in some way in this journey, but we continue to hold tightly. We've had times where we have heard the precious voice of the Lord, deep in our spirit...and we know Whose voice it is. He is trying to redirect our steps, but we choose instead to keep following the person in front of us. After all, they have only misled us a couple of times. We cannot see how we would make it unless we were following them. As Jesus said, we are "like sheep without a shepherd"...or "if the blind lead the blind, both will fall into a ditch".

When we look to people, instead of looking to God...who is the only Source of strength, direction, and hope ..we can wind up being terribly misled. We were excited once about our life in Christ, but now we live in confusion and uncertainty. We begin to not trust ourselves. Even worse, we begin to lose trust in Jesus. We question Him. We question His word. We question ourselves. We WANT to question the person walking in front of us...but we wouldn't dare.

175

We have been made righteous by the blood of Christ beloved brothers and sisters... 2Cor.5:21.

An exchange has been made...our sin for His righteousness...and when we begin to realize this wonderful truth, we can begin to walk on our own. We can begin to take steps in faith, knowing that His sheep hear His voice...and we follow Him! He becomes our leader! We now walk in confidence. We now walk with a boldness that we have never experienced before. We are stable with an unshakable foundation!

My question to you today is simply...Who are you following...and why? Do the people in your life help you to have a better understanding of who you are in Christ? Do they encourage you in your walk with God? Do they help you to see that you're an overcomer? Do they help you to know and believe that you are deeply loved, and that all of the promises of God apply to you? Or are you walking in a circle? Are you following the person in front of you simply because that is what you have done for a long time and it's become familiar? Have you chosen to follow Jesus...your Righteousness? Maybe it's time to get out of the circle. Your Shepherd is calling you. He is calling you to follow Him, and Him alone. Take that first step. You will never regret simply following Christ!

We Can Trust The One Who Qualifies The Unqualified

Psalm 103:4 *"Who redeems your life from destruction, Who crowns you with loving kindness and tender mercies."*

There are four women who are mentioned in the genealogy of Jesus. One might think they would be Sarah, or Rebekah...or even Rachel or Leah...the wives of the Old Testament patriarchs. But instead, they are Tamar, Rahab, Ruth and Bathsheba...three of whom had morally questionable backgrounds.

Tamar resorted to deception and prostitution to produce children through her father in law. Yet, it was from her line, the tribe of Judah, that the Messiah came. Rahab was a gentile, and a prostitute in Jericho, who became a believer in the God of Abraham. She also became the mother of Boaz, who married Ruth.

Ruth was morally upright, but as a Moabitess, she was a gentile, and was therefore considered unclean. Yet, she became the grandmother of David, whom the Jews regard as a great King. Bathsheba committed adultery with David. Later, she gave birth to Solomon, from whose royal line Jesus was descended.

When I see these stories in the scriptures, I am reminded that He...Jesus...is greater than our sins. Where sin might abound, Grace much more abounds. Even when the world might want to disqualify us, He qualifies us to be His...and to be blessed...and to be loved!

God is a God of second chances. He is actually a God of many chances. The stories of these women aren't that different from many of our own stories. They show that even when we have troubles...even when we've had a past...even when it's been of our own making...these events in our lives do not have to be final...or fatal. The Lord receives us...just the way we are...He loves us right where we are at. He can work in any situation...but more importantly, He changes US. He makes US new. He redeems our life from destruction. He loves. He restores. He forgives. He is the Friend Who is closer than a brother...Who would never leave us.

Friends, do not look at your present circumstances and be discouraged. Trust the One Who has redeemed your life from destruction, and Who crowns you with loving kindness and tender mercies. Trust the One Who qualifies the disqualified.

Perfect Love Drives Away Fear

1 John 4:18 *"There is no fear in love. But perfect love drives out fear, because fear involves torment, so the one who is afraid is not perfected in love."*

The word *perfect* means "complete" or "mature". The love that is referred to is God's selfless *agape* love.

One of the most amazing characteristics of our God is that He IS love. He cannot and will not act outside of Who He is. When we begin to understand not only the love of God, but the character of God, we will realize that love and fear cannot exist together. Once we begin to believe this, fear will not be able to stay in any capacity in our lives. It cannot remain alongside this extraordinary and triumphant love.

One of the keys to overcoming fear is total and complete trust in God. Trusting God is how Shadrach, Meshach, and Abednego faced the fiery furnace, without fear. It is how Daniel faced the lion's den. Trusting God is how Stephen stood before his killers fearlessly. To trust God is to refuse to give in to fear. Even in the darkest times, we can trust in our Lord to love us, to guide us, to protect us, and to keep His promises. This trust that we experience comes from knowing God, like you would know your spouse. If someone came to me and said something unkind about my husband, I would know his heart well enough to know that there could be no truth to it. We should be and can be that convinced about Who God is, and how much He loves us.

Another key to overcoming fear is found in verse 12 of 1 John:4, which reminds us that "If we love one another, God abides in us, and His love is completed and perfected in us!" Have you ever noticed that if you are having a challenging day, it really helps to get your mind off of yourself? One of the best and most practical ways to overcome fear is to love one another...and change your focus. Focus on God. Focus on His Word. Look for someone that might need a word of encouragement and go visit them or write them a note. Bake them some cookies. It sounds like a small thing, but simply changing what you're looking at that day can change your reactions to the day's events, and you can go from fear...to love!

Fear is associated with punishment, but the believer has been fully forgiven of any and all sin, past, present and future. The one who knows the heart of Christ lives in true fellowship with Him and can fully trust the Lord with his heart, knowing that God IS love.

Beloved, I believe that if you stand on the following truths, you will be ready, and armed for battle!

1. I will keep my mind on Christ. (Isaiah 26:3)
2. The Lord will give me strength. (Isaiah 41:10)
3. God will not fail me. (Deuteronomy 31:6)
4. The Lord is my Salvation. I have nothing to fear. (Isaiah 12:2)
5. God is on my side. (Psalm 118:6)

Multiplied Blessings to you all!

No Negative Force Can Occupy The Same Place As His Spirit

1 Corinthians 15:57 *"Thanks be to God who gives us the victory, through our Lord Jesus Christ"*

Most beloved child of God – Has the Lord ever failed you? Of course He hasn't. He has never forsaken you or turned His back in any way. He is emphatically FOR you. He is on your side...in your corner. He has been and will continue to be your place of refuge and strong defense.
He is your place of protection. In this amazing place, He guards you from the things of the world – from sickness and ill health. He is with you even now. There is absolutely nothing for you to fear because His plans for your life are being fulfilled as you rest in Him and rely on His strength. You can trust Him fully.
You may count on the One who is righteous – who not only works in cases that are seemingly impossible... where the obstacles appear to be insurmountable...but He incredibly overrules whatever prevailing circumstance you may find yourself to be in. He takes pleasure in bringing victory in those places where there is no victory in sight.

Count on Him. He is always there. Whenever faith is being stood upon, things begin to change. Darkness is turned to light. Grief is turned to joy. Sickness to health. Poverty to supply...doubt to faith...anxiety to trust.

No type of negative force or oppression can stand in His presence. It cannot occupy the same space where His Spirit resides. In His presence, all that is not of Him MUST leave!

You've asked for the victory. He says you are a victorious overcomer. But don't just look for that victory...look for HIM...and you will see the victory that He brings with Him.

You Have All The Strength You Need For This Moment Of Your Life

Isaiah 40:28 *"Have you not known? Have you not heard? The everlasting God, the Lord, the Creator of the ends of the earth, does not faint or grow weary"*

Lift up your eyes beloved child of God. Look to your Creator. He has formed you, this Master Craftsman, this amazing Artist. All things beautiful have evolved from Him. You were made perfectly by the Source of all life. To fathom means to go deeper and deeper...and you are continually exploring the limitless depth of His profound love for you.

He has implanted power into your Spirit. When you have no might, He increases your strength. He causes it to multiply, and brings joy to your spirit, causing strength and might to abound in you. The joy of the Lord truly does become your strength. He gives you more power and ability than you would ever be able to manifest in your human capability. He has given you energy as well...more than that of a skilled athlete who might compete for the gold medal. He gives you all the strength you will need for this moment of your life. Yet, He Himself does not grow weary!

Because you are in Christ, you not only have physical strength, but emotional endurance along with strength of character. Your spirit soars with this astounding strength. The excitement of new possibility propels your life into plenty of wonderful new directions.

You may have once been a slave to sin and weakness...but you have been made clean by the blood of Christ, and your sins have been blotted out.

May we always remember that in Christ is everlasting strength, eternal hope, and never-ending power. Let us not forget that the Lord never grows faint, and He does not get weary. You are in Him. Therefore, you live, and move, and have your being in Him.

He strengthens you day by day. Glory in Him, and rejoice with Him every day. His joy is your strength.

We Remember His Sacrifice

Hebrews 10:17 *"And their sins and iniquities will I remember no more."*

Child of God, have you ever really thought about the fact that you have been forgiven? You are not only forgiven...but your amazing Father CHOOSES to remember your sins no more! This is almost difficult to understand, since we so often rehearse things over and over in our minds when people have hurt us. We remember their unkind words. We hold on to injustice...and play it like a broken record...over and over in our minds...while knowing that our own sin has been forgiven...and forgotten!

In the Old Testament, animal sacrifices were made because without the shedding of blood, there was no remission (forgiveness) of sin...but Hebrews 10:3 says " but in those sacrifices, there was a REMEMBRANCE made again of sins every year." It wasn't possible for the blood of goats and bulls to remove sin. It only covered it. What people needed was forgiveness...the permanent, stain erasing, powerful, amazing forgiveness that Jesus would offer!

Hebrews 10:10 says that we are sanctified through the offering of the body of Jesus Christ...once...for all! The word sanctified means to be cleansed, purified, made holy, separated from profane things, dedicated to God. This is what the sacrifice of Jesus has done for YOU beloved! Jesus offered one sacrifice (Himself) for our sins forever! Where there is remission (forgiveness) of sin, there is no more offering needed!

Child of God, you have been forgiven...and you can trust that your Heavenly Father will not call to remembrance that thing that may haunt you. He has chosen not to. As the scripture says, "Blessed is the man to whom The Lord will not impute sin." Christ laid down His life for us, while we were yet sinners....and the blood of Jesus has washed our sins away. We are clean...because of Jesus! He remembers our sin no more...but we remember His sacrifice...and we are so grateful to be so completely loved.

Our Heavenly Father Always Leads Us In Triumph

2 Corinthians 2:14 *"But thanks be to God who always leads us in triumph in Christ, and through us spreads and makes evident everywhere the sweet fragrance of the knowledge of Him."*

Pause and think about this. We are triumphant, at ALL times, because we are in Christ! No matter what your situation may look like on the outside, you are IN Jesus, and He will always lead you in triumph! That is something to hold on to, beloved. It is such a good verse to think on, especially when we are dealing with a difficult circumstance. We can remind ourselves as we go through, that this too shall pass, and we will come out on the other side!

The other thing that I love in this verse is the fact that because we are in Christ, there is something in us that people will pick up on. It is the sweet fragrance of the knowledge of Him. Paul's bold confession of God gave witness of a life that had died to self and lived only for Christ. It demonstrated him to be a man who followed in the footsteps of the Lord Jesus, by presenting his life as a living sacrifice (burnt offering) that is holy and acceptable to God.

Perhaps the sacrifice in the Old Testament that most typifies the life of Christ and the life of Paul, was that of a burnt offering. It was a freewill offering, given to the Lord out of love, and not out of duty. Because it was given out of love, it showed a deep loving respect for the Lord and a passion to carry out His will. The Burnt offering was a gift, freely given, joyfully presented and lovingly offered to God, and it became a sweet smelling savor to Him.

Paul explains that when we are able to trust God, even during what can be a difficult season, when we are pressed out of measure, what comes forth is a sweet smell, an aroma that blesses the heart of God, but it blesses the heart of those around us as well.

May our lives become a living sacrifice, holy to the Lord and honoring to His name. May we be willing in all circumstances to give thanks to our heavenly Father, knowing that He always leads us in triumph in Christ, and manifests through us a sweet smelling aroma of the knowledge of Him.

Spiritual Strength Is Stored In The Very Depth Of Our Being

I Chronicles 26:27 *"Some of the plunder taken in battle they dedicated for the repair of the temple of the Lord."*

I believed for years that God brought trials into our lives, to test us. But, then what do I do with James 1:13 that says that God Himself tempts no one. He is not the One who brings trials into our lives to see how we will react. He already knows us. It would not be in His true nature to bring trouble. We live in a fallen world. I believe that most of the trials we endure stem from that. But I do believe that He has given us tools to stand against the forces of evil when those difficult situations come our way.

Great physical force is stored in the depths of the earth, in places such as coal mines. Coal was produced by the tremendous heat that burned ancient forests many years ago. In the same way, spiritual force is stored in the very depth of our being and because that is the case, we are ready, spiritually speaking, to stand in the face of adversity.

A woman that I know about sent her husband out one morning to wash their car. When he didn't come back for a while, she went out to see what was taking him so long. She found him lying still in their driveway, not breathing, no pulse. She could have panicked. But she believed that God had given her the tools to act in this situation. She dug deep into the Spiritual resources that she knew she had. She began to command death to leave her husband's body. She believed that she had authority in Christ. She declared her husband to be alive and well, made whole by the blood of Jesus! The next thing you know, his eyes opened and he sat up!

Someday we will see that the "plunder taken in battle" can actually prepare us to become like Great-Heart in the book *Pilgrim's Progress*...so that we too could lead our fellow pilgrims triumphantly through trials and difficulties...and eventually end up at the city of the King. May we never forget that we are victorious, not because we've been home doing our push-ups, but because God says we are victorious. We are strong in the Spirit!

Paul never carried around a discouraged attitude...but a chorus of victorious praise. The more difficult his trial, the more he trusted and rejoiced.

He said, "Even if I am poured out like a drink offering on the sacrifice and service coming from your faith, I am glad and rejoice with all of you". Phil. 2:17...

Lord, today help us to recognize You in every situation. Help us to know that seeking You first can at times seem like a battle...a battle for time, a battle of trust...but it is a battle worth fighting because the plunder we recover in having a deeper knowledge of You is what will Help us to stand firmly no matter our circumstances.

This Battle Belongs To The Lord

2 Chronicles 20:15 "He said, listen carefully all of you people of Judah, and you inhabitants of Jerusalem, and King Jehoshaphat, the Lord says this to you, 'Be not afraid or dismayed at this great multitude, for the battle is not yours, but God's. '"

Did you know that courage is not the absence of fear? It is pushing past the emotions, trusting God despite the circumstances, and taking steps in faith to seek the Lord in whatever you may be going through. That is what Jehoshaphat did. He sought God.

In any situation, no matter how overwhelming, you can determine ahead of time what you are going to do, and how you are going to obtain victory. If you have already decided to trust God no matter what, then when things come at you that you weren't expecting, you are able to remain stable and solid, seeking God, who is always on your side. You can set your mind on victory...or defeat. Jehoshaphat was afraid. He had the armies of the sons of the Ammonites as well as the Moabites coming to invade Judah. He realized that without God's help, the Israelites would be powerless against the enemy. But, they were not without God's help. Jehoshaphat heard from the Lord, and his mindset changed, to one of victory.

In our day, just as in Jehoshaphat's day, the Lord is present. He is willing to fight our battles. He wants us to increasingly find freedom from fear, and to walk with courage through any situation. Real freedom is the deep-seated confidence that no matter what, God has provided everything we need, and we are not going into this thing alone.

There are times when God instructs us to take our positions, stand still, and see His deliverance. There are also times when we need to take our hands off, stand back, and let God fight for us. We needn't fear what comes against us. We need to simply stand firm in our faith. We can't always see the whole picture from where we are in the situation, but the Lord can, and He knows the way through for us. When we call on Him, I believe that He responds to us in the same way He did to the people of Israel, by instructing them to "Be not afraid nor dismayed, for the battle is not yours, but God's."

He further instructed the Israelites to take their positions, but stand STILL, and watch the Lord, who would fight for them.

All of Israel fell down before the Lord and worshiped Him...and began to praise God with a loud voice. When the people began singing and praising, the Lord set ambushments against the enemy, and they were struck down in defeat.

If you are facing a battle today that seems overwhelming, give it to God, and allow Him to fight for you. Meanwhile, you continue to rest in Him, trust Him, and Praise Him! Then watch...as He makes a way where there seemed to be no way!

I Am The Way And The Truth And The Life

Jesus answered, *"I am the way and the truth and the life. No one comes to the Father except through me. If you really knew me, you would know my Father as well. From now on, you do know Him and have seen Him."* John 14:6-7

It can't be said any plainer than this. In this very familiar statement, the Lord Jesus silences all the naysayers, all the critics, and forever answers our questions about the nature of God. I say that it is very familiar because it is often quoted but seldom really understood.

The Lord's statement that He is the way answers a very serious question..."How?" When He said that He is the Truth, He answers the age old question, "Why?" And in His revelation to us that He is the Life, He speaks to the familiar question "What?" These questions, "how", "why" and "what" seem to come up often in our hearts. Since the fall, "how", "what", and "why" have dominated the thinking of man. Many have tried to answer these heartfelt questions over the centuries. Rows of books fill libraries and bookstores all over the world. These inquiries have been debated by great leaders and teachers. They have been written about, sung about, and discussed openly. Sadly, it seems that for many, there has been little understanding or revelation on the matter.

Yet in this one brief conversation with His disciples, Jesus says that He is the answer to each. He doesn't say, "I have the answer to each", or "I know how to find the answer to each", but rather, "If you know me, you now know God", and "If you've seen me, you have seen God." He is the answer to every question and every uncertainty. He is the answer to our concerns about the meaning of our very existence.

How is this possible? It is because our Lord and Savior embodies each of us. He is God in human form, He is the very *way to God*. As the *Logos*, the very Word of God, *He Himself is the truth*. And because He is eternal, and the creator and sustainer of all that exists, both seen and unseen, *He is the life*.

It is a continual challenge of our faith to gain and hold to the understanding that all we need is in Jesus. He is God's provision to mankind, in every area and in every way. God the Father has given us His Son. When we have a need, it must awaken our heart to again confess as did Paul the apostle, "That I may know him."

This Land Is Your Land!

Joshua 2:24 "And they said unto Joshua, 'Truly, The Lord hath delivered it into our hands all the land; for even all the inhabitants of the country do faint because of us.'"

This is another verse that really speaks to me. Two of the men whom Joshua had sent to scope out the land of Jericho, came back with this report. They had spoken to Rahab, who was a harlot...but a woman who had a heart for God. She was willing to risk everything she had for a God she barely knew. We can never gauge a person's love for God based on what their background might be, or their lifestyle...or even their appearance. She spoke of the concern and downright fear that her people were experiencing because of the stories they were hearing about the children of Israel. They had heard of God's extraordinary power in defeating the armies across the Jordan River. Her people knew that God had given Israel the land. Rahab expressed that all the inhabitants of the land "faint because of you."

I am thinking today about who...and/or what...may be attempting to inhabit YOUR land. Who or what is it that seems to want to occupy what you know God has given to you? Rahab spoke to the men that she knew God had given the land to. I believe that God has done the same thing for each one of us. He has given us the body that we live in...our land! He has given us the soul that we possess...the mind that produces our thoughts and emotions...the desires that we long to see come to fruition...our gifts and talents...our ministries...in other words...our land! This land has been given to us...by an amazing God! And I believe that the "inhabitants" of OUR land have to bow to us. That discouragement that you may be dealing with FAINTS...because of YOU! That tiredness has to go...it is an intruder in YOUR land. Any type of despondency or despair cannot stay. This is YOUR land! Reasoning and unbelief must vacate!

When we all start to have an understanding that what we have has been given to us is by The Lord, and that He meant for every one of these gifts to be specifically ours, we can more easily begin to stand firmly against the things that try to invade what is ours. The land is yours! God delivered it into YOUR hands! Any other "inhabitants" faint because of YOU!

The Foundation Of Our Faith Is Unshakable

II Peter 1:16-18 *"For we did not follow cleverly devised stories or myths when we made known to you the power and coming of our Lord Jesus Christ, but we were eye witnesses of His majesty. For when He was invested with honor and (the radiance of the Shekinah) glory from God the Father, such a voice as this came to Him from the Majestic Glory (in the bright cloud that overshadowed Him, saying), 'This is My Son, My Beloved Son, in Whom I am well pleased and delighted.' We actually heard this voice made from heaven when we were together with Him on the holy mountain."*

If ever you are struggling in your walk of faith, read this verse! Read it several times, and let it sink in! I can only imagine what it must have been like to have been there. To hear Peter actually say to all of us now, "Listen people...this was not just a cleverly devised story. This was no myth". In other words, this was not a hoax! Peter was letting us know that he wanted us, long after he was gone, to be able to call to remembrance the truth, that these three disciples, Peter, James and John, had walked with Jesus. They had seen the Shekinah glory from God the Father. They had heard the voice from heaven. They were eye witnesses. Peter was very intentional about what he was saying. He wanted those of us who would come after him to know that the very foundation of our faith is unshakable!

Peter was clear that this was not a vision or a dream that only he himself had seen. Rather, it was an actual experience that Peter, James and John all saw and heard. In that day, as in every age, there were religious frauds, even con artists, who made a living by claiming to have some new revelation that would help their followers to get whatever they wanted. These false teachers invariably would charge a substantial fee for services rendered. They would lure people in by promising them something, such as freedom from their problems. But their teaching was false, and so their promises were never truly delivered.

Paul referred also to the false teachers of that time. He told Timothy to "instruct certain men not to teach strange doctrine, nor pay attention to myths and endless genealogies, which give rise to speculation, rather than furthering the administration of God, which is by faith." He also instructed Titus to reprove his hearers "so that they may be sound in the faith, not paying attention to myths and commandments of men who turn away from the truth."

John also confirmed the words of Peter when he wrote, "And the Word became flesh, and dwelt among us, and we saw His glory...glory as of the only begotten from the Father, full of grace and truth."

We have the testimony of a man here who spent over three years with the Son of God. He saw Jesus hungry, tired, and rejected. He saw him feed the 5,000. He saw Him walk on water, heal the sick, and raise the dead. He saw Jesus in His glory on the mount of transfiguration. And He saw Him risen from the dead, ascending into heaven, and with the promise that He is coming again! This amazing witness to Jesus Christ is part of the foundation of our faith...and I believe! How about you?

If Forgiveness Could Be Bottled, It Could Change Your World - Yet God Gives It Freely

1 Timothy 1:16 *"Howbeit for this cause I obtained mercy, that in me first Jesus Christ might shew forth all longsuffering, for a pattern to them which should hereafter believe on him to life everlasting."*

Longsuffering...a word you don't often hear...and perfectly descriptive of our God. It means forbearance, patience, constancy, perseverance, and even to be slow in avenging wrongdoing! Paul had stated in verse 15 that he was the chief of sinners. He had been a Pharisee...one who lived by the law and upheld it. He had been schooled under a man named Gamaliel...who was the leader of the Sanhedrin...the Jewish council who made up what would have been the Supreme Court in Judea during the Roman period. Paul described himself as a blasphemer...a persecutor...and injurious. He went from house to house arresting Christians and dragging them to prison. He even obtained letters of permission from the Jewish leaders to bring Christians to Jerusalem for punishment. He was also consenting to the stoning death of Stephen...an amazing man of God...and yet after all that, Paul obtained mercy from God...and the grace of God was exceedingly abundant with faith and love, which is in Christ Jesus (vs.14).

Beloved, Jesus came into this world to save sinners, and through the life of Paul, Jesus showed incredible forbearance, patience, and a beautiful constancy in Paul's life in His pursuance of him...that Paul might know Jesus! He was a man completely changed by the love of God...and we are blessed to read his story, not only so that we might see the heart of God, but that we might see the pattern laid out for all of US...an outline for OUR lives...an example, if you will...for all who would hereafter come to believe on Him.

Paul had received forgiveness. What a powerful thing! If it could be bottled, forgiveness could move mountains, mend relationships, heal the broken...and change the world. Yet, God gives it...FREELY! All we need to do is receive it!

Paul had to go forward after he received salvation (sozo)...(to be saved, forgiven, to have been rescued from danger, to be healed.). If Paul had continued to look back at what he'd done, he might have stayed in the past. He might have never fulfilled the amazing future that God had planned for his life! He could have been rendered useless...incapable of moving ahead.

192

Also, if Paul had tried to add to his salvation...to the finished work of Jesus...then a question arises...why did Jesus die? Why did He lay down His life for Paul?

Why did He lay down His life for you...for me...if it wasn't enough...if we have to add to it? Beloved, nothing could be further from the truth. Salvation was meant to be a gift to all of us...and it's a gift that is a complete gift. In other words, salvation was finished at the cross, and nothing needs to be added to it. We simply receive it as we would receive any gift...with gratitude, and a heartfelt thanks to the God of mercy. He has provided this gift because He loves us!

Paul's life should encourage us. Beloved...no matter what may have happened in your past, you can move forward, like Paul did. We don't have to keep looking back, dragging the past along into the future. We've been given a gift that was meant to bring life in abundance to every partaker. It's a gift that brings hope when life throws us a curve in the road, peace in the midst of any and all circumstance, supernatural strength when all human strength is diminished, joy that flows like a fountain...and the list goes on and on. The grace of our God is exceedingly abundant with faith and love in Christ...for every one of us. Receive it today. Partake. Rest. You will never regret the decision to shake off the past, and to put ON the fullness of God!

God is WITH us!

Matthew 1:22-23 *"Now all this was done, that it might be fulfilled which was spoken of The Lord by the prophet, saying, 'Behold, a virgin shall be with child, and shall bring forth a son, and they shall call His name Emmanuel, which being interpreted is, God with us.'"*

Jesus' name is not only... Jesus. His name is Emmanuel...and it has such an incredible meaning! It was not chosen haphazardly. It was prophesied by the prophet Isaiah...and it means the God Who is with us! That is Who Jesus is! He is the God Who is with us! He IS God. He IS with us! Amazing!

Years ago, I had a friend whose husband struggled with all kinds of problems. Eventually, he went to jail because he had gone so far in his debauchery. It looked like he would spend a long time there. It looked like his marriage was probably over. It looked like he would not be allowed to raise his children and that they would never know their dad....but God was WITH him. One day, God sent someone to this man to tell him about Jesus. And from that day nearly forty years ago, that man's life changed. His marriage relationship was healed. His relationship with his children...healed! He did not spend years in jail, but was soon released. He has spent his life serving The Lord...loving his Savior...and if he could tell you one thing, it would be that he knew...that God was with him!

Everything we struggle to get through...all of our own self effort...cannot produce what the presence of God can do in an instant! It can change hearts. It can bring healing. It can restore and bring wholeness to the most challenging situation. And, the truth is...it is not struggle or self effort that brings transformation. It is beholding the Savior. It is trusting in the fact that He is with us...because He said so.

It is an amazing thing to have God with us. Look back at some of the Old Testament passages that speak of God being with them. When God was with them, they won battles. When God was with them, they were never defeated. When God was with them, they were victorious, and successful. Even when they were outnumbered, it did not matter...because God was with them.

It is no different for us today... Except for one thing. God is IN us. We take Him with us wherever we go.

We simply need to believe it, stand on it, and walk by faith, taking every step trusting...that He is with me! He is our Helper, and He will not only work for us... He will work through us!

If you are wondering how to change what you expect in your life...so that you aren't looking back, and expecting more of the same...look forward...and plant your life firmly in His word, beholding Who He is in your life, beholding His promises...and you will begin to see change...a greater manifestation of what...and WHO...you are focused on. Surely...You can EXPECT this to happen!

You Will Never Be Forgotten

Isaiah 49:16 *"behold, I have graven thee on the palms of My hands"*

The children of Israel had been taken captive in Babylon. They began to feel as though God had deserted them...but Isaiah pointed out that just as a mother would never leave her child, God had "engraved" or" inscribed" His beloved children on the palms of His hand.

Every one of us has, at some point in time, gone through some type of bondage...something that seemed to hold us captive...and it's very likely that many have questioned where God was in that situation. Beloved, it is not even in God's nature to leave one of His children. He has made provision for us in every way through the finished work of Jesus at the cross, to not only be with us in time of trouble, but to live IN us. You live in a body. You have a soul...a mind, will and emotions...but you also have His Spirit living in you. You have become the temple of the Holy Spirit. For Him to desert you in any way would mean that He didn't hold to the incredible covenant that we are part of in Christ, and God would never break covenant. His love is too great. Hebrews 8:12 speaks of that covenant when it says "for I will be merciful to their unrighteousness, and their sins and iniquities will I remember no more." Verse 10 says, "I will be to them a God, and they shall be to me a people." Precious child, YOU are His! He says that all shall know Him from the least to the greatest.

He has made a way for us to know Him. He lives in the heart of the believer. He wants to reveal Himself to you. He longs for intimacy with you. He will not leave you. He has engraved you on the palm of His hand.

If you look up the word engraved, it means to permanently inscribe. Hundreds of years ago, there was a practice that involved one burning, or permanently puncturing... "inscribing" something that was of great value, onto the palm of one's hand. It signified that whatever had been inscribed was so important, that the wearer wanted to be continuously reminded of it.
Beloved, God has the image of YOU indelibly etched into His hand. You are always in His sight. You are always on His mind and in His heart. His eyes are fixed on you. You are always near to Him.

I think sometimes of the nail pierced hands of our Savior....that prove His victory over death...that validate His authority as Lord and Savior...that confirm how great a love He has for every one of us...and I am reminded again that the hands that were pierced for me...for you...are the same hands that hold my life, and that carry my inscription. Beloved, you will never be forgotten!

Launch Out Into The Deep River Of Life

Luke 5:4. *"Launch out into the deep water"*

Jesus instructed the fishermen to launch out into the deep. That is where the boatload of fish were to be found. The depth of the water into which we embark really depends on several things...have we completely let go at the shoreline? How great is our need to "launch out", and even...how significant is our fear of the deep water?
I believe that it is the same with us as it was with Simon. It is in the deep places of God where our needs are met. It is in the depth of His Word that we will find new meaning.
When we launch out Into the depth of the atonement, we begin to have such a beautiful understanding of Who Christ is...and How greatly we are loved. This alone will carry us through the deepest waters that we could ever maneuver. When we begin to have a deeper understanding of Who He is, we also start to have a deep understanding of who we are in Him. Our trust begins to increase. Our hope grows...and we find ourselves floating along the deep and furious water...not really concerned about the depth...because we know the One Who carries us, the One Who provides...and the One to whom we are anchored.

We can put out into the deep of God's purpose for us. We will be strengthened to walk in that purpose, and to face every detour with boldness and confidence that God is holding on to us, and that we will not sink. We will be more courageous about whatever is set before us...whether it's our ministry, or simply sharing the good news that is the gospel. The depth of our vision unfolds until we can begin to imagine the brilliance of His presence, and our heart is overwhelmed with joy!
The waters of Ezekiel's vision were at first ankle deep. Soon, they were knee deep. Then they were waist deep. Eventually, they were so deep that they could not be passed over. I heard a teacher one time who said that once the waters are over our heads, it really doesn't matter how deep they become...because we are simply floating along...trusting God on this voyage...knowing that He will never let go of us.
Beloved...launch out into the deep river of life! I believe the Holy Spirit desires that our SELF be completely submerged. In that way, we are hidden...and even bathed.in His life giving stream. Let loose of whatever you may be holding onto at the shoreline...and sail with Him into the deepest of waters. This is a great adventure!

You Can Truly Bless The Heart Of God!

Jeremiah 2:2 *"I remember you"*

Our precious Savior, Jesus Christ, delights in thinking about His bride, and to look upon Her beauty. Just as a bird would often return to his nest, or a traveler far away from home longs to see his home again, it would seem that the heart continually pursues the object of its' affection. Think of the person that you long to see, the child, the spouse, the mother or father...you can never look too often upon the face of someone that you love. We desire always to have what is precious to us in our sight.

I believe it is so even with our Lord Jesus. From all eternity, "His delights were with the sons of men", and His thoughts rolled onward to the time when each of us were born. He has viewed each of us in the mirror of His foreknowledge. "In your book, all my members were written, which in continuance were fashioned when as yet there was none of them." When the world was set upon its pillars, He was there, and He knew you before you were ever formed in your mother's womb.

I heard a true story many years ago about a woman who was imprisoned for murder. She spent day after day alone in her cell, thinking about what she had done. One day an evangelist came to the prison, and she was allowed out of her solitary confinement to go see him. He told her that day about the love of Jesus, and that He had laid down His life for her, even while she had been living in sin. This woman could hardly believe that a love like that existed. But she realized, that Jesus had remembered her. She received Christ that day, and her life was changed!

Her family, however, did not know about this change in her life. They were hurt and angry over what she had done, and refused to ever visit her. Because she was in solitary confinement, she saw no one, except the guards who brought her food each day. She began to wonder how she would get through the next 20 years with no one to share Jesus with. She wanted to encourage others with this new way of life in Christ. She wanted to bless, as she had been blessed. Then it came to her one day. She would bless God. Since she had come to the realization that He would never leave her or forsake her, she determined to never leave or forsake Him. She began to minister to the Lord!

199

Beloved, He remembers you. He knows every thought you've had. He knows your heart. He knows how you might have reacted to someone's hurtful words. He remembers. And, you can trust that He will never let you go. As you go through your day, may you remember Him. May the Lord indelibly paint on the eyes of your soul, the image of His Son. Picture Him holding out His arms to you. Picture yourself sitting with Him, and then pour out to Him from your heart of gratefulness and thanksgiving. You can truly be a blessing to HIS heart today!

His Presence Is Sufficient In The Storm

Galatians 2:20 *"I am crucified with Christ; nevertheless I live; yet not I, but Christ liveth in me; and the life which I now live in the flesh I live BY the faith of the Son of God, who loved me, and gave himself for me."*

The heritage of the cross is a life lived in trust. It frees us from the bondage of sin that drives us to compensate for that, and provides for us the certainty that we are loved by the God of the universe. This is the faith He wants us to live by, and even that faith is His gift to us.

Few versions of the Bible translate Galatians 2:20 exactly as it appears in the original Greek. Paul wrote: "I have been crucified with Christ, and I no longer live, but Christ lives in me. The life I live in the body, I live by the faith of the Son of God, who loved me and gave Himself for me"

The vast majority translate it, "The life I live in the body, I live by faith IN the Son of God." They could not conceive of what Paul might have meant by living the faith OF Jesus...so they translated it as "faith IN the Son of God" because certainly there are so many wonderful scriptures that speak of the importance of putting our faith IN Him. I believe Paul was speaking about something different however in this verse. I believe that Paul was saying that he lived by Jesus' faith...not by mustering up enough of his own.

We know that when we are born again, it is not a physical rebirth, but a spiritual one. The very Spirit of God comes to live inside us. There are many verses that attest to this, but one of my favorites speaks of the fact that we have become the temple that the Holy Spirit now dwells in. It's amazing to think that in the Old Testament, there was a temple built that had an outer court, an inner court, and a Most Holy Place, where the Spirit of God dwelt. Now, WE have become that temple. The outer court is our body. The inner court is our soul. The Most Holy Place is our spirit.

The Bible then instructs us to walk in the Spirit, not in the flesh. We have been made new creations in Christ. He lives IN us. And when we are walking in the Spirit, one of the things we are experiencing is a new sense of His direction, His hope, His purpose...and His faith. Because He lives IN us, we no longer have to look to the heavens and reach out for answers because the One Who IS the answer, lives IN us.

201

When the Lord showed me this recently, it changed my life. Time after time over the years, I have wondered what was "wrong" with me. Why I couldn't muster up more faith? For years, I saw myself as a failure to God because it seemed so hard to stand strong during the difficult times. But beloved...God does not see us as failures. We are not disappointments to Him. This verse is incredible. How often do you feel "weak" in faith? Try as hard as you might to believe, belief still escapes you. How do you muster up what you lack? People tell us to simply trust Jesus more...and while they may be right, it is rarely helpful to hear without practically understanding the how part. How do we trust Him more than we already do?

I believe the answer lies here. Paul didn't live by his own human faith. He knew that Jesus lived IN him, and he let Jesus' trust in the Father stand...IN HIS OWN LIFE.

It's amazing how simple it is, knowing that we don't have to muster up more faith. We can stand in Christ's faith, Who lives in us. It releases a power beyond our own abilities or intellect. We can see a little more clearly. Our hearts find greater endurance. Answers we thought we needed no longer seem that important. It is His presence that proves to be sufficient in the storm...and we recognize once again...that we are loved.

Move Past Your Roadblocks, Like David Did

2 Samuel 5:7-19 "But when the Philistines heard that they had anointed David King over Israel, all came to seek David, and he heard of it, and went down to the stronghold. The Philistines also came and spread themselves in the valley of Rephaim. And David inquired of the Lord saying, "shall I go up to the Philistines? Wilt thou deliver them into my hand?" And the Lord said unto David, "Go up…for I will doubtless deliver the Philistines into thy hand."

David had been anointed King of Israel. This was his destiny. However, now the enemy was trying to capture him. Has it ever seemed that just as you were making progress toward something…just as you are able to look back at that huge hurdle you overcame, there is another obstacle right around the corner? It's like you can almost see the finish line to your dream. You're so close, you can nearly reach out and touch it…but the opposition that would prevent you from seeing it come to fruition is looming right in front of you…and this time it seems to be too massive to overcome.

David would have understood what you are going through. He would have appreciated what you are feeling…because he had been there. He had been anointed, but now his enemies were trying to stop him. They were trying to steal his destiny.

When Jesus was born, Herod tried to kill Him. He tried to steal his destiny. When Jesus had been baptized and then fasted 40 days, while He was in the wilderness, Satan came to tempt Him, in an effort to derail His destiny. Probably every person we can read about in the scriptures had a roadblock of some kind…from Abraham to Moses, from Esther to Ezekiel, from Daniel to Joshua, from Jesus to Paul.

David, in these verses, paints a clear picture of his response to the situation. First, he retreated to the stronghold. A stronghold was similar to a castle, a place of defense and protection, a fortress, a quiet place.

Today, we run to Jesus. He is our Strong Hold! David said, "He is my Rock, my Fortress, my Stronghold." He is also our Shield and Deliverer. He is the One in Whom we take refuge. What a fortress or fortification might be to a city, Jesus is to us. We are kept by His power, as in a garrison or barricade. We are secure in Him.

The second thing that David did was to inquire of the Lord. He asked God what his next move was to be. He needed to hear from the Lord before he could proceed…and in that place of quiet…that place of protection…that Strong Hold…the Lord spoke. He revealed to David not only what his next move should be, but also the outcome!

When we are facing circumstances that appear to be overwhelming…that threaten to steal our destiny…when we are teetering on the path to our future…we can learn from the life of David. It is in that place of refuge…that quiet place in Christ, where we seek Him…and then listen for His answer. Then, we can continue in the plan and the purpose that God created us for.

God Is Pleased With You

Luke 3:21-22 *"Now, when all the people were baptized, Jesus was also baptized, and while He was praying the heaven was opened, and the Holy Spirit descended on Him in bodily form like a dove, and a voice came from heaven, 'You are My Son, My Beloved. In You I am well pleased'."*

God was well pleased with His Son, Jesus. And it's wonderful to me to think about the fact that He was pleased with Jesus before He did any miracles or mighty works. This must have painted a picture in the heart of Jesus that He was loved. He was God's Son, and His Father was delighted with Him. His Father was overjoyed...just because His Son existed! He didn't have to do anything to prove Himself before God. The fact that Jesus was born was enough for Him. He loved His Son!

Think about this for a moment. Jesus allowed God's word to be true in His life. If you read John 5:19-20, He told the Jews that He (the Son) could do nothing of Himself, but whatever things the Father did, He would do in the same way, because the Father dearly loves the Son and would show Him great things. Jesus believed it. He knew Who He was, the Son of God, and He never allowed the people around Him to create any type of doubt about that.

My question today is, "What about you?" All of us who have received Jesus, are children of God. But how do you see yourself? I have never read anywhere in the scriptures that God considers us to be His grandchildren. No. We are His sons and daughters. We are His kids. And He is pleased with us. So many verses would back this up, but let's look for a moment at John 17:22-23 "I have given to them (us) the glory and honor which You have given to Me, that they may be one, just as WE are one; I in them and You in Me, that they may be perfected and completed into one, so that the world may know without any doubt that You sent Me, and that You have LOVED THEM, just as You have loved Me!" There are so many other verses I could go to. Ephesians 1 talks about how God would never leave us as orphans. Colossians 2 reminds us that we were removed from the kingdom of darkness and translated into the Kingdom of God's dear Son!

Do you see it? And will you, like Jesus did, believe His Word? In Luke 4:2-15, the enemy challenged the identity that had been formed inside Jesus by attacking the Word of God.

205

If Jesus had given in to that temptation to doubt, history as we know it, would have been changed completely. The devil wanted Jesus to develop a wrong picture of Who He truly was, and to let go of the nature of Who He was...the Son of God. But Jesus believed God's Word to be true.

I implore everyone who reads this to consider something. We need to let go of self, and take hold of the Word of God. We need to believe what He says about us! Believing Him is what ushers us into His power and grace. Beloved, let His Word paint a picture on the inside of you, just as Christ did. God is pleased with you! Behold the truth, and stand firmly. It will change your life!

Your Light Is Shining Brighter and Brighter

Matthew 2:16 *"Then Herod, when he saw that he had been tricked, was extremely angry, and he sent soldiers to put to death all the male children in Bethlehem and in all that area, who were two years old and under, according to the date which he had learned from the magi."*

Satan was the real motivator of Herod's actions. Ever since the Lord first prophesied that a man would bruise his head, Satan has been seeking out this "seed" of the woman (Gen. 3:15).

It appears that Satan is able to perceive when the Lord is making a major move in the earth. In the days of Moses, Satan moved Pharaoh to kill all the male children of the Israelite slaves, and here he motivates Herod to kill all the male children in Bethlehem. No doubt he was seeking to eliminate this "seed" who was going to bruise his head.

Once again, we see children being slaughtered today. This time it's through abortion. Our youth are also being attacked in unprecedented ways. Is it possible that Satan thinks this is the generation that is to bring in the second return of the Lord? Is he, in desperation, trying to stave off his doom by destroying this generation?

We need to have enough spiritual perception to recognize that just as in the days of Moses and Jesus, this slaughter of the innocent children today is an indication of an even more important struggle in the spiritual realm. As I write this, the entire world has been affected by the corona virus. Stores and businesses are closed. Sports teams are off the field. Even doctors offices are closed, which seems strange. Whatever has been deemed by the government as "non-essential" has been shut down. The church has been put in that group. And while churches have remained closed now for weeks, the abortion clinics are open for business and are thriving. It is unthinkable to me that murdering innocent babies is considered "essential", while worshiping the Lord is thought to be non-essential. The world is certainly getting darker and darker. But there is a light in this world. And though the world is growing dark, the body of Christ are shining brighter and brighter. Praise God! We could be the generation that sees the Lord come back. Hallelujah!

God Seeks Until He Finds

Ezekiel 34:16 *"I will search for the lost, and bring back the strays. I will bind up the injured and strengthen the weak".*

Can you see from this verse how loved you are? Do you know that you have been pursued? Do you realize how much God desires to love and protect you? Do you understand that He is your Shield and Defender?

The word "strays" really stands out to me in this verse. It means...those who are wandering aimlessly...those who are seen as outcasts by the world. These are they who are pursued...who are mended...whose hearts are healed...by the LOVE of the Father. LOVE HEALS! God IS love!

Many of us have not experienced this kind of love from our earthly fathers. It may be hard for you to imagine a father who is that committed...that loyal...that dedicated to the unfolding of your life. But God is just such a Father, and you can invite Him into your situation, into your pain...and then watch as He begins to "bind up" the broken places in your life. He begins to strengthen your weaknesses and restore your confidence...not only in who He is...but in who He has made you to be in Him!

Where other eyes choose blindness, God's eyes seek until He finds. As far as you could ever run away, He will find you and bring you home. As chipped or broken as your heart might have been, He binds up and mends. it. As dark as the world around you may appear to be...He comes with healing light to lead you to safety.

There is no gap too large for His love to bridge, no failure that He has not redeemed, no plague of spirit that He cannot cure. Don't run from Him today. Run TO Him...and allow Him to love you back to wholeness.

He Was Victorious In All Things - And We Are In Him

Hebrews 4:15 *"For we have not an high priest which cannot be touched with the feeling of our infirmities; but was in all points tempted like as we are, yet without sin. "*

Have you ever wondered if The Lord really understands what you are going through? When you are dealing with rejection, loss, being misunderstood...or even loneliness? Beloved, you are not alone...and your Savior was no stranger to hardships. He understands the deepest pain.

The religious leaders of Jesus day challenged His authority (Matthew 21:23), and they tested His teachings (Matthew 19:3). They called Him a glutton, a wine bibber, a friend of tax collectors and sinners (Matthew 11:19), and a blasphemer (Mark 2:7). They said He was demon possessed and mad (John 10:20). They put Him on the spot when they brought an adulterous woman to Him ((John 8:2-11). They attempted to stone Him (John 8:59 and 10:31-39). They accused Him of perverting the nation (Luke 23:2).

When you have been ridiculed because of your belief, Jesus understands. When you feel as though you are standing alone...He is standing with you...and IN you! When you've been rejected, Jesus understands the experience of being denied by a loved one (Luke 22:54-62). He also understands about the sickness you may be suffering...because He bore your sickness on the cross (Isaiah 53:4).

He knows the pain of betrayal, as He was betrayed by one close to Him (Luke 22:47-48).
Our precious Lord and Savior certainly understands all that we are going through. He endured much in His own life here on earth. He endured much in His own death...but beloved, He came that we might have life...and have it in abundance. He came that we might be able to walk in peace...no matter the storm surrounding us.

We can not only be comforted by the life that Jesus lived...we can be inspired by the example He is to us...not only in His life...but in His death, burial and resurrection. He was victorious in all things...and we are in Him!

209

The New Man Is A Pretty Exciting Person

Ephesians 4:22-23 *"And be renewed in the spirit of your mind; and that ye put on the new man, which after God is created in righteousness and true holiness"*

Are there things about the "old you" that you weren't crazy about? Maybe you felt you were too manipulative, too weak, too compliant, too regimented, too rebellious...too bossy, too afraid, too inhibited, too critical, too opinionated, too unfocused, too indecisive, too willing to settle for less...

I have great news! You are invited by the Lord to shake off all the dust from the old you, and reveal what He has been working on deep inside. Welcome to the new you! PUT ON the new man and come forth for the big reveal! You have not just been renovated...it's better than that...you have been completely made new!

When you begin to experience those memories of what the old you was like...just remind yourself that this isn't who you are any more. At salvation, your spirit was completely changed. And your soul is being renewed moment by moment. Those memories? That's all they are is memories. The REAL YOU has been recreated in the likeness of God. You have been made righteous, and you walk in true holiness! Put THAT on each day, like you would put on a new outfit!

Throw open those doors, grab a pair of scissors, grab that ribbon, and cut away...The bottom line is that you don't forget to celebrate who God has made wonderful YOU to be! You don't have to look back and see yourself as the sum of your old definition. You are not who anyone has told you, you are. You are who God says you are. Your old self has been made new and the new man is a pretty exciting person! Congratulations!

Jesus Laid Down His Life For The Sheep

John 10:7 and 11 *"then said Jesus unto them again 'Verily, verily I say unto you, I am the door of the sheep'".* Vs 11. *"I am the good shepherd. The good shepherd giveth His life for the sheep"*

Sheep were often gathered into a sheepfold to protect them from the elements...such as thieves, wild animals, weather, etc. The sheepfolds were often in caves, sheds, or open areas surrounded by walls made of stone or branches. The shepherd generally slept at the opening of the sheepfold, and he actually became the door...the way in for anyone wishing to enter!

Jesus said, "no one comes to the Father but by Me". He is not only the door to the Father...He is the door to the sheepfold...and we...you and I...are the sheep that He cares deeply for.

In these verses, we hear an echo of John's words, "This is the sacrificial Lamb of God, Who takes away the sin of the world." We catch a glimpse of the approaching cross , where the good Shepherd will lay down His life for the sheep - not only for the lost house of Israel, but also for those who are yet outside the fold. Our good Shepherd is not only the One Who guards and guides, feeds and protects us, but He is also the sacrificial offering, Who laid down His life for the sheep.

A hired man would tend the sheep for money...a salary. Jesus does it out of love! He has bought the sheep and owns them. He is committed to them. He isn't merely doing a job. He has laid down His life for the sheep! Just as a shepherd protects his flock, Jesus protects us...and nothing can pluck us out of His hand! He came to give us life...in abundance! He knows those who are His. He knows the sheep by name. He knows what you may be dealing with and everything about you...and He calls you His own. He leads you...and when you stumble, He carries you. He goes before you, and you follow Him because you have become familiar with, and know His voice.

Today, you can rest in Him. You can stand firm in the fact that you are being cared for...by the Good Shepherd.

You Are Alive With His Presence

Leviticus 6:13 *"The fire shall be ever burning upon the altar. It shall never go out."*

The book of Leviticus mentions this fire several times. The fire that burned upon the altar was to burn continuously. The Lord wanted a perpetual fire there, and He had a reason for it. According to the scriptures, this fire was directly lit by the hand of God. The fire symbolized the guiding presence of the Lord. It portrayed God's power, holiness, and protection over His people. Every morning, the priest was to add firewood and arrange the burnt offering, so that it would not go out.

Before the giving of the Law, God had appeared to Moses in flames of fire, from a burning bush. Moses recognized that though the bush was on fire, it did not burn up. This fire was far from ordinary. The closer Moses got to the burning bush, the more incredible this scene became. But Moses himself went on to say that the "angel of the Lord" was manifested in the burning bush. God chose the appearance of a continuous fire when calling Moses to lead the people out of Egypt to a new land. Later, when God was leading the Israelites out of Egypt, He appeared as a pillar of fire at night. The Israelites would recognize His presence among themselves, and they would know His leading and protection.

The fire on the altar was to be kept burning, never to be extinguished. It had been started directly by God. It served as a constant reminder of His presence. No other source of fire was acceptable to God. So...when Nadab and Abihu, the sons of Aaron the priest, offered a strange fire before the Lord, they died. This was a fire that they had started themselves. It was not a continuation of the fire started by God. What they didn't realize was that there is no other God. There is no copy. Anything that isn't original, truly is not of God.

The sacred fire endured for 40 years in the desert and most likely beyond that. When King Solomon built the temple, the temple was dedicated and once again, God lit the fire on the altar.

Beloved, do you realize that you are now the temple of God? When you received Christ, the fire of the presence of God came to live in you. And this fire is a continual reminder of the presence of God in your life, of His protection, and of His Life in YOU!

212

When each of us were born again, there was a perpetual fire that began in our spirit. The Holy Spirit of God has become one with your spirit, and nothing...NO THING can quench it. There is NO substitute for it. There is a fire burning in the heart of every believer. Acts 2:2 tells us that as each believer received the Holy Spirit, there were tongues of FIRE that sat upon each one of them. Beloved, You are ALIVE with His presence! Hallelujah!

You Have Great Worth In The Heart Of Your Maker

1 Peter 5:7 *"Casting all your cares upon Him, for He careth for you."*

It is such an immense comfort to know that "He careth for me". Come. Cast your burden upon the Lord. If you are staggering beneath a weight that your Heavenly Father would love to carry for you, give it to Him. What seems to you to be a crushing burden would be to Him, as dust. Beloved, God has not passed you over in His care for you. He Who is the feeder of sparrows will also furnish what you need. Do not sit down in despair. Hope on. There is One who cares for you.

The eye of God is fixed upon you. The heart of God beats for you. The hand of God is able to reach down into your situation. Isaiah 53 confirms that God has healed your wounds, carried your burdens, and bound up your broken heart. Do not doubt Him because of your tribulation, but believe that He loves you in every season. If you are in a time of trouble, know that you are loved. If you are in a time of prosperity and joy, know that you are loved. You don't need to hang on to any kind of burden or worry. God Himself is concerned for your welfare. God Himself wants you to be whole, healthy and happy. And God Himself has paid the penalty for your sin and has set you free from condemnation.

God concerns Himself with the things that interest you. Whether they be great or small, they matter to Him because they matter to you. When we are casting our cares, we are recognizing that we have great worth in the heart of our Maker. Our God is not a distant God. He is a very present help in time of need. He will withhold no good thing from you.

You can trust God with every detail of your life. He would never refuse to carry your burdens. He will not faint under their weight. Come then. Leave all of your concerns in the hand of your most capable and gracious God.

Its' A Glorious Thing When A Heart Is Changed

1 Corinthians 5;11 *"But actually, I have written to you not to associate with any so-called brother if he is sexually immoral or greedy, or is an idolater, devoted to anything that takes the place of God, or is a reviler, who insults or slanders or otherwise verbally abuses others, or is a drunkard or a swindler - you must not so much as eat with such a person."*

This is a difficult verse to digest. It is actually pretty clear, but we rarely hear it taught. First of all, let me say that we are still called upon to forgive. When someone has truly wronged us, we should be praying for them. We pray and then we let it go by giving it to God. But I do not believe that we can always jump back into a relationship that has been toxic...where time and again someone has purposely hurt us.

I've heard it said that unforgiveness is like drinking poison and hoping that the other person dies. So often, folks don't even realize that they have hurt us. But I believe that forgiveness is for us as well as for them. It's turning over someone, or some situation to Jesus and taking your own hands off. It's not looking back. It's believing that God has a purpose and a future for us that we don't want to miss because our focus is on situations rather than the Lord.

The above verse gives us quite a list. It might not be that difficult to miss a meal with somebody who is a drunkard, or sexually immoral...but why is it as believers that we so often tend to put up with people who insult and slander other people? And worse, sometimes we join them.

I was in a friendship for years with a person who continually gossiped. She and her husband talked about every person we knew. I listened and heard every word of it. It affected me, and not in a good way. But I didn't walk away. Then one day, I had a thought. I realized that if this person was talking about everyone else we knew, what was to stop her from talking about me? And that thought became a reality as I overheard she and her husband one day, not just gossiping about me, but making fun of me, and it was in front of a room full of people. I still didn't immediately walk away, but over time, I pulled out of that friendship completely.

215

Beloved, I believe that we should take this verse as seriously as any other. I am in no way saying that you should walk away from a marriage, or even a friendship where there has been an incident or two. But I also believe that this verse was meant to protect us as well as the other person, as Paul reminds us that it may bring them to repentance. And what a glorious thing it is when a heart is changed!

Dig A New Well

Genesis 26:15 *"Now all the wells which his father's servants had dug in the days of Abraham, his father, the Philistines stopped up by filling them with dirt."*

Isaac was Abraham's son. He had gained great wealth, owning flocks and herds, and a large household, along with a number of servants. The Philistines envied him. Because of their disdain for Isaac, and his father Abraham before him, they had filled up their wells with dirt, rendering them useless.

We all know that wells contain life sustaining water. We need them now, just as they did in Isaac's day. I grew up in the same house until I was about 18 years old. One day, my dad was out mowing the lawn, and the lawnmower hit something in the ground. My dad started digging to see what he might unearth. It was a well. For years we had lived in this house, not knowing that right there in the back yard, was a well. It had been filled in with dirt years before, rendering it useless. But my guess is that at some point in time, someone had used this well and probably depended on it. If in the depth of a well you can tap into a living spring, the water will flow continually, and you wont have to dig as deep or as wide because the water is constantly coming in, refreshing and renewing.

Jesus is our Living Spring. He is the Living Water that flows through us freely as believers. When He is allowed to penetrate every area of our hearts, the water is continual, and it is fresh. But just as the Philistines had thrown dirt into the wells of Abraham and Isaac, there are natural things that can come into the life and heart of a believer that clog our spiritual well. It can be doctrine or unbelief. It can be natural things that we are involved in, or even being overly involved with work or ministry, that starts to fill our well. God wants our spiritual well to flow freely, and He wants to be the One we look to in all things.

If you looked at the shoreline of many of the rivers in the world, you might find those areas filled with a lot of trash and filth. But if you go closer to the source of a river, it is likely to be pure. You can actually drink from some. But the further you get from the source, the more dirt fills the water. You need to stay near the source.

If you read further into Genesis 26, you find that Isaac had a remedy for the well situation. He dug another well. He actually had to dig several wells, before he found water, but he didn't give up.

Many folks have been treated cruelly by life. Maybe we were treated unfairly somehow. Maybe there was some kind of injustice done that we just can't seem to move past. Maybe we've waited for answers from God that we haven't seen happen yet.

Here is my thought to you. Dig another well. Don't quit. I am completely convinced that many times we just give up too soon. What did Isaac do? He grabbed a shovel and dug a new well. It's not always big things that rip our lives apart. Many times it is smaller things that just keep adding up and throwing a little more dirt in the well. Isaac kept digging, and he found a place where there was no contention, no hatred, and where the water could flow freely. Don't give up, beloved. Don't look to the world for answers that can only come through the Living Water that penetrates your heart. Grab your shovel. Keep digging!

The Holy Spirit is Only The Beginning Of What Is Yet To Come

Ephesians 1:13-14 *"Ye were sealed with the Holy Spirit of promise, Which is the earnest of our inheritance until the redemption of the purchased possession, unto the praise of His glory"*

That word "earnest" means down payment. The Holy Spirit is the down payment of the inheritance we have as born again believers in Christ. He is the Foretaste, and the Beginning of so much more to come. How exciting is that?

Anyone remember the Old Testament story of the spies being sent into the Promised Land? They came back with some of the most beautiful grapes that anyone had ever seen! Those grapes were the earnest of the inheritance that was to come for the Israelites. They were only the beginning of so much more. They were a sample of what still awaited them. In the same way, the Holy Spirit is the earnest, and the foretaste of what awaits us!

What is the seal that this verse speaks of? In Paul's day, seals were used in at least four ways. They were sometimes put on letters to guarantee that they were genuine and written by whoever claimed to be the writer. They were often placed on goods or merchandise that traveled from one place to another, to indicate who it belonged to and where it was going. A seal indicated ownership. A seal was used to show authenticity or even that something had been approved or inspected by someone. Lastly, seals were used as a warning or protection...as when Jesus was placed in the tomb, and the tomb was sealed. This was to protect it and keep others out. So...since we know here that a seal has been placed upon us, I believe it is to show that we are genuine. It shows ownership, who we belong to. It shows that we are approved, and it provides us with protection and security.

He is the earnest of our inheritance...and we are left to imagine...what will the fullness be like? However rich our experience with God is in this life...it is only the beginning of what is to come! It's the inheritance that was described by Peter as being, "incorruptible and undefiled...that fadeth not away, and is reserved in heaven for us"

What a beautiful way of expressing to us that the best is yet to come! However amazing our life in Christ has been in the here and now...there is more to come and it will be even more amazing! All that the Holy Spirit has ever been able to do in and through us, including the peace He has given and the joy we have walked in...for every one of us...this has only been the beginning. What a beautiful picture has been painted for what awaits us!

Neither Do I Condemn You

John 8:7 "So, when they continued asking Him, He raised Himself up and said to them 'He who is without sin among you, let him throw a stone at her first.'"

This is probably my favorite story in the New Testament. For some reason, often when I've read it, the tears start to flow. I think it's because I identify with the heart of this woman. I'm guessing that she was probably scared, for one thing. She had been caught in something for which the law demanded that she be stoned to death. It was very possible that she might lose her life. I'm also guessing that her life may not have been easy. Women in those days were often seen as having less value than men. And for some reason that we don't know, the man that she had been with wasn't with her when she was brought before the Lord. The scribes and Pharisees had brought her to Jesus.

When these Pharisees told the Lord that she had been caught in the act of adultery, and that the law of Moses demanded that she be stoned for it, Jesus did something rather strange. He stooped down and wrote on the ground with His finger. Someday when I'm in heaven, I want to ask Him about that. I've heard a lot of different opinions about why He did what He did, and the truth is, I have no idea. Here's what I do know. His answer to these men stopped them dead in their tracks. He said, "He who is without sin among you, let him throw a stone at her first." Wow.

These men probably looked at each other, stunned. Most likely, every one of them thought about their own lives, their own sin, their own mistakes...and they knew that they couldn't be the one to cast that first stone. The Bible says that they were convicted by their own consciences and they left, one by one. The wisdom of Jesus had changed the entire situation. Now He was left alone with the woman. He spoke to her, "Woman, where are those accusers of yours? Has no one condemned you?" The most amazing part of that question is that the only One Who could have condemned her was Jesus! He was the sinless, spotless, Lamb of God. If He had wanted to pick up that first stone and throw it at her, He could have. But He didn't. Instead, He told her, "Neither do I condemn you."

Most of us have been taught all our lives that if we clean up our lives, God will forgive us. But we can see in the life of this woman that we've had it backwards, because the Lord forgave as she stood before Him in her sin, and then He told her to "Go, and sin no more." I've heard it said that He gave her a gift that day. It was the gift of "No condemnation".

Did you know that He has given you that same gift? My question to you today is, have you received it? Do you know that you can come to God in whatever state you are in, and He will love you, accept you, and honor that gift in your life, just as He did in the life of the woman caught in adultery? You don't have to clean yourself up to approach God. Come to Him, beloved...just as you are. Let Him pour His love into your life. Allow Him to speak to your heart, "Neither do I condemn you." Invite Him in. And then watch the change begin from the inside out.

Lord, forgive us when we have thrown stones at others who don't live up to our standards. Thank you for showing us how to embrace people the way You would. Thank you for this beautiful demonstration of Your love. Amen.

Do You Need A Spark Of Hope? Keep Reading.

Deuteronomy 4:29 *"But if from thence thou shalt seek the Lord thy God, thou shalt find Him, if thou seek Him with all thy heart and all thy soul."*

What an incredible promise. To me, it's as if God is sweetly saying, "I'm here...and I want to help." I had a thought as I was writing this. So often when we are seeking something, or someone...it's because they are lost. We frantically search the house because we can't find our keys. I have emptied out my purse all over the table more than once in a mad search, only to find out that the elusive keys were right in my pocket. I have been at some type of event, and even written my name on the cup that I was using...and STILL lost the cup! More than once, I've used several cups because I kept losing them.
But it's different with God. He isn't missing. God isn't lost, beloved. He is right where He said He would be. He is alive and well...and living in your heart.

The verse says..."but from thence...or from 'there'"...And where is 'there'? It is that point that you're at, when you've come to the end of yourself. It is from there that you begin to seek the Lord your God...and when you search for Him with your whole heart, you not only find Him, you find out something else. You discover that He was pursuing YOU! You will understand that God is not, and never has been finished with you. This verse, in my opinion, is about revival. It's about God revealing His heart to us.

Sometimes people feel that they have to get their act together before they can seek the Lord. But this verse is telling us to seek Him from there...wherever 'there' is for you. When you have come to the end of yourself, He will never reject you.

Years ago, I was going through the most difficult things I had ever faced. I opened my Bible one morning to this passage.
The words came to life! They seemed to jump off the page and into the deepest place in my heart. I knew that this was a promise...and I knew that God never breaks a promise. I took it as mine! I received it...like you would receive a gift. And there was a spark of hope that was birthed in me that day!

I did not have all the answers in that very moment, but I knew that God had spoken to me...and so began my quest. I wanted to know this God. I wanted to understand Him.

I wanted to walk daily in what He died to give me...in the joy, peace, strength, trust, and the amazing hope that I was beginning to get a taste of.

I share this today for the reader who is at the end of your rope...for the person who doesn't think they can keep going...for the one who doesn't know how to go forward any more. I can promise you the same thing that He promises to all of us. If you, from this day forward, begin to seek Him with all your heart, you WILL find Him! And you WILL begin to understand that He has been pursuing YOU all along. And you will know how long, how wide, how deep and how high the love of Christ truly is for you. You will also begin to fully understand His sacrifice for you, and who you have become when you are in Him! God's grace to you is greater than your temptation to give up.

I am praying for you, beloved. I may not know you by name, but our God does. Please don't quit . The Lord is speaking to you, my friend. Hopefully you will be encouraged as well as inspired to continue in your own quest. Multiplied blessings to you!

The King Of Kings And Lord Of Lords Has Chosen Us

1 Corinthians 6:19 *"Do you not know that your body is a temple of the Holy Spirit who is within you, whom you have received as a gift from God, and that you are not your own property?"*

There is an expression that I've heard recently that says, "I'm completely gobsmacked!" That pretty much describes how I feel when I read the above verse. The word means to be utterly astonished and/or astounded! To think that the precious Holy Spirit of God lives IN ME! Why, it's positively wondrous!

Beloved, your body, this earthly vessel that you have been given, is a container. The Bible says it is the Temple for the Holy Spirit to reside and dwell in. Think about it. In the Old Testament, the temple had an outer court where people would gather. The outer court of our temple is our body, our flesh. Then there was an inner court, where the furnishings were a reminder of the deeper relationship that God drew His people into. Our inner court is our soul. It's where we do our thinking, where our will and emotions live...those things that draw us into a deeper walk with God.

Lastly, there is the Holy of Holies, or Most Holy Place. It was the deepest part of the temple, the inner sanctum, the place where the presence of God resided. For us, the Holy of Holies is our Spirit. It is the place where the presence of God dwells, in us...in His temple...GOBSMACKED!

Do you see that this verse goes on to relate to us that we have received the precious Holy Spirit as a gift? The King of kings and Lord of lords has chosen us. He will never leave us or forsake us...we are His dwelling place, His abode. And we carry His presence proudly.

Beloved, you were bought with a price, with the precious blood of Jesus, and you are not your own. You belong to the Lord. May we all, as the scripture says, honor Him, and bring glory to His Name as we live our lives, so that others may see Him in us. Hallelujah!

Take Hold of What Jesus Has For You

Genesis 19:26 *"But Lot's wife, from behind him (foolishly, longingly) looked back toward Sodom in an act of disobedience, and she became a pillar of salt."*

Lot had been warned by the Angel of the Lord. He and his wife were to leave Sodom immediately, because it was about to be destroyed. The outcry for judgment had been heard by God due to the evil there. But something unbelievable happened. Lot's wife stopped, and she looked back at Sodom...and she became a pillar of salt.

This story has always intrigued me because I didn't understand why she became a pillar of salt. I mean, why not a pillar of sugar, or flour? Then I read one day in Genesis that the area of Sodom which was near the Dead Sea, was rich with salt. All of a sudden, it made sense to me. Lot's wife looked back, and she became what was in her past. The Amplified Bible says she looked back longingly. Maybe she regretted having to leave? Maybe she had memories that triggered joy and happiness. Maybe she had friends or family that she just didn't want to leave behind.

In any case, she looked back at this salt rich, but evil city, and she turned into a pillar of salt. I remember one time when my husband and I had to move. We had to leave a city that we loved, but we had reasons that no one at the time knew about. There was some influence in that place that just wasn't the best for us. It was a difficult move because we loved the people there, but we knew it was necessary. It was a long time before I could stop looking back. And as long as I kept looking back longingly, thinking about what I'd given up, it kept me bound up in the reason that I'd left. I struggled to overcome the past, and I couldn't embrace the amazing future that God had for me, as long as I was still caught up in the past. I learned something during this time. You can't go forward and backward at the same time!

What about you? Is there something you need to let go of? Is there something that keeps pulling you back when you know that what you really need is to go forward? Paul gave us something pretty valuable to think about. In Philippians 3:12-13, he said that he had learned to press on, so that he might take hold of that for which Christ had for him. He went on to say that he forgot what was in the past, so that he could reach forward to what lay ahead.

Letting go can be hard. Whether it's a place, a job, or just a memory, there are times when God wants us to move forward. I didn't know what the future held, but I knew the One Who held the future. And so do you. Trust Him, beloved. He will certainly go with you. And you can walk fully in the purpose and the wonderful plan that He has for your life without looking back.

The Path To The Cross Tells You How Far He Will Go To Show His Love

1 John 4:10 *"In this is love, not that we loved God, but that He loved us, and sent His Son to be the propitiation for our sins."*

It may be *difficult* for you to believe that God knows your name...but He does. *Written on His hand. Spoken by His mouth. Whispered by His lips.* Your name.

You have *captured* the heart of God. He cannot bear to live without you. When you are asleep, He is still watching over you.

God's love for you is *patient.* God's love for you is *kind.* God's love for you never comes from a heart filled with envy or jealousy. It comes from a heart that *bears* all things, *believes* all things, *hopes* all things, and *endures* all things. And it is a love that will never fail.

God's dream is to have relationship with You. And the path to the *cross* tells us exactly how far God will go to call you back.

It is not our love for God: it is God's love for us that reveals HIS heart for each and every one of us. He sent *His Son* to be the way. If you want to touch God's heart, use the name He loves to hear. Call Him "Father".
He thinks you're wonderful!
And says, "I have written your name on My hand".

The price that He paid for your redemption was a heavy price. But, what would One give...for the *love* of their life...their Bride. They would give everything...and He DID.

You Are The Salt Of The Earth

Matthew 5:13a-14 *"You are the salt of the earth; but if the salt loses its flavor, how shall it be seasoned?"* Vs 14 *"You are the light of the world. A city that is set on a hill cannot be hidden."*

You may need to read these verses again. They are speaking of us, as believers. We are salt, and we are light. I live in the United States, where salt is used most of the time to season food. But in other countries where they have no refrigeration, salt is used as a preservative. If a butcher, for instance, wanted to send a large piece of meat to someone, it wouldn't go in some type of refrigerated box. Therefore, it would have to be preserved. That's where the salt comes in. Meat, left on its own, will begin to decay. That is what meat does. But adding the salt, slows down the decay, enough that it could safely reach its location, and be eaten without any problem.

Jesus left us here to occupy till He comes back. He instructed us to go into all the world and preach the gospel to all people. When we do so, we are acting as salt, preserving nations and people all over the world so that the spiritual decay not only slows down in the lives of people all over the world, but also to bring a spiritual seasoning to their life, that it might be richer and more fulfilling.

We are also light. Being children of Christ, who is the Light of the world, we are full of the brightness of our Savior. When a believer walks into a room, things should change. Darkness has to flee. When darkness is gone, you are only left with light, and light is what truth will begin to shine through.

As children of God, we are meant to shine His light, and the gospel of His grace into a world that is steeped in darkness. We are to be people who radiate the light of God's love and truth into the lives of those with whom we come in contact. We are not to hide the light of God that burns brightly in us from a world that desperately needs Him. We have been empowered by the indwelling of the Holy Spirit to shine forth truth and to expose evil when we see it. We are called to intercede for people, and we are privileged to partner with God as we carry out these endeavors. People should be drawn to us because of the love of Christ that radiates from our hearts to theirs.

Jesus entrusted the church with the privileged position of being His ambassadors here on the earth. He instructed us to "let your light so shine before men, that the world may see your good works, and glorify your Father Who is in heaven." Today, there is a life that you can touch. You are salt to someone. You are light. Right now, allow the light of your "new life in Christ" to shine steadily into the darkness of this world, so that all who see it will catch a glimpse of Christ reflected into their lives.

Allow Yourself to Receive What Jesus Died To Give You

Psalm 116:12-13 *"What shall I render to the Lord For all His benefits toward me? I will take up the cup of salvation and call upon the name of the Lord."*

We have an incredible Lord and Savior. Jesus left His perfect home in heaven, and became Man - for us. He was born into poverty - for us. He lived a perfect life - for us. He was rejected - for us. He was mocked and tortured - for us. He was crucified and died - for us. He descended into the place of sheol - for us. He got the keys to hell and the grave - for us. He was raised from the dead - for us. He ascended into heaven - for us. He sent His Holy Spirit - for us. And by the power of that same Spirit, He has given His body and blood for the forgiveness of our sins. It is certainly no wonder that the psalmist muses, "What shall I render to the Lord for all His benefits to me?" And what about us? It's interesting to think, as the psalmist did, about how we could somehow repay God for all He has done for us. I think the most amazing part of the verses are in the statement, "I will take up the cup of salvation and call upon the name of the Lord." You see, if you truly want to bless the heart of God, then let yourself receive what He died to give you. Nothing would please Him more than to know that His children are walking in the blessings that He wanted you to have.

I remember when my mother died. She had some saved some money that was specifically for me. I'm sure she did the same thing for my sister. We never talked about it. But my mom had hidden this money somewhere in the house, and gave me instructions about how I was to locate it and what I was to do if anything happened to her. This meant a lot to her, and she brought it up more than once to make sure that I would honor her request. She wanted to bless me.

The Lord is simply wanting to bless His children. He would love for us to honor His request. And the best way to thank the Lord for "all His benefits" is to make use of those benefits, to claim them as our very own and walk in them daily. We have been redeemed from sin and death so that we might walk in this world as a living testimony to the goodness of the One Who, in His mercy, redeemed us. When we have received the Lord's benefits, people who know us should be able to notice the "benefits" of the Lord's goodness in us. They should know us as people who love because we know that we are loved, people who forgive because we know that we have been forgiven, and people who give because we have received so much. The best way for us to give thanks to Him, and to glorify His name is to receive what He has given, and to put it to use in our lives. It's the most beautiful gift we could give to Him.

Our Hope Is Firmly Anchored - In Christ

Hebrews 6:19-20 *"We have this hope as an anchor for the soul, firm and secure. It enters the inner sanctuary behind the curtain, where Jesus, who went before us, has entered on our behalf."*

It seems that at times our souls are easily tossed about when waves of uncertainty rush over our lives. We feel vulnerable occasionally when the tides of circumstance wash over us, while we are struggling to keep paddling out in the open water. If we are to rely on our own navigational skills, we may even feel unprotected at times.

But an anchor, firmly tethered, will keep the boat steady regardless of high seas. Remember, waves are on the surface, and the anchor sits calmly on a deeper level.

Our anchor (hope) is firm and secure. It is steadfast and reliable. The anchor is lodged within the veil. We need to know that! This is a reference to the veil that hung across the inner sanctuary of the tabernacle, where it concealed the Ark of the Covenant. This was where God in His glory met with the High Priest once a year as the priest brought a blood sacrifice to atone for the sins of the people. And this is where Jesus has gone as a forerunner for us. He entered the Holy of Holies once for all with his own blood, which was and is infinitely precious and indestructible!

It is our hope in Jesus that anchors our windswept soul, and keeps us in the perfect spot...despite how unmanageable navigation seems to be during a storm. Sometimes a storm is no time to try to navigate at all, but a time to get still.

This hope permeates us, through all our many thick, high walls and complicated layers. Jesus cuts through all of that like a hot knife through icing. He goes directly to the secret, sacred places and ministers to us there by holding us firmly. Our lives at times may seem tossed about by the waves around us, but our hope is always firmly anchored in the depths of the rising waters...in Christ.

His View And Opinion Of Us Is Our Reality

Matthew 6:33 *" but seek ye first the kingdom of God, and His righteousness, and all these things shall be added unto you."*

Seeking Him first in all things...in our personal lives, at our jobs, in our relationships, in decision making. This simply means keeping our minds and our hearts set on Him - on the things above, not the things here on earth, not on our problems or our situations. Abide in Him daily, moment by moment...by taking every thought captive, to not only who you have become in Christ, but in His all encompassing love for you.

The way to experience, walk in, and LIVE in perfect peace, is to stop giving any kind of consideration to the lie that you are not who God says you are. In Him, we live and move and have our being...and He rejoices over us!

Jesus had told His followers not to worry about provisions, such as food, drink, or clothing. That's because God would provide for their needs. We are to keep our focus on the Lord...to seek the things of God as a priority over the things of the world. The salvation that IS His kingdom, is of greater value than all the world's riches.

The glory (doxa) of God, is His view and opinion of us...and His view and opinion is amazing! You see, He knows us inside out. He knows every thought we will have, every word we will speak, and everything we will do...and His love remains...and His love is all encompassing...because He IS love.

His view and opinion of us IS our reality. So, if you catch yourself starting to see yourself outside of what His opinion of you is...you simply need to adjust your perception. He only sees you through the blood of His Son...whole, healed, loved, worthy., righteous, perfect. Keep your heart set on Him, beloved...and whatever else you may need will be added unto you.

Let The Word Of God Dwell In You Richly

Isaiah 41:17-18 *"The poor and the needy seek water, but there is none. Their tongues fail for thirst. I, the Lord, will hear them; I, the God of Israel, will not forsake them. I will open rivers in desolate heights, and fountains in the midst of the valleys; I will make the wilderness a pool of water, and the dry land springs of water"*

Child of God, you are held firmly in the strength of His hand. In the very moment that you lift your voice to cry out to Him, and you raise it to praise and magnify His Name, *then* His glory has gathered you up. He has wrapped you in the garment of joy, and His presence will be your great reward. What a beautiful reward it is!

Lift your heart to His. You will know without a doubt that He loves you. Let your voice sing to Him in praise. As you do so, a spiritual fountain will be opened within you, and you may enjoy its' refreshing waters.

Speak to Him. From the deepest place of your heart, let your love flow to Him. Let your lips praise Him. Let your praises rise in the daytime and in the night. Then you will lie down in peace, and rise up in joy, and you may indulge in the endless fountain of His love. As it is written..."Out of his heart will flow rivers of living water" John 7:38

Let the Word of God dwell in you richly; for His Words, they are Spirit, and they are Life. They are living and powerful, and you will brandish them in faith effectively against the powers of darkness.

You are held in His embrace. Allow yourself to rest there. His Spirit, and His ways are not acquired by intellect, but His love is received by those who long for Him. As faith receives His promises, and those who seek Him are the recipients of the gift of faith, even so, to those who desire a closer relationship with Him, are drawn close, so that they may drink deeply from the Living water that He offers them. They have received the power to love Him, in return as He has loved them.

He gives Himself, and His love fully, His love is not measured out in portions. He has opened His heart to you completely. It is His desire that you continually experience His peace and joy. You will no longer go in and out...but you will dwell in Him as He has dwelt in you.

Keep His Word in the Midst of Your Heart

Proverbs 4:21-22 *"Do not let my words depart from your eyes; keep them in the midst of your heart; For they are life to those who find them, and health to all their flesh."*

Could this verse be saying what I think it is? I believe so. The Word of God is alive, and it carries life within it, to those who find it. The Bible is the only book ever written that can say that. There have been many amazing and wonderfully creative words written by millions of talented authors over the last few centuries, but no one can manage to claim that what they have written will bring life to the reader, or that it will bring joy or peace. The difference with the Bible is that although it may have been penned by the hands of men, it was authored by God Himself.

Your eyes not only help you to see the things around you, they are what bring focus to those things. If a teacher says to "Keep your eyes on the goal", it is understood to mean that everything in that person's life should be directed toward the chosen objective. It doesn't mean that the student should stare without blinking at something visual. Focused sight on one goal, with all choices serving that goal, is a great road to success, as well as staying on the best path for your life.

Just as it is with your eyes, your heart must also be single - it must be focused on one goal. Since wisdom and seeking God are contrary to all that is in this world, going after both goals is not possible. James said to purify your hearts from being double minded, so that you can go forward in stability, with a single goal in your heart. Solomon told his son to keep his words and sayings in the midst of his heart. Your physical heart is the basis of life for your body. It pumps the blood that is the life of your flesh. Your heart is also the place of your affections, the place where hope is birthed, the place where strength is multiplied, the place where you choose what you love and value. A wise man will choose to love wisdom and to value it highly. He will choose to keep, and hold on to and live by the Word of God, and to keep that Word in the midst of his heart.

But there is one more thing I want to mention from this verse. Keeping the Word of God always before your eyes, and in the midst of your heart brings health to your flesh.

I know that some will find this hard to believe, but it's in the Bible. Remember that the Bible is truth...all of it...whether or not we understand it. I believe that the heart of God is always for His children to be in good health. And this verse gives us a glimpse into how we can do that. Keeping the Word, which has life in it, always before us, always in our hearts, will bring health to our bodies. I have seen this to be true in the lives of some of the people I know who believe this and live by it. I could share so many testimonies. Maybe that will be a book for another time. What I can say to you now, is you can trust that the Word of God is true...EVERY word! Feed on it daily. Let it reach into those deep places in your heart to bring life, and your future will be changed forever.

Your Faith Is Precious To God

1 Peter 1:6-8 *"In this you greatly rejoice, even though now for a little while, if necessary, you have been distressed by various trials, that the proof of your faith, being more precious than gold which is perishable even though tested by fire, may be found to result in praise and glory and honor at the revelation of Jesus Christ"*

Suffering is something that that none of us look forward to. Even in recent days, I have seen some of the people I love facing some of the most difficult things imaginable. Though suffering is not of God, we all seem to go through it at some point in our lives. As the God-man, even Jesus suffered, and as His children, we also suffer at times.

I've heard it taught that when we are suffering, God is using it to teach us. While it is certainly possible to learn from the Lord while we are in a season of suffering, (because quite frankly, I believe we seek Him more at those difficult times), I do not believe that God brings suffering to teach us. I believe that He uses His word to teach us. He can certainly teach us at all times. It does seem that we pay more attention when we are feeling desperate.

We must remember that we live in a fallen world. And because all of us have been given free will, some are a little slower to respond to the heart of God than others. Much of the suffering that people endure comes unfortunately, at the hands of other people. Some of it comes through the devil, who is real, and some of it can and does even come through our own mistakes.

When I am going through a trial, it is always a comfort for me to know that I am not alone, and that there will be an end to this. This too shall pass. The Bible says that there is a glory that is going to be revealed in each one of us. One of the definitions of the word "glory" is God's view and opinion of us. Someday that will be FULLY revealed. And the things of this earth will no longer matter! Romans 8:18 says "For I consider that the sufferings of this present time are not worthy to be compared with the glory that is to be revealed to us"

Saints, may we all begin to see every trial for what it truly is. We know that God did not send it. If we believe that He did, then we would have to also believe that what Jesus did on the cross was for nothing. And we know that isn't true. Jesus fulfilled the old covenant. He came to restore. He came to break the power of sin.

He came to give LIFE. And He did just that. We are His children, in Christ, and live under a new covenant with better promises.

The kingdom of God operates by faith. The faith of God's people is more precious to Him than that of gold, or anything found here on this earth. When we trust God and take Him at His Word, then act on it, I believe it blesses the heart of God. Think of how you feel when your children trust what you tell them and then respond accordingly.

The question that confronts each of us is simply...how will we respond to difficulties? Will we let them embitter us, or will we allow them to transform us? Can we begin to see that even while we are going through a trying situation, we can live...TRULY LIVE...and help bring hope and help to others? Can we believe God, that He is good all the time, and that He cares for us?

God IS love...and He loves you with a love that is everlasting. That will never change!

God's Word Is Held In High Esteem

1 Thessalonians 2:13 *"And we also thank God continually for this, that when you received the word of God which you heard from us, you welcomed it, not as the word of mere men, but as it truly is, the word of God, which is effectually at work in you who believe."*

The precious people in Thessalonica had received the word of God. They had accepted it as truth, as the doctrine of God, not as anything fabricated by men. And that word, under the power and influence of the Holy Spirit, had worked powerfully in them, bringing light, understanding, and life.

We know and understand the Word of God in the same way today. It is not of human origin, but a divine revelation. And we do not merely embrace it by human reasoning, but by the conviction that this was and is a revelation of God. This is the truth of God, which came from the love of God, and when we embrace it, the faith that it generates is like that of the Thessalonians. It will endure every trial.

This Word is alive...and it is alive in us. Paul's confidence in the Word of God wasn't a matter of wishful thinking or blind faith. He could see that it worked *effectively* in those who believe. God's Word doesn't just bring information or produce feelings. It is power filled, and it can change lives. It births in us saving faith, laboring love, and a steadfast hope in Jesus. It fills us with the Holy Spirit's power and deep conviction.

The Word of God is to be held in high esteem. In Psalm 138, God said that He would honor His Word above His name. Jeremiah the prophet said that if a prophet has a dream, let him tell his dream..."but he that has My Word, let him speak it faithfully". When a woman called out of the crowd to Jesus at His teaching the Word, she said, "Blessed is the womb that bore Thee...", to which Jesus replied, "Rather, blessed are they that hear the Word, and do it." Those who receive the Word are promised to be blessed. According to Jeremiah 17:7 "They shall be like trees planted by the living water, bringing forth fruit in their season. Their leaf shall not wither, and whatsoever they do will prosper."

Jesus is the Living Word of God, and is traced to every page of the written word. His are the words of eternal life. His word is miraculous because the Spirit of the Living God is the eternal source of power.

His Word has the ability to cut into the deepest recesses of all that is spiritual, and divide it from that which is of the soulish realm. It has the power to separate the soul of man from the born-again Spirit. It is able to judge the deepest thoughts and intentions of the heart.

May we continually thank Him, and rejoice in the fact that His word is alive in us. May we embrace it daily. And may we allow Him to complete the good work that He has begun in each of us.

Don't Live "Less Loved"

Luke 15:20 *"And he arose, and came to his father. But when he was yet a great way off, his father saw him, and had compassion, and ran, and fell on his neck, and kissed him."*

I have heard the story of the "prodigal" or "lost" son taught many times over the years. I have heard it preached from some of the godliest men I know. I have been in Sunday School classes where it was taught. I have heard my own husband teach it several times because it is one of his favorite Bible stories. I have heard many different slants on the story from the younger son being the main focus, to the older son, being the one who is often overlooked as we study this parable.

Recently, I was reading a book, and the title of the next chapter was "A Father Like No Other". As I began to read the chapter, I realized it was going to be teaching about the prodigal son. I hate to admit this, but I almost skipped the chapter. I truly thought that I'd had so much teaching on this over the years, that there couldn't possibly be anything that had been overlooked. I really didn't think that I could learn anything more from the story.

Boy, was I wrong. As the chapter began to unfold, the story came to life for me...and I saw something that I had never seen before. The author asked the question...At what point in the story do you think the father loved the son the most? My answer would have been that he didn't love him more at one point in the story than at another point...but the author shared that when he asks that question, almost always the first answer is that it is the moment where the Father met the son on the road. Some also suggest it might be when the father gave him his inheritance and let him go. Only then does it become clear. There is no point in the story where the father loves his son more than at any other point. He loved his son completely through the whole process. That love from the Father is the constant in the story.

The events in the story cannot be accounted for by the varying love of the father...only the varying perception of it by the son. Though he was not less loved at any point, through most of the story, he lived as if he were. When he took the money from his father and left home, free to pursue his own way, he lived less loved. When he spent this money in a foreign land, wasting it on his own pleasures, he lived less loved. Even when he started for home, practicing his plea of repentance, and willing to be a slave, he lived less loved.

But finally, when he was home in the robe, the sandals and wearing the ring, sitting at his father's table, it seemed to sink in. He was loved...but he always had been! It was just that then he could stop living as if he weren't.

I wonder how much of our lives today are spent living "less loved". We worry that God will ask us for some difficult sacrifice...and we live "less loved". When we "fail" in some way that we know is against the will of God...we live "less loved". When we give in to anxiety during the difficulties of our circumstances, we live "less loved". When we try to earn God's favor by our own efforts, we live "less loved". Even when we get caught up in trying to become more like Him...we live "less loved".

The truth is that God wants a relationship with you. He wants you to know how He feels about you all the time. He wants you to know that the love He has for you isn't going to change or vary because of your circumstances.

Jesus ended the story at an interesting point. The younger son was in the house enjoying his newfound relationship with the father. The older son was still outside angry and deciding what to do. Would he come to know just how much he was loved and join the celebration, or would he remain convinced of his father's unfairness and stay angry and alone outside?

The choice was his...and it is ours. Everything in our life really hinges on one question...Do you know how loved you truly are? If you don't know or aren't sure...isn't it about time you found out?

His Light Will Dispel The Darkness

Exodus 14:21 *"All that night, the Lord drove the sea back"*

I see something in this passage that shows me something beautiful about the Lord. He is at work during the night, during the dark seasons in our lives. So, much of the real work of God for the children of Israel did not happen when they realized at some point during the day that they could not cross the Red Sea. It occurred "all that night".

There may be a great work occurring in your life when things seem their darkest. You see no evidence yet, but God is at work. God was just as much at work "all that night" as He was the next day when the Israelites finally saw the evidence. The next day simply revealed what God had done during the night.

Often, when I'm looking at a situation in my life, it is difficult to see my way through. I don't always see the path clearly. But, when I have taken several steps into whatever the situation might be, I can look back and see that God clearly made a way. When, by faith, I kept walking, I realize that God was parting the waters in my life for me, when I didn't know or see that He was doing it. I have come out on the other side of some difficult situations knowing that even in the darkness, God had directed my steps.

Are you reading this today from a place in your life where everything seems dark? Do you have faith to see, but aren't seeing yet? Are you lacking continual victory in your spiritual growth? Is your daily quiet communion with your Lord seemingly growing smaller?

"All that night, the Lord drove the sea back". Don't forget it. God is at work in your life, even when you can't see. He works through the night until the morning light dawns. Through the dark times in your life, God is Light. And that light will dispel the darkness. Trust Him. He is there.

We Can Rest In The Power Of Stillness

Mark 15:3 *"He answered nothing"*

I don't know if there is a more compelling story anywhere in the scriptures to me. I really don't like injustice. Therefore, this story, which speaks of Jesus, the precious Savior of the world, being reviled by men, and then remaining silent, pulls at the strings of my heart. He answered nothing. With one quick burst of divine power, or one fiery word of rebuke, He could have caused His accusers to be laid prostate at His feet. Yet...He answered not a word, allowing them to say and do their very worst. He stood in the POWER OF STILLNESS...this beautiful Savior, this completely blameless Light of the world...God's holy, silent Lamb.

The Bible reminds us in Isaiah 30:15 that in quietness and confidence shall be our strength. That is what we witness here in the life of Christ. The Savior of the world walked in perfect peace, despite what was going on around Him, because His confidence was in the Father, and that confidence WAS His strength.

I think of the many times that I have been tempted to speak up, to mouth off, to stand up for myself, to let people know my opinion. And yet, as one of His, there is a place of stillness deep in my heart. It is a place of trust. It is a place where the presence of Christ exists and dwells, in me. It is a position In Him, which when we operate from, it allows God to direct our steps, and guide us through. It is a place where peace abides. It is a stillness that stops our scheming, self-vindicating, and the search for a temporary means to an end through our own wisdom and/or judgment. Instead, it lets God provide an answer, through His unfailing and faithful love, to even the most cruel blow that we may have suffered.

I wonder how often we take things into our own hands, kind of like Sarah did in the Old Testament. God is reminding us that He was there. He was standing quietly waiting for Sarah to call on Him, and He awaits our call as well.

May each of us remember the silent power that has been instilled in us as a believer and child of God. May we remember that just because we might move the hands of a clock, it doesn't actually change the time...and sometimes our actions may only make the situation worse. But we can surely rest in His power of stillness...and trust that He will carry us. We are in very capable hands.

242

Jesus Wants Us To Use The Inheritance He Left Us

Psalm 6:6 *"I am weary with my groaning; all the night, I make my bed to swim'. I water my couch with tears"*

The cry of David is surprisingly startling to me. He was the King of Israel. He carried a lot of authority. People respected him. Even the Lord said that David was a man after His own heart. And so I find it strange that David struggled with his thought life. But it seems the biggest battles I have in my own life are in my mind...the same thought life that David dealt with. Often, right before I go to sleep, when I am laying there thinking about the events of the day, or what I need to do the next day, the biggest part of the battle takes place. Frequently, before we are fully awake in the morning, the devil is bidding to send troubling thoughts, to deceive us, and to plant defeating ideas in our minds. We see from the scripture that even David struggled with this...David, who loved God and trusted Him deeply...still wrestled at times with his thoughts.

Satan wants us to be hopeless, faithless, and negative. He has done his job when he can plant doubt and unbelief in the mind and heart of a child of God...because then we are rendered useless for the Kingdom. He definitely does not want us to have a positive outlook when we get up in the morning. He would rather see us have a bad attitude and to be self-centered, rather than God centered, offering our lives and our day to Him.

Thank God, that through Jesus, we have been redeemed...and we don't have to live, just accepting every thought that pops into our head. This is not God's best for the believer. When a thought comes that we recognize as not being from the Lord, we should immediately cast it down, and begin to think on whatsoever things are good. (Phil. 4:8) The Lord loves us. He has a plan for our lives. He wants to be able to use us. He left us with joy and peace, as part of our inheritance from Him. When my father died, he left me an inheritance. He would have been crushed if he thought that I never used it. Think about it. Jesus wants our lives to be hope-filled lives...because He is the God of hope. Even when we are facing the most challenging times we could imagine, we should be walking in hope. This is what was left to us.

Isaiah 26:3 says "Thou wilt keep him in perfect peace, whose mind is stayed on thee...because he trusteth in thee"

To be "stayed", means to remain...to steadfastly think on the things of God...to not lose focus. We can never avoid all the problems that this life has to offer...but we can take control over our thoughts. We can choose to accept or dismiss every thought that comes our way. When we are steadfastly thinking about the things of the Lord, trust develops, and peace comes...perfect peace. When we are trusting Him, our whole attitude changes...and we become stable, supported by God's unchanging love for us, and by His mighty power, we are not shaken...but remain firm.

Today, begin to resist whatever negative thoughts the devil may hurl at you...and start to trust God's power in order to live a wonderfully victorious life!

Silently and Without Conscious Effort, You Can Be Changed

Psalm 37:4 *"Delight yourself also in the Lord, and he shall give you the desires of your heart"*

Child of God, do not be anxious concerning the growth of your soul. Leave it with Jesus. Hasn't He said that the lilies grow without taking thought of themselves? So will you, both in the natural and in the spiritual.

Jesus is delighted with you. He loves everything about you. He longs to give to you the hopes of your heart. Delight in Him, beloved.

Occupy yourself with becoming acquainted with His character and person. He delights in you knowing His true nature. Celebrate in fellowship with Him. Your very association with Him will bring about changes in your soul that will surprise you when discovered, just as you have so often experienced the joy of seeing a beautiful sunrise.

Turn your face toward Him, as well as your heart. Leave to Him the responsibility of probing your soul. He is truly the Master Surgeon. He is skilled in all the cures of the soul as well as those of the body. Let Him care for your health.

Delight yourself in Jesus, and He will bring about what you desire to see in your character and personality. Feed upon His Word. You will begin to notice change. It is there that you will come to a clearer understanding of His Person. Only as you know Him can you come to be more like Him.

Silently, and without conscious effort, you will be changed.

Your Needs Will Be Met...According To His Riches In Glory

Philippians 4:19 *"And my God shall supply all your need according to His riches in glory by Christ Jesus"*

The world these days seems helpless as the systems of the nation and of the entire world go up and down. Just to watch the news can cause fear and uncertainty to rise up. We hear about war, recession, crime, unemployment, inflation, political debauchery, and on and on it goes.

Beloved, God does not want you to feel helpless. You are not of the world. John 17:16 says "They are not of the world, even as I am not of the world". Whatever the world's situation is, fear not...because your God shall supply all your need according to His riches in glory by Jesus Christ. I am not saying that you will get everything you want. That is not what the verse is talking about.

The verse says that God shall supply all your NEED. What is it today that you NEED? It doesn't say that He will supply sometimes. It doesn't say He will supply if you behave yourself. It doesn't say that He will supply if He feels like it. It doesn't even say that He will supply sometimes. The verse says that He will do it, according to His riches in glory. It is not according to this world's system...or according to the riches of the company you work for. It is not according to your budget or your promotion. It is according to God.

When you are feeling anxiety, because everything around you seems uncertain, fix your eyes on Him...the One who is unshakable, unwavering...the One Who cannot lie, Who never breaks a promise...the One Who died for you...the One Who loves you. Keep your eyes on Him...not on what is going on around you. Don't continue to saturate your mind with all of the "bad news" around you. Instead, look at the unshakable and eternal Word of God. Your heart will become unshakable as well, and stable. God supplies for you...on that you can trust... whatever the need might be...according to His riches in glory, in Christ Jesus.

The Holy Spirit is Our Trustworthy Guide

John 16:13 *"But when He, the Spirit of Truth comes, He will guide you into all the truth. For He will not speak on His own initiative, but He will speak whatever He hears from the Father, and He will disclose to you what is to come."*

The emphasis in this passage is on the word "guide". The Holy Spirit is our Guide! The Bible refers to Him as such, NEVER a controller. He will not "drive" His sheep. He never forces. He gently leads.

Because He is the Spirit of Truth, He guides His believers into that truth. This makes Him a trustworthy Guide. He helps us to discern what is true and what isn't. He helps us to detect what is wise, and what is foolish. He helps us to see what is best, and what is simply o.k. He goes before us, and opens our understanding to make things clearer, and as He leads men in the way they should go, He does so without turning to the right hand or to the left, which, without a guide, we would all be tempted to do.

He is One with the Father and the Son. He will not teach anything contrary to either of them. What He hears of the Father, that shall He speak, thereby showing the intimate consent between Himself, the Father and Christ. It is one conjoined testimony, in which the honor and glory of the holy Trinity, and man's salvation are equally concerned.

Each day is a day of decisions. As you are barraged with the details of everyday living, remember Who is with you, living in you, giving you that extra on-the-spot sense of discernment that you will need to make both big and small decisions. And the wonderful thing is that as you develop a greater sensitivity to His guidance, you will worry much less about those decisions that you've made. Why? Because the Holy Spirit is a trustworthy Guide.

He Is Present With You...NOW

Psalm 68:19 *"Blessed be the Lord, who bears our burden day by day, the God who is our salvation!"*

He is our salvation, and He carries our burdens day by day. He is with me daily. He is very present. He walks through this life with me, and when tomorrow comes, it will be today...and He will still be with me. When yesterday was here and I walked through, it was today. Pretty interesting to think about, isn't it? He is always with us...IN THE PRESENT.

He spoke this to me several years ago when my precious husband was about to go in for surgery. I was already thinking about what tomorrow might hold. What might the complications and/or problems be? I was remembering what had gotten us to this point that we found ourselves in. I was remembering the pain, the uncertainty. In other words, I was worrying.

Worry is an absolutely useless emotion. It drags its buddies along with it - and the next thing you know, you are dealing with fear, and anxiety as well. Many countless hours are wasted when we give over to it, especially when we know that it is the Lord who day by day carries our burdens.

God is a very present help. He is not caught up in time or limited by it in any way. He is not looking ahead to tomorrow, wringing His hands or wondering how He will deal with the events of the day. He isn't looking back at yesterday, wishing He would have handled something differently.

No, His presence is with us...NOW. And when tomorrow comes, it will be today. And He will be ever present. You can hang your faith on this truth. There will never be a time when you have to go through a crisis alone. Your very present Father will still be there, relieving you of the load that you've been trying to carry yourself, and bearing your burden day by day.

Our Only Goal Is Christ

Philippians 3:8 *"I count everything as loss compared to the priceless privilege of knowing Christ Jesus my Lord, for whom I have suffered the loss of all things, and count them as rubbish that I may gain Christ."*

Just hearing those words from the heart of Paul stirs so much in me. If you read the verses before and after this one, you can certainly learn a lot about the life of Paul. He was of the stock of Israel, circumcised the eighth day, a Pharisee. But the things that were gain to him, he counted as loss for Christ. His confidence could have been in the flesh. It could have been in his accomplishments. It could have been in people...those surrounding his life. But he was willing to walk away from everything he had known...in order to know Christ.

The Greek word for "know" is the word "gnosis", and it means so much more than just to know someone or to have information about them. This word is talking about intimacy. In fact, it indicates the same type of relationship that a husband and wife would have. This was Paul's desire, and I believe it is many of yours as well. We want to know Him! We want to be close to Him. We want to understand and have communication with Him. We want oneness!

Paul was willing to give up anything, his past life, his future life, his reputation...and he would count those things as dung, that he would win Christ and be found in Him. 25 - 30 years earlier, Paul had a life changing and glorious experience on the road to Damascus, the result of which caused him to see all of his past accomplishments as loss. The ONLY thing that mattered to Paul was his relationship to Jesus, to be found in Him! He wanted to share in the fellowship of Christ's sufferings and to continually be conformed into the likeness of the One he loved. Further on in the passage, we can see that Paul was now looking forward.
He could have easily been looking back. He could have focused on his past mistakes, the fact that he had persecuted believers, and had even consented to the stoning death of Stephen.

But Paul knew something. He knew who he now was in Christ. And he was wise enough to realize that you can't go forward and backward at the same time. God had called him forward. So, he forgot what the past held, and he reached forward to what lay ahead. He pressed on because his only goal was Christ.

Beloved, God does have a purpose for your life, just as he did for Paul's. God is no respecter of persons. Verse 15 in this passage reminds us that we should all have the attitude that Paul had. We should follow his example and observe those who live by the pattern that he has given us. And one last thing, that desire that Paul had to "know" Christ intimately...well, Christ had that same desire for Paul. And, He has it for you. You are deeply loved, and highly favored. Don't ever forget it.

You Are Connected To The True Vine!

John 15:1 *"I Am the true Vine...You are the branches."*

A couple of hundred years ago, if you were walking through a vineyard, you might notice something pretty impressive. The vines were connected, not just to each other, but to one particular vine that was amazingly strong, healthy and probably quite old. It was the vine from which all of the other vines grew. It was called the true vine. Every plant in the vineyard received life and sustenance from the true vine. It was their source of nutrition. If any of the vines became contaminated in any way, they could easily be removed without any of the other plants being affected. No disease could come their way because they were attached to the true vine.

I saw this depicted in a movie once. A family who owned a vineyard looked out one day to see smoke and flames. The entire vineyard was on fire. The family all rushed out to retrieve water, in an attempt to put the fire out. But they were too late. The entire vineyard had burned and was completely destroyed. Then someone remembered the true vine. Had it been touched by the flames? They all ran up the hill to find it was still intact. They could start over.

Jesus is the True Vine, and we are all connected to Him. We remain in Him and because we do, we are able to bear much fruit. He is the Life and the Strength in us, and His provision in us continually sustains us, bringing the nutrition that we need. We are part of Who He is, and because of that, even when something has come against us, we can start over.

Jesus is the True Vine and there is no carbon copy. He is the only One from which true life is received. And Jesus was emphatically letting us know in the usage of the words "I AM" that He is the One who is eternal, self existent, and unchanging, omnipotent, omniscient, and omnipresent. And this wonderful, unchanging God desires to have an intimate relationship with those who are His...the branches!

Saints of God, you are connected to the TRUE, life giving Vine! Give thanks to His Holy Name!

The Lord Has Made Provision For Every Area Of My Life

Psalm 27:1 *"The Lord is my light, and my salvation. Of whom shall I fear?"*

I've really grown to love words. I know. That sounds like a strange statement. What I mean is that I love looking into the original meanings of words in the Greek or Hebrew. I find that often a verse will take on a much deeper meaning that I wouldn't have otherwise seen.

"The Lord is my light." The word "light" means a concrete illumination. Not only is The Lord lighting our way, and illuminating our path, but He is the bright, clear light of instruction, prosperity, and even happiness! He wants us to be successful and He leads us on a direct path and shows us the way.

..."And my salvation"... The word "salvation" here is a different word than the one we often find in scripture for salvation. Here it is the word "eysa" which means liberty, freedom, deliverance, safety, and victory. If you are in a situation where you feel held back, held down, or even oppressed...The Lord is your salvation. He is your deliverance. He is your safety, and He will lead you through...to victory!

"Of whom shall I fear"...the word here for "fear" means to dread or terrify...to be made afraid. Beloved, this verse is letting us know that we don't have to fear anyone...because The Lord IS our light. He IS our salvation. It's not that He might be! It's that He IS! Another version even refers to Him as our stronghold, which is a tower or fortress. It's a fortified refuge where one can be protected from the enemy. This is what your God is to you! When you are dealing with difficult or challenging people, The Lord is your place of refuge! You have nothing to fear because this refuge...this tower...this strong HOLD...lives...in YOU!

Remind yourself of it. Say it out loud. The Lord IS my light. He illuminates my path in life. He IS my joy! He has made provision for every area of my life to be successful. The Lord IS my salvation! He IS my freedom, my deliverance, and my safety. He IS my victory! Whom shall I fear? No one! Nothing! Because The Lord IS my place of refuge. He IS the strong HOLD in my life.

If you read on further in this passage, David said that when his enemies came, they stumbled and fell. Beloved, remind yourself today of this truth...and as you speak it out loud, let the words sink back down into your own ears, into your soul. You will not only be comforted...you will have confidence to face whatever you need to face today...not because of anything you've done, but because you can completely trust in and rely on Jesus!

Cast Yourself Upon His Mercy

Psalm 89:1 *"I will sing of the mercies of the Lord forever; With my mouth will I make known Your faithfulness to all generations"*

Precious child of God, He has loved you with an everlasting love, and with strong cords He has bound you to Himself. In the day of adversity, He has been your refuge, and in the hour of need, He has and will continue to hold you up. You have found your strength in Him. You have seen His goodness on the right hand and on the left. You have beheld His power, and His glory has not been hidden from you.

He has blessed you out of the overflow of heaven, and has not withheld from you whatever your heart desired. And He stands at the ready, waiting for you. He waits to hear your heart. His promises are always yes and amen. Wasn't the blood applied to the lintel and the doorposts for the salvation of the entire family? So, He can be trusted with those you love and cherish deeply.

So know that He is working with you and for you. For most certainly a light will shine out of the darkness, and the faith you have exercised through the years will be rewarded one hundredfold. And your faith will be turned to sight, for you will see with your eyes and hear with your ears, and rejoice in your heart over what will come to pass.

The love He has for you is wonderful, and you will both praise and glorify His name. For He that keeps you neither slumbers nor sleeps. The Lord your God is your strength, and in Him is no weariness. He never tires of you coming to Him, and your cry is welcome to His ears, however frequent.

Cast yourself upon His mercies; for His loving kindness never fails, and His grace and compassion are inexhaustible. His faithfulness is extended to all generations.

Too Blessed To Be Stressed

Ephesians 1:20-23 *"He raised Him from the dead and seated Him at His right hand in the heavenly places, far above all principality and power and might and dominion, and every name that is named, not only in this age but also in that which is to come. And He put all things under His feet, and gave Him to be head over all things to the church, which is His body, the fullness of Him who fills all in all."*

In Biblical times, defeated enemies were brought back in chains and the victorious king would sit on his throne and put his feet up on the back of the enemy as a sign of victory. Similarly, Jesus sits on His throne, and His father brings all of His defeated enemies and puts them under His feet. We, the church, are the body of Christ. This means God Himself is making our own enemies to be OUR footstool. We can rest in Jesus because with each passing day, the defeated enemies of sickness, hopelessness, depression and many others, are under our feet.

The old testament priests stood daily, ministering because their work was never finished. But the Lord Jesus sat down at the Father's right hand because His work was finished through His one sacrifice on the cross. He conquered all of our enemies. Praise God! And after He sat down, He is "from that time waiting till His enemies are made His footstool."

We are also told in the Word that God "raised us up together, and made us sit together in the heavenly places in Christ Jesus." We are in Christ, seated with Him at the right hand of God. As He is, so are we in this world. Jesus is resting as lack, anxiety, poverty, hopelessness, are all put under His feet. Because we are in Him, these enemies are under our feet also.

God didn't say that we could rest when all our enemies have been destroyed. He didn't say that rest comes when all of our problems are resolved. He is saying that He wants us to sit down, and rest FIRST. We can rest in the finished work of Jesus, and we can remain in that rest no matter what is going on around us. We can 'let not our hearts be troubled'. Whatever may be going on in the world, or in our personal lives, we have been called to rest. Our enemies have been defeated and the Lord even fights our battles for us. Our job is to trust the Word of God - and rest.

254

Any enemy that comes against you, or your family is already defeated. The Lord has already won the victory.

The ways of God are quite different from the ways of the world. He instructs us to allow ourselves to rest now. The Bible tells us to labor to enter in to that rest. It is laborious to rest when we find ourselves wanting to do something about the challenges we see. The children of Israel struggled to rest and to believe in God's promises because they focused on the obstacles. We certainly can learn from their story. We are called to rest, because we are too blessed to be stressed!

You Are a Container For Victory

Mark 6:49-52 *"But when the disciples saw Jesus walking on the sea, they thought it was a ghost, and cried out; for they all saw Him and were shaken and terrified. But He immediately spoke with them and said, 'Take courage! It is I (I AM)! Stop being afraid.' Then He got into the boat with them, and the wind ceased; and they were completely overwhelmed, because they had not understood the miracle of the loaves, but in fact their hearts were hardened, (being oblivious and indifferent to His amazing works)."*

These disciples, followers of Christ, had just witnessed another miracle. They had seen Jesus multiply the loaves and fish that He had, to feed a multitude. How quickly they had forgotten. Now they were eye witnesses to yet another miracle, and the Bible says that their hearts were hardened, being oblivious to His amazing works. I remember seeing a miracle one time after I had prayed for someone. I was stunned by what I was seeing with my own eyes. Like the disciples, I was not quite comprehending it.

The word "hardened" in the verse actually means "unresponsive". It means to be completely lacking sensitivity or spiritual perception. How is it that the disciples' hearts lacked spiritual perception, or that any of our hearts lack sensitivity after having spent time with Him? I believe that it's because we haven't allowed for the revealed love of God to become personal. We can read the Word, be present every week at church, attend Bible studies, and our hearts may still not be tender to the reality of Jesus. Unfortunately, our own hearts can grow hard, even as born again believers, when the relationship that we are developing with Him is compromised in any way.

Romans 12:2 reminds us to be transformed by the renewing of our minds. It is that shift in thinking that begins to bring true change. As our minds begin to know and realize that God truly is a good God, Who wants the best for His children, as any father would, our hearts begin to soften as that truth becomes reality.

Jesus miraculously walked on water to come and save His disciples who were in the middle of a terrible storm. But they didn't recognize Him right away, thinking He was a ghost. They had heard Him and were aware of His promises, but didn't grasp them. They needed Him, but didn't immediately reach to grab hold of His provision. How often have we not sensed His presence ourselves? These disciples cried out in fear, instead of calling out in faith. They were terrified.

The word "terrified" means 'to set in motion what needs to remain still.' What they set into motion, was fear, anxiety, desperation. In all of our lives, when we trade in God's truth for what the world says is a better plan, we can easily 'set in motion what needs to remain still.' Resisting His promises can cause us to forget His presence; and it is His presence that fills us with confidence, acceptance, and peace.

Proverbs 10:11 says that "the mouth of the righteous man is a well of life". Do you know what can carry your victory? You can! You can declare a thing! You can speak over your life. When your mind is renewed and your heart is fully persuaded of the goodness of God, you can begin to see change! You can accept, walk in, and declare the truth of God over your life! Thank you Lord for the sweet revelation of your love for us, followed by change that is effortless!

Christ Is Shining Radiantly Into Your Life

Exodus 16:10 *"the glory of The Lord appeared in the cloud"*

Each of us should get into the habit of looking for the glory of The Lord in our lives...in every situation...even in the storm cloud that may seem to be hanging right over our life. Once we have seen Christ in our situation, our hope comes alive, and our path begins to change. We stop looking at the dark center of the cloud, and we fix our eyes on the Light of the world.

The cloud of the Lord was what the children of Israel followed daily to direct their steps. God was in that cloud. The glory of the Lord appeared in the cloud, and went before them daily! There was more than a common brightness in it. The glory of God shone from it. Christ, the brightness of His Father's glory, and the express image of His person appeared in the cloud, in a beautiful display of His majesty. This made it very observable to the Israelites.

We were created to live victoriously...and every day, we can look up...and see the glory of God in our situations. When we make the decision to wholeheartedly turn from any symptoms of doubt, lack of trust, or discouragement, and in turn to believe God...to stand firmly in what we know to be true, our faith will be reawakened...and the very breath of God's divine strength will begin to permeate our souls. We may not even notice it at first...but as we get determined to shun every tendency toward doubt and unbelief, we will begin to experience peace...even a sense of being carried.

If we could see into the unseen world, and gaze at the mighty armies of strength and power that are always with us, there wouldn't be any desire at all to "give in" to the enemy's ploy to push us down...or keep us discouraged...or to riddle us with guilt...or even to question God.

Child of God, look up! Christ, the brightness of His Father's glory...and the express image of His person, is shining radiantly in your life. Look for the visible display of His majesty in even the smallest details of your life. You will certainly see Him.

Jesus Was No Fairy Tale

1 John 1:1 *"(I am writing about) what existed from the beginning, what we have heard, what we have seen with our eyes, what we have looked at and touched with our hands, concerning the Word of Life (the One Who existed even before the beginning of the world, Christ)"*

I can't begin to imagine what John and the other disciples saw. He is letting us know here that what he along with others saw and heard, was real...and it was incredible. What a glorious thing! They heard the voice of God when He related to Jesus "You are my Beloved Son in Whom I am well pleased." To have been there must have been amazing . John looked on Jesus. He saw the miracles. He was there when Jesus walked on water. He was in the boat. He was there with Him in the garden. He was there when Jesus washed the feet of the disciples, including Judas. He saw the heart of Jesus. He touched Jesus, not only with his hands, but he touched the heart of Christ. John knew the love of Jesus. He knew that He was cared for, the beloved of the Lord. It must have been an amazing thing to have walked with Jesus for over 3 years.

John knew that Jesus was the only begotten Son of God. He knew that He was the Way, the Truth and the Life. He knew Him as the True Vine, the One Who is the Sustainer of life to all the branches. John was probably very familiar with the Old Testament. He knew that Jesus, as the Lamb of God sacrificed His life, once, for all. In the Old Testament, when people would bring a lamb for a sacrifice, the priest would inspect the lamb for any type of blemishes or defects. The lamb had to be perfect in order to be the sacrifice. Jesus was perfect. He would lay down His life, the Redeemer, and bring hope to many generations to come. No one asked Him to do it. The love that He had and HAS for each and every one of us is what compelled Him to do it. The Bible says that He did it for the JOY that was set before Him. I believe that the joy was US. I believe it was the love He had for you, and for me.

Jesus was Immanuel, spoken of in the prophetic book of Isaiah. He was the Bread of Life, the One Who came from heaven to bring and sustain life. He was the Prince of Peace, on Whom we cast our care. I'm sure that John cast his cares on Christ, knowing that there was no need to be worried or anxious about anything, but that in every circumstance, he could make his requests known to God, and then thankfully receive and walk in the peace of God that passes all understanding.

Jesus was the Word, made flesh. The Word is a translation of the Greek word "Logos". He was the principle of divine reason and creative order. He was the Son of God, sent to earth to reveal the heart of the Father to the world. Jesus was that Eternal Life, Who was at the side of His Father, in communion with Him...that Life on which all other existence, physical and spiritual, depends. John solemnly testified as an eyewitness to every one of us that this Jesus was no fairy tale. This was real, and it was written to every one of us as a message of hope. Grab onto it, beloved. Grab hold of the truth of Who Christ was, and never let it go!

Christ Has Fulfilled The Law

Romans 10:3 *"For not knowing about God's righteousness (which is based on faith), and seeking to establish their own (righteousness based on works), they did not submit to God's righteousness."*

Paul was speaking here of Israel. His heart's desire was for their salvation. He knew that they had a certain zeal for God, but that they did not have the correct and most vital knowledge about Him. The Israelites did not understand God's righteousness. Because of generations of people who not only followed the law, but also added to it, folks had no idea that true righteousness was based on faith, not works.

Verse 4 goes on to remind us that Christ fulfilled the law. He was the end of it. In fact, the law was to lead people to Him, which it did. Now, righteousness is freely given to those who believe in Him as Savior. Paul showed throughout Romans that the law could never save anyone. No one could keep it! And if you broke even one of the over 600 laws given, you had essentially broken them all! He wrote in Romans 3:23 that "all have sinned and fallen short of the glory of God." The only One Who could follow, keep and fulfill the law was Jesus.

And Paul shows that the law was never meant to stand on its' own forever. It always pointed to Christ. He kept it perfectly and fulfilled its' righteous requirements once and for all.

Christ's righteousness is available now to everyone who believes in Him. The book of Hebrews, especially chapter 8, speaks in greater detail about a new covenant, one that was established by Christ, and in Christ...one that was meant to end man's dependence on rituals and animal sacrifices. Jesus became our perfect sacrifice, and He, the Lamb of God, died once, for all.

To this day, precious people continue to strive for righteousness, based on their own works. I have spoken to people who do not feel like they are good enough to one day go to heaven. Many have simply given up believing that God could ever love a "sinner like them", when in fact, it was while we were yet sinners that Jesus died for us. We need not submit to a list of rules or regulations to find our way to heaven. We only need to understand the truth. When we receive Christ, we are In Him, and He is righteous. That makes us righteous too. We have been granted, as a gift, the righteousness of the Lord...the most amazing gift I can ever imagine receiving. How about you? Will you receive it today?

How Valuable You Are

Psalm 139:17 *"How precious are Your thoughts to me, O God! How vast is the sum of them! If I could count them, they would outnumber the sand. When I awake, I am still with You."*

Beloved, as you begin your day, think for a few moments...about how valuable you are in the eyes of God. You have been uniquely created...to be the amazing you that no one else can be! There is no other "you" anywhere! Your presence in this world, in the time frame that you are living in, and to the family that you were born to, is significant. You were no accident. You were planned! You are a gift, sent by God. You've been wonderfully wrapped in a beautiful package...just waiting to be unwrapped...and unveiled!

There is so much in you that the people in your life need. Every word spoken, every thought you have, every gift you've been given, every hug that you have shared... are all placed in you by your Creator...and you are an amazing treasure to Him! He is acquainted with all your ways. You were made in secret...yet not hidden from God!

The Lord understands you. He knows you intimately...in fact more intimately than anyone here on earth. He knows when you are hurting. And when you are struggling because you feel alone or misunderstood. Remember that He is the One Who knit you together in your mother's womb. His works are wonderful! And YOU are one of His amazing works.

His thoughts regarding you are numerous and precious. They are too many to even count. And He longs to spend time with you! He knows you inside and out...and His love for you is immeasurable. You are not only His gift to the world, but you are His gift to Himself...amazing!

So...believe it...and let yourself be unwrapped...to a generation who need to experience The love of Jesus...through you!

Forgiven - What A Beautiful Word

Hebrews 10:18 *"Where these have been forgiven, there is no longer any sacrifice for sin."*

Forgiven. What a beautiful word. To know that we have been forgiven is to rest fully in the promise that God will no longer remember our sin. It has been cast from us, as far as the east is from the west. Our spiritual slates have been wiped clean. This verse reminds us that there is no longer any sacrifice for sin. Jesus died once. It was over 2000 years ago. But His sacrifice purged all of our sin, past, present and future.

Why then, do we persevere in carting around the heavy load of remembered sin? It isn't that God is reminding us. It's that we remind ourselves. We hang on to things that God has released. Perhaps it is our lack of believing and standing firm in His promises that prevents us from enjoying the liberty that comes from simply being forgiven. Maybe in some strange way, we are hard on ourselves because we don't believe we are who God says we are.

If anyone in the scriptures had a reason to feel bad about his past, it was Paul. He persecuted believers and was even consenting to the stoning of Stephen. Paul could have let his past affect his future. But he had an encounter with Jesus and he was forever changed. If he had continued to look back instead of forward, we wouldn't have a large part of the New Testament, and some of the most incredible and encouraging teaching imaginable.

Jesus died so that we as believers could live victorious, reconciled, liberated, joyful, productive, and beautiful lives. Give thanks to the Lord for your clean slate by enjoying the freedom that He died for you to have. Let go of your past, and put the load down. When you have gone to Jesus with a repentant heart, and invited Him in, you never have to look back.

We Glory In Christ Jesus, In Our Service To God

Romans 15:17-18 "Therefore I glory in Christ Jesus in my service to God. I will not venture to speak of anything except what Christ has accomplished through me in leading the Gentiles to obey God by what I have said and done – by the power of signs and miracles, through the power of the Spirit".

One of life's great mysteries is that God chooses to use human beings as instruments of His work. Though He has given man the earth to care for and watch over, it seems it would be so much easier and quicker if He would just do what needs to be done! In reality, He has done all that needs to be done through His Son. Now it needs to be lived out and brought to bear on this fallen world. That is where we as men, and as His new creation come into view.

Paul had no difficulty understanding that He was only a vessel of God. The value is not in the vessel, but in the treasure the vessel holds. We are earthen vessels, Paul wrote, who contain a great treasure. The treasure is the life of God, the power of the risen Christ.

Because Paul understood this so well, he would never consider boasting in what he had accomplished. He knew that it was God who was working in him and through him.

In a day when men are not content to serve in secret, when people clamor and strive for "ministry", we must return to the words and heart of Paul. He said, "I glory in Christ Jesus in my service to God." His glory was always in the Son of God; in His life, in His salvation, and in His grace. He desired nothing of worldly fame. He wanted only to be faithful to the Lord.

He also knew that it was the Lord he served first. He served many churches, many people, in countless ways, but ultimately it was the Lord alone that Paul served. The power of his servant's heart was that he had encountered the cross and the finality of its dealings with the self-life. The self-life must end so that Christ may be revealed. Paul understood that and had embraced it many years before.

Ultimately, the only thing that can change a man's heart is the power of the gospel of Jesus Christ. It was this message Paul preached and demonstrated, the Holy Spirit testifying to the truth of his message with signs and miracles.

There is a great separation in the work of God. The source of the life is God's alone, but the vessel is human clay. He is the treasure, we are the clay pot. But we are allowed the privilege of containing this treasure and of sharing that which is of infinite value with a lost and dying world. As did Paul, we too glory in Christ Jesus in our service to God.

Jesus Is Causing You To Soar

Psalm 1:1-3 *"Blessed is the man who walks not in the counsel of the ungodly, Nor stands in the path of sinners, Nor sits in the seat of the scornful. But his delight is in the law of the Lord, and in His law he meditates day and night. He shall be like a tree planted by the rivers of water, that brings forth its fruit in its season, whose leaf also shall not wither; And whatever he does shall prosper."*

Psalm 1 presents two ways to live; the way of the world, or the way of the Word. We can so easily walk in the way of the world, and not even realize it. The "ungodly" are those who seek independence from the Lord, who have a human or earthly perspective on life. At times, this way of life appears to be the way of success, acceptance, and prosperity. But, Psalm 1 helps us to see things in a true perspective...the prosperity of the wicked will be fleeting, but for those who delight in the Lord, living a life of faith, it will lead to blessing, fruitfulness, and fellowship with God, both now and forever.

Pay attention to the progression in verse 2. We delight in the Lord, and then we meditate in His Word. Delight is a response of the heart to the value and the beauty of something or someone. In this case, it is to God's Word. Meditation then involves sustained thought. It actually takes work because it is so easy to be distracted, but it is the meditation on His Word that strengthens and allows the Word to penetrate our minds and hearts more deeply. Through it, we are "transformed by the renewal of our minds".

I recently heard a story about a pilot who was flying a small plane. He was on a short flight, alone, when he heard some kind of gnawing sound behind him. He couldn't leave the cockpit to figure out what the noise was, but then his instrument panel began to act up. He turned to look back, and noticed a rat, gnawing at some of the wires that were connected to the instrument panel. He knew that if the rat chewed all the way through the wrong wire, his instrument panel would go down, and more than likely the plane would crash. He couldn't land the plane right then, and he couldn't leave the wheel. He had only one choice. He would fly higher. He would take the plane up where the air was thinner, knowing that more than likely the rat wouldn't be able to breathe at that altitude, and it would die. From the altitude of about 10,000 feet, the view was amazing. The pilot was enjoying seeing the mountains and the beautiful evergreens that were right underneath him. Eventually, he noticed the gnawing stopped. He turned around to see that the rat hadn't made it. It was laying on its' side. The oxygen level was insufficient, and it didn't survive.

There are times in this life when we have to deal with ungodly situations, or even people, and at times we don't know exactly what to do. May I advise you, just go higher. Continue to delight yourself in the Lord, and be a light to those around you who are walking in darkness. Continue to meditate in His Word and allow it to strengthen and sustain you. You will be surprised to find that there will be some who want to go with you. There may be some who will not survive going higher with you, but for you...your eyes are fixed on Him, and you are continuing to soar. You have the most beautiful vantage point, above all of life's issues and problems. May you lay hold of the blessing of Psalm 1 as you delight in the beauty and the value of God's revealed Word. May you continue to bring forth fruit, and may all that you do be prosperous.

One Piece At A Time, We Will Be Given A Whole New Picture

Revelation 21:5 *"He who was seated on the throne said, "I am making all things new"*

ALL things. Not just some things...everything! "Eye hath not seen, nor ear heard, nor have entered into the heart of man the things which God has prepared for those who love Him."

The old creation had long groaned under corruption, but is delivered by a new creation. The earnest expectation of the creation eagerly waits for the revealing of the sons of God. The creation itself will also be delivered from this bondage of corruption.

Everything in your Spirit was made new when you were born again. You are an original creation. The old man is dead! But there is more to look forward to. Everything about your LIFE can be renewed. God began with the renovation of your heart and now works outward, touching every aspect of your life.

You've been made to be authentic, and completely genuine. Your Creator can breathe life into things that you have thought dead. He can restore relationships. He can cast your circumstances in a new light. He can renew your energy to ensure you have enough endurance, and courage to soar! He can re-invigorate your faith. He can give you clear eyes to see His majesty in everything and everyone. He can give you fresh understanding and an awakening of appreciation. He can help you to walk in the Spirit, and to see things completely differently than you may see them now.

The redemption set forth in the book of Revelation is much broader than the individual redemption of sinful men. It extends to the redemption of the earth and the entire creation.

A small smile will spread into a full blown grin as you watch Him work in your life. He fits it all together, one puzzle piece at a time, giving you a whole new and amazing picture! And you realize that all along, you have been so incredibly blessed!

Epilogue

The situation that I spoke about earlier in this book never did change...but the Word of God has changed me. There is so much I could say here. I want to encourage those of you who are waiting for answers to keep seeking Him. The answers that I was looking for were not exactly the answers that I got. But, the answers that I got were better! I've shared many of them in this book. The Bible makes us an amazing promise in Deuteronomy 4:29. It says, "But if from thence, you will seek the Lord your God, you will find Him, if you seek Him with all your heart, and all your soul." Beloved Saints...if I could encourage you in anything, it would be not to quit. Don't give up! I believe that the Lord is speaking to you, and He wants to pour into your life, even more than you want Him to! I can't give you an exact date, or a moment when it happened...but I can tell you that the Lord has healed my heart, my life and the pain that I lived with for such a long time.

One day, I simply realized that the pain that had been so familiar to me for so long...was gone! And it was time for me to start LIVING again! Jesus came that we might have life...and have it in abundance. I realized that this was part of the inheritance that He left for me...but that I had to CHOOSE it.

It was in spending time in the Living Word that the change began to occur. As I sought Jesus...and truth...it was that very truth that did make me free! And why not? God promises that He came to set the captives free - to cause the blind to see - to release from prison those who are bound. I fit every category. I was in a prison (of my own making), although I didn't see that at the time. I was held captive by a wrong belief system and was thereby blinded to the truth.

It really did feel like a prison. The thing was - the door was open, and I was free to walk out at any time. You are too! You can walk out into the Light - the Light that is Christ.

One step at a time, you can walk into the freedom, the goodness - the truth, the HOPE - that God has for you.

My prayer is that you will find healing in the pages of this book. And I WILL be praying for you. I love Paul's power filled prayer for the Ephesians. May the God of our Lord Jesus Christ give you the spirit of wisdom and revelation in the knowledge of Him. May the eyes of your understanding be enlightened. May you know the hope of His calling and the riches of the glory of His inheritance to you. May you understand the exceeding greatness of His power toward you and IN you. And may you KNOW the love of Christ, walk in it, and receive it as your own...because it IS yours!

Multiplied Blessings to you all.

Made in the USA
Middletown, DE
18 February 2021